MATTHEW AS STORY

**Other Fortress Press Books by
Jack Dean Kingsbury**

Matthew: Structure, Christology, Kingdom

Matthew (Proclamation Commentary)

Jesus Christ in Matthew, Mark, and Luke
(Proclamation Commentary)

The Christology of Mark's Gospel

*Conflict in Mark:
Jesus, Authorities, Disciples*

*Conflict in Luke:
Jesus, Authorities, Disciples*

Second Edition, Revised and Enlarged

JACK DEAN KINGSBURY

MATTHEW AS STORY

FORTRESS PRESS   **PHILADELPHIA**

To
John Schmidt †

FIRST EDITION COPYRIGHT © 1986 BY FORTRESS PRESS
SECOND EDITION COPYRIGHT © 1988 BY FORTRESS PRESS

Library of Congress Cataloging-in-Publication Data

Kingsbury, Jack Dean.
  Matthew as story.

  Bibliography: p.
  Includes index.
  1. Bible. N.T. Matthew—Criticism, interpretation, etc. I. Title.
BS2575.2.K48 1988   226'.206   88-3718
ISBN 0-8006-2099-2

Printed in the United States of America   1-2099

12   13   14   15

Contents

vi   Contents

Preface

This book is a completely revised and enlarged edition of its predecessor. It, too, is a study in literary, or narrative, criticism. As a subdiscipline of Gospel research, narrative criticism has surged to the fore in the 1980s in a way reminiscent of redaction criticism in the 1950s and 1960s. The appearance of an ever-increasing number of articles, monographs, and doctoral dissertations devoted to narrative-critical study is but one measure of the potential scholars find in this method for gaining fresh insight into the meaning of the Gospels. The advent of narrative criticism has already brought about considerable change in the way courses on the Gospels are being taught in colleges, universities, and seminaries.

The purpose of the book remains the same: To explore the world of Matthew's thought by focusing on the plot (or flow) of the gospel story being told. Nevertheless, this second edition constitutes, in both major and minor ways, a significant revision of the first one. Thus, two new Chapters have been added: one that deals with the great speeches of Jesus (Chapter 6); and one that traces the story-line of the religious leaders (Chapter 7).

The need to devote a separate Chapter to the religious leaders had become increasingly apparent to me. Careful study of Matthew shows that it contains not just two story-lines (those of Jesus and of the disciples) but three, since the story of the leaders, too, is told. This story, however, is, like Matthew's characterization of the leaders as well, exceedingly harsh. The world Matthew creates in his Gospel is one of cosmic conflict between good and evil. In it, Jesus Son of God, as the bearer of the Kingdom of Heaven, vies with Satan and his kingdom of evil. Since the religious leaders stand forth in the human realm as the principal antagonists of Jesus, Matthew aligns them with Satan and paints them in the darkest of colors. Matthew's portrait of the religious leaders, therefore, is unabashedly polemical, and of this the reader needs to be forewarned.

While this second edition has been enlarged, it has also been revised. Chapter 5, on Jesus' use of "the Son of man," has been substantially rewritten. The aim is to explain not only more fully but also more clearly both the meaning and the function of this self-designation. In the case of all the other Chapters, care has been taken to refine and enhance them. New topics are addressed or new insights developed, the argument has been streamlined, or the text has simply been made more readable. Finally, significant new additions have been made to the literature cited both in the footnotes and in the bibliography.

The debt of gratitude I owe in revising this book is largely to the same persons without whose assistance the original edition, too, would not have seen the light of day. My heartiest thanks go to Harold W. Rast of Fortress Press for approving and supporting the project; to John A. Hollar, also of Fortress Press, for once again turning manuscript into book; to Martha Aycock, reference librarian here at Union Seminary, for securing articles and books not readily available; to Mark A. Powell, now assistant professor of New Testament at Trinity Lutheran Seminary in Columbus, Ohio, for supervising the preparation of the index; and especially to my wife, Barbara, whose spirit and good humor always add spark to every project.

JACK DEAN KINGSBURY

Union Theological Seminary in Virginia
Easter 1987

Abbreviations

AnBib	Analecta biblica
AThD	Acta Theologica Danica
BETL	Bibliotheca ephemeridum theologicarum lovaniensium
BEvT	Beiträge zur evangelischen Theologie
BJRL	*Bulletin of the John Rylands University Library of Manchester*
BU	Biblische Untersuchungen
BWANT	Beiträge zur Wissenschaft vom Alten und Neuen Testament
CBA	Catholic Biblical Association of America
CBQ	*Catholic Biblical Quarterly*
CBQMS	Catholic Biblical Quarterly—Monograph Series
ConBNT	Coniectanea biblica, New Testament
EKK	Evangelisch-Katholischer Kommentar zum Neuen Testament
FFNT	Foundations & Facets: New Testament
FRLANT	Forschungen zur Religion und Literatur des Alten und Neuen Testaments
GBS	Guides to Biblical Scholarship
HNTC	Harper's New Testament Commentaries
HTKNT	Herders theologischer Kommentar zum Neuen Testament
HUCA	*Hebrew Union College Annual*
Int	*Interpretation*
IR	*The Iliff Review*
IDB	G. A. Buttrick, ed., *Interpreter's Dictionary of the Bible* (Nashville: Abingdon Press, 1962)
Ign. *Eph.*	Ignatius, Letter to the Ephesians
Pol.	Ignatius, Letter to Polycarp
Smyrn.	Ignatius, Letter to the Smyrnaeans
IRT	Issues in Religion and Theology
JAAR	*Journal of the American Academy of Religion*

JBL	*Journal of Biblical Literature*
JR	*Journal of Religion*
JSNT	*Journal for the Study of the New Testament*
JSNTSS	Journal for the Study of the New Testament Supplement Series
LXX	Septuagint
Neot	*Neotestamentica*
NLH	*New Literary History*
NovT	*Novum Testamentum*
NovTSup	Novum Testamentum, Supplements
NT	New Testament
NTAbh	Neutestamentliche Abhandlungen
NTL	New Testament Library
NTS	*New Testament Studies*
OBO	Orbis biblicus et orientalis
OT	Old Testament
PRS	*Perspectives in Religious Studies*
RB	*Revue Biblique*
RRel	*Radical Religion*
RSR	*Recherches de science religieuse*
SANT	Studien zum Alten und Neuen Testament
SBL	Society of Biblical Literature
SBLDS	SBL Dissertation Series
SBM	Stuttgarter biblische Monographien
SBS	Stuttgarter Bibelstudien
ScrMin	Scripta minora
SNTSMS	Society for New Testament Studies Monograph Series
ST	*Studia Theologica*
TDNT	G. Kittel and G. Friedrich, eds., *Theological Dictionary of the New Testament* (Grand Rapids: Wm. B. Eerdmans, 1964–76)
TI	Theological Inquiries
TS	*Theological Studies*
TynBul	*Tyndale Bulletin*
WUNT	Wissenschaftliche Untersuchungen zum Neuen Testament
ZNW	*Zeitschrift für die Neutestamentliche Wissenschaft*
ZTK	*Zeitschrift für Theologie und Kirche*

1
Understanding Matthew: A Literary-Critical Approach

INTRODUCTORY REMARKS

The goal of this book is to explore the story that is found in the Gospel according to Matthew. To guide this exploration, the method to be used is that known as literary criticism. Since literary criticism has many guises, the method itself begs to be discussed (Chap. 1). This discussion, in turn, stands in the service of the principal task of the book: to trace the story-lines of Jesus (Chaps. 2–4), of the religious leaders (Chap. 7), and of the disciples (Chap. 8). In addition, there are also special topics that call for attention. These have to do with Jesus' designation of himself as the Son of man (Chap. 5), the disposition and character of the great speeches Jesus delivers (Chap. 6), and the social and religious circumstances in which the Christian community that stood behind Matthew's Gospel apparently lived (Chap. 9).

As presently practiced, much of literary criticism focuses on the Gospels as narratives. It involves a study of the content of these narratives and of the rhetorical techniques by means of which they are told. One literary theorist, Seymour Chatman, has provided a useful outline for discussing the constituent parts of narrative,[1] and David Rhoads has shown with what profit this outline can be employed in investigating the Gospel of Mark.[2] My investigation of Matthew's Gospel will also draw from Chatman's outline, and supplement it as well with the work of others.

Literary-critically, the Gospel of Matthew is a unified narrative, or "artis-

---

1. Cf. Chatman, *Story and Discourse*.
2. Cf. Rhoads, "Narrative Criticism," 411–34; also Rhoads and Michie, *Mark as Story*.

tic whole."[3] The story it relates is governed, as will be seen, by a single, overarching "evaluative point of view." Moreover, the action, thought, and interactions of the characters are all organized by means of a coherent plot. This plot has a beginning, middle, and artful ending.

As a unified narrative, Matthew invites the reader or interpreter to concentrate precisely on the gospel story being told. In this respect, literary-critical method differs noticeably from the historical-biographical, the form-critical, and the redaction-critical approaches to Matthew. Interpreters taking one or the other of these approaches have tended to regard the gospel story chiefly as a source from which to obtain information about historical, social, or religious realities that existed beyond the boundaries of the story in the "real world" of the first century. Thus, uppermost in the minds of certain nineteenth- and early twentieth-century proponents of the historical-biographical approach was the use of Matthew to establish a factually sound portrait of the life and ministry of the historical Jesus.[4] Following World War I, form critics viewed Matthew as a compilation from which to derive sayings or stories of Jesus that could be made to provide a sketch of the rise and development of the gospel tradition between Easter and the time of the writing of the Gospels themselves. And in the years since World War II, redaction critics have largely scrutinized Matthew so as to reconstruct the theology of the first evangelist or the social situation of the community to which he belonged.

To approach Matthew's Gospel as a unified narrative, however, is to attend to the very story it tells. When one reads Matthew, one temporarily takes leave of one's familiar world of reality and enters into another world that is autonomous in its own right. This world, which possesses its own time and space, is peopled by characters and marked by events that, in varying degrees, are extolled or decried in accordance with this world's own system of values. By inhabiting this world one experiences it, and having experienced it, one leaves and returns, perhaps changed, to one's own world.[5]

THE STORY OF THE NARRATIVE

Like other narratives, Matthew's Gospel may be said to comprise two parts. Chatman designates these two parts as the "story" and its "dis-

3. On the canonical Gospels as being "unified narratives," note the following remark by Frye ("Literary Perspective for the Criticism of the Gospels," 220 n. 42): "The conviction which I gain from studying the Gospels is that each is a narrative of considerable literary merit, in which diverse materials have been so effectively integrated that each Gospel should be treated as a literary work in its own right." Cf. also Combrink, "Structure of the Gospel of Matthew as Narrative," 66–68; Petersen, Literary Criticism, 20–23, 28, 40; Rhoads, "Narrative Criticism," 412–14.

4. Cf. Kingsbury, Matthew (Proclamation Commentaries), 1–9.

5. Cf. Uspensky, Poetics of Composition, 137.

course."[6] The "story" of Matthew is of the life of Jesus from conception and birth to death and resurrection. The "discourse" of Matthew is the means whereby this story of Jesus' life is told. In simple terms, the "story" is "what" is told, whereas the "discourse" is "how" the story is told.

Events

The story of a narrative like Matthew's Gospel encompasses, according to Chatman, three elements, namely, "events," "characters," and "settings."[7] "Events" are the string of incidents, or actions, which stretches the length of the story. They comprise the "plot," or flow, of a story. To create a "plot," the author arranges the events of a story in a particular temporal and causal sequence so as to elicit from the reader some desired response.[8] In Chapters 2–4, the plot of Matthew's story will be traced in detail. The concern here is to discuss the element of conflict.

The element of conflict is central to the plot of Matthew.[9] Jesus is the royal Son of God in whom God's end-time Rule is a present, albeit hidden, reality (3:17; 12:28). He is thus the supreme agent of God who "thinks the things of God" (16:23e; 11:27). The conflicts in which he becomes embroiled are with Satan (4:1–11), demons (12:28), the forces of nature and of illness,[10] civil authorities (such as Herod and Pilate),[11] Gentiles (including Roman soldiers),[12] Israel,[13] and, above all, Israel's religious leaders.[14] On those occasions when the disciples, too, "think the things not of God, but of humans," Jesus likewise engages them in conflict.[15] In one instance, in Gethsemane, he even struggles with himself (26:36–46). In the time following the resurrection, the exalted Jesus, through his missionary church, will also enter into conflict with the nations (24:14; 25:31–46).

Noteworthy about these conflicts in which Jesus involves himself is the fact that whereas he freely employs his incomparable authority to vanquish Satan, demons, and the forces of nature and illness, he chooses not to

6. Chatman, *Story and Discourse*, 19–27.

7. Ibid., 26 (chap. 2).

8. On the topic of "plot" in general, cf. the fine survey by Matera ("Plot of Matthew's Gospel," 235–40).

9. Rhoads ("Narrative Criticism," 415) discusses this point with reference to Mark, but it is, of course, no less true of Matthew.

10. Cf. 4:23–24; chaps. 8–9; 11:5; 12:9–13, 15, 22; 14:14, 15–21, 22–33; 15:21–28, 29–31, 32–38; 17:14–21; 19:2; 20:29–34; 21:14–16, 18–22.

11. Cf. chaps. 2, 27; also 14:1–13.

12. Cf. 8:28–34; 27:27–31, 32–37.

13. Cf. 11:16–19, 20–24, 25; 13:10–13; 27:25.

14. Cf. 9:3, 11, 34; 12:2, 10, 14, 24–37, 38–45; 15:1–14; 16:1–4; 19:3; 21:12—23:39; chaps. 26–27.

15. Cf. 8:21–22, 23–27; 14:28–32; 16:5–12, 21–23; 17:14–20; 19:13–15; 20:20–28; 26:25, 30–35, 36–46.

compel humans to do his bidding (23:37; 26:37–45, 53).[16] On the contrary, he calls humans to repentance in view of the gracious nearness of God's kingly Rule (4:17). The upshot is that the conflict on which the plot of Matthew's story turns is that between Jesus and Israel.

Israel in Matthew comprises two larger groups: the Jewish crowds and their leaders. As the reader quickly discovers, until the passion the crowds are generally well-disposed toward Jesus. Jesus' conflict with them is over whether he can bring them to hear his message of the Kingdom and to give him their allegiance (4:17). At the outset, the prospects that Jesus will attain his goal appear to be bright, for John the Baptist readies the crowds to receive Jesus, the Coming One (3:5–6, 11).

On a negative note, however, the reader also encounters from the beginning "warning passages" implicating the crowds. All Jerusalem is startled when it hears that the King of the Jews has been born (2:3). With no one in Israel does Jesus find the great faith a Gentile exhibits (8:10–13). Jesus commissions the disciples to a mission in Israel but predicts only failure and persecution for them (chap. 10). In an address to the crowds concerning John, Jesus censures them as "this generation" that turns away from both John and himself (11:16–19). And in an interlude during his discourse in parables, Jesus refers to the crowds in harsh terms, characterizing them as being blind, deaf, and without understanding (13:2, 13). The effect of these warning passages is to lead the reader to anticipate that Jesus will not, finally, succeed in winning the crowds over to his side.

As if to grant Jesus time to woo the crowds, it is not until his arrest that they oppose him as enemies (26:47–56). In fact, their attitude toward him changes so abruptly as to occasion surprise for the reader. At 21:45–46, it is yet reported that the crowds trigger fear in the religious leaders, thus prompting the latter to forgo any attempt to arrest Jesus on the spot. At 22:33, the crowds respond to Jesus' teaching with the same amazement with which his sermon from atop the mount had earlier been received (7:28). At 23:1, the crowds join with the disciples in forming the audience to whom Jesus addresses his words of woe against the scribes and Pharisees. And at 26:4–5, the crowds are still regarded by the religious leaders as a threat to their guileful plans to capture Jesus and kill him. Despite all this, however, at Jesus' arrest the same crowds whom he had daily been teaching in the temple, armed with swords and clubs and acting on orders from the chief priests and the elders, suddenly appear with Judas in order to take Jesus by force (26:47, 55). Indeed, what is yet more ironic is that these people, to whom God had sent Jesus as Shepherd and King (2:6), should also shout aloud to Pilate, the Roman governor, "His blood be on us and on

16. This observation, made by Rhoads ("Narrative Criticism," 415) relative to Mark, applies also to Matthew.

our children!" (27:25). The repudiation of Jesus by the people of Israel is complete.

Not the crowds, however, but the religious leaders are the implacable adversaries of Jesus.[17] Jesus' conflict with them is to the death. Entrusted by God with the oversight of Israel (21:33), the leaders are the appointed guardians of the law and the tradition on the one hand and of the temple cult on the other, the essentials that make Israel distinct as a nation. In Matthew's story, the leaders are the epitome of what it means to "think the things not of God, but of humans" (15:6–8, 13). From the outset, they are resolutely opposed to Jesus, for the first offense with which they charge him, blasphemy against God, is at the same time the offense for which they finally condemn him to death (9:3; 25:65–66).

Although Jesus' conflict with the religious leaders is invariably grave, the factor that changes dramatically as one moves through the story is the level of tension. At the beginning this is at a low ebb, but after a time it rises perceptibly. For example, in the first part of the story (1:1—4:16) the reader senses only imperfectly the tension that will later tax so severely Jesus' relationship with the religious leaders. Fundamentally, the purpose of this first part is to introduce the reader to Jesus on the one hand and to the religious leaders on the other. Nonetheless, in three scenes the specter of conflict suddenly appears. At 2:3–6, the religious leaders, in making their debut in the story, stand forth as the allies of wicked King Herod. In 3:7, the leaders are denounced by John the Baptist, the forerunner of Jesus, as being as evil as a "brood of vipers." And in the pericope on Jesus' confrontation with Satan, the groundwork is laid for a later point in the story at which the reader will recognize that the religious leaders, in their confrontations with Jesus, show that they have affinity with Satan (4:1–11).[18]

In the second part of the story (4:17—16:20), the reader looks on as the tension between Jesus and the religious leaders gradually mounts until it reaches the breaking point. In the first half of the second part (4:17—11:1), the reader is initially led to anticipate conflict, and then takes note as conflict finally erupts. To lead the reader to anticipate conflict, sayings of Jesus and of Matthew as narrator occur casting the religious leaders in a negative light. In the Sermon on the Mount Jesus variously predicts persecution for the disciples at the hands of Israel (5:11–12; cf. 23:29–36), declares that the righteousness of the scribes and Pharisees is insufficient for gaining entrance into the Kingdom of Heaven (5:20), and enjoins the disciples to practice their piety, not after the manner of the hypocrites in the synagogues whose aim it is to win public acclaim for themselves, but in true worship of God (6:1–18). Following the sermon, Matthew remarks,

17. Cf. below, Chap. 7; also Powell, "Religious Leaders."
18. Cf., e.g., 4:3 with 16:1; 19:3; 22:18, 35.

with a sidelong glance at the scribes, that they, unlike Jesus, are "without authority" in their teaching (7:28–29). Later, Jesus, after praising a Gentile because of his great faith, asserts that whereas the sons of the Kingdom will be cast into the darkness outside, Gentiles will sit at table in the future Kingdom with Abraham, Isaac, and Jacob (8:11–12). And later still, Jesus, approached by a scribe who would arrogate to himself the authority to become his disciple, replies with a word that turns the scribe away (8:19–20).[19]

Led by these sayings to anticipate conflict, the reader watches as the first controversies between Jesus and the religious leaders flare up (chap. 9). Nevertheless, serious as these controversies are—the first complaint lodged against Jesus charges him, it will be recalled, with blaspheming God (9:3)—they are still "preliminary" in nature: their function is to prepare the reader for the more intense conflict soon to come. Three observations make this apparent: (a) The conflict the reader observes here in chapter 9 is not so acutely confrontational as subsequent conflict, for Jesus is not himself directly attacked for something he himself says or does. (b) This conflict does not have to do with the Mosaic law as such. (c) And however acrid this conflict, it does not incite the religious leaders to make the fateful decision to kill Jesus.

If the conflict of Matthew 9 is still preliminary to the more intense conflict to come, this more intense conflict bursts forth in the latter half of part two of Matthew's story (11:2—16:20). What distinguishes this conflict is the fact that the three features that were so conspicuously absent from earlier conflict now stand out prominently: (a) Debate becomes acutely confrontational, which is to say that for the first time in Matthew's story Jesus is himself directly attacked for an act he himself intends to perform (12:9–13). (b) Debate concerns the Mosaic law itself (12:1–8, 9–13). (c) And debate gives rise to such rancor in the Jewish leaders that they conspire to take Jesus' life (12:14). With this sharp turn of events, Jesus' conflict with the religious leaders has now become irreconcilably hostile and the tension between Jesus and them extreme. Moreover, as a sign that the situation is not likely to improve, Jesus and the religious leaders continue to clash in fierce debate throughout this latter half of the story's second part (12:24–37, 38–45; 15:1–11; 16:1–4).

In the third part of Matthew's story (16:21—28:20), the reader observes the conflict between Jesus and the religious leaders run its course to resolution. In this part, too, the conflict remains irreconcilably hostile and the level of tension high. As Jesus journeys to Jerusalem (16:21—20:34), only once do the religious leaders engage him in controversy. They ask him whether the law allows for a man to divorce his wife for any cause, and he,

19. On the interpretation of this disputed passage, see below, pp. 133–34.

replying in the negative,[20] makes use of this controversy to instruct his disciples (19:3–12). Once he is in Jerusalem, however, Jesus spends the bulk of his time in the temple (21:1—23:39). Immediately preceding his passion, therefore, the temple becomes the site of a climactic, two-day clash between him and the religious leaders (21:12—23:39).

To highlight the climactic nature of Jesus' clash with the religious leaders in the temple, Matthew makes effective use of several rhetorical devices. The most notable of these are the following: (a) The controversies in the temple are all acutely confrontational in tone, for Jesus is himself directly attacked in each instance over some matter having to do with his own actions or views.[21] (b) The questions put to Jesus are all of the weightiest kind, for they touch on such issues as his right to be acclaimed as the Son of David (21:15–16), or the source of the authority on which he acts (21:23), or his understanding of the law[22] or of scripture (22:42–45). (c) The atmosphere in which these controversies take place is one of intense hostility, as is evident from the desire of the leaders at one point to seize Jesus (21:46). (d) Debate between Jesus and the religious leaders in the temple continues virtually unabated, as one after another the various groups that together comprise the whole gamut of Jewish officialdom step forward either to challenge him or, at the last, to be challenged by him: the chief priests and the scribes (21:15), the chief priests and the elders of the people (21:23), the disciples of the Pharisees with the Herodians (22:16), the Sadducees (22:23), a lawyer of the Pharisees (22:35), and the Pharisees (22:41).

What is the outcome of this two-day clash between Jesus and the religious leaders in the temple? The outcome is that the leaders, unable to best Jesus in even a single debate, are at the last reduced by him to silence. As Matthew, the narrator, comments at 22:46: "And no one was able to answer him a word, nor from that day did any one dare to ask him any more questions." Defeated in debate, the leaders withdraw from Jesus in the temple, just as Satan, also defeated by Jesus in debate, had earlier withdrawn from him (4:11). Having exhausted all options but one, the leaders meet together and conspire on how to bring about the arrest and death of Jesus (26:3–5).

From the passion account itself, the reader learns of the resolution of Jesus' conflict with the religious leaders (chaps. 26–28). Ironically, both Jesus and the leaders act to achieve Jesus' death, but for radically different

20. Specifically, Jesus' reply in 19:9 (cf. also 5:32) reads: "And I say to you that whoever divorces his wife, *parektos logou porneias,* and marries another, commits adultery." The words in italics comprise the so-called "exceptive clause," and scholars have had difficulty determining the exact meaning of Jesus' reply because they are not certain of the meaning of this clause. For a discussion of it, see below, p. 66, n. 12.

21. Cf. 21:16, 23; 22:16, 23, 35; also 22:41.

22. Cf. 22:17, 24, 36.

reasons. From the leaders' standpoint, they believe that by bringing Jesus to the cross, they are doing the will of God and purging Israel of a false messiah, or "deceiver" (26:65–66; 27:63). From his own standpoint, Jesus also embraces the cross, but he does so because he understands himself to be God's royal Son sent to shed his blood for the forgiveness of sins (21:37–38; 26:28). Since both Jesus and the leaders act to achieve the same goal but with contradictory motivations, God is the one who ultimately decides the conflict between them. By raising Jesus from the dead and investing him with all authority, God vindicates Jesus and thus decides the conflict in his favor (28:5–6, 18). Ironically, therefore, the cross of Jesus in Matthew's story serves not as the symbol of his destruction, but as the means whereby God accomplishes the salvation of all humankind, Jew and Gentile alike (1:21).

As we noted above, the conflict on which the plot of Matthew's story turns is that between Jesus and Israel, especially the religious leaders. In addition to Israel, however, Jesus is also depicted as entering into conflict with the nations and with the disciples.

Because the focus of Matthew's story is on the life of Jesus between conception and resurrection, Jesus' conflict with the nations is not part of the story's plot. This conflict, not narrated in story form, is instead sketched by Jesus in prophetic utterances about the future (cf. chaps. 24–25). This means that as Jesus tells of this conflict, he no longer sees himself as the earthly Son of God but as the exalted Son of God whom God will invest with all authority in heaven and on earth (28:18–20). As the exalted One, Jesus will dispatch his missionary church to make all nations, including Israel, his disciples (23:34; 24:14). The point at which Jesus' conflict with the nations will finally be resolved is at the consummation of the age (24:3). At that time, the exalted Jesus will return in power and splendor to preside over the final judgment to the salvation or condemnation of all (16:27; 25:31–46). Indeed, Jesus' sudden appearance will signal the coming of God's great Kingdom in glory, and he will reign supreme (19:28d; 24:29–31).

By contrast, Jesus' conflict with the disciples is a fully embedded in the plot of Matthew's story as is Jesus' conflict with Israel. At places in the story, the disciples, too, "think the things not of God, but of humans" (16:21–23). Nevertheless, the conflict Jesus has with them is of a fundamentally different order from that between Jesus and Israel or between Jesus and the nations. The disciples, after all, are not enemies of Jesus but his followers. The source of their conflict with Jesus is their periodic failure to comport themselves in a manner that befits sons of God (5:9, 45) and disciples of Jesus (10:1, 24–25) who live in the sphere of God's end-time Rule (13:11, 38). In like fashion as Jesus calls them to come after him, entrusts them with a mission to Israel, and makes of them the recipients of divine revelation (4:17—16:20), so he must also engage them in conflict as they show themselves to be persons of "little faith,"[23] or fail at once to grasp his words (15:15–16; 16:5–12), or do not avail themselves of the authority he has imparted to them.[24] Moreover, as Jesus journeys to Jerusalem and embarks on his passion (16:21—28:20), his conflict with the disciples intensifies noticeably. They do not, and in fact will not, comprehend the truth that servanthood is the essence of discipleship. The resolution of Jesus' conflict with the disciples is that he does finally lead them to grasp this truth (28:16–20; 10:38). As proof of this, he commissions them at the last to their worldwide ministry (28:18–20; 24:1—25:46). Because the Matthean portrait of the disciples is the subject of Chapter 8 in this book, further comment on Jesus' conflict with the disciples can await that discussion.

To summarize, "events" have been defined as the incidents that occur throughout a story and the "plot" as the peculiar temporal and causal sequence according to which the author has so arranged the events as to elicit from the reader some desired response. Central to the plot of Matthew's story is the element of conflict. The principal conflict pits Israel against Jesus, and the death of Jesus constitutes the primary resolution of this conflict. On another level, Jesus also struggles with the disciples. Here the conflict is to bring them to understanding, or to enable them to overcome their "little faith," or to invite them to avail themselves of the great authority Jesus has given them, or, above all, to lead them to comprehend that the essence of discipleship is servanthood.

Characters

In Chatman's scheme, the story of a narrative encompasses not only "events" and the "plot" to which events give rise but also "characters."[25] Typically, "characters" are the persons who appear in a narrative work such as Matthew's Gospel.[26] Groups of persons, like the "crowds," for example, may function as a single character. "Characterization" has to do with the way in which an author brings characters to life in a narrative.[27] To bring characters to life, an author has at least two methods available to him or her:[28] (a) The author can "show" the reader the characters by letting them speak and act for themselves or by having other characters talk about them or react to them; or (b) the author can arrange to have a narrator simply

23. Cf. 8:26; 14:31; 16:8; also 6:30; 17:20.
24. Cf. 14:16; 15:33; also 17:16, 19.
25. Chatman, *Story and Discourse,* 107–38.
26. This definition is basically that of Abrams (*Glossary of Literary Terms,* 20). Chatman (*Story and Discourse,* 108) believes that it is stating the obvious; he defines a "character" as a "paradigm of traits" (ibid., 126–27).
27. Cf. Rhoads, "Narrative Criticism," 417.
28. Cf. Abrams, *Glossary of Literary Terms,* 21; Rhoads and Michie, *Mark as Story,* 101.

"tell" the reader about them. In Matthew's story, both methods are used, but "showing" is preferred to "telling."

One can distinguish among kinds of characters on the basis of the traits they possess. Chatman defines a "trait" as a personal quality of a character that persists over a part or the whole of a story.[29] Thus, Jesus is described in Matthew as being "obedient" toward God[30] and "compassionate" toward the crowds (9:36; 14:14; 15:32). But although both traits are clearly ascribed to him, the fact that he is compassionate is explicitly stated, whereas the fact that he is obedient must be inferred. But if there are some character traits that the reader must infer, what is to prevent the type of unwarranted "psychologizing" of characters in the gospel stories that was so prevalent in nineteenth-century lives of Jesus? The answer Chatman would give is that the traits attributed to characters must be reflective of the narrative work in question and the contemporary culture in which it arose.[31]

To distinguish among kinds of characters, E. M. Forster[32] posits the first two of the following three categories and M. H. Abrams[33] makes mention of the third. (a) "Round" characters are those who possess a variety of traits, some of which may even conflict, so that their behavior is not necessarily predictable. Round characters are like "real people." In Matthew's story, Jesus and the disciples count as round characters. Jesus is a round character because although he is always cast in a positive light, he nonetheless exhibits such a great number and variety[34] of traits that he effectively becomes a "real person" for the reader. And the disciples are a round character because they exhibit strongly contrasting traits throughout the story. (b) "Flat" characters are those who tend to possess only a few traits but who in any case are highly predictable in their behavior. In Matthew's story, the Jewish crowds and the religious leaders prove to be flat characters. (c) And "stock" characters are those who possess only one trait. In Matthew's story, the minor characters rate as stock characters. The "leper" whom Jesus cleanses, for instance, exhibits the single trait of "faith" (8:1–4).

As these remarks indicate, therefore, the principal characters of Matthew's story are Jesus, the disciples, the religious leaders, the crowds, and the minor characters. Since the protagonist, or leading character, is of course Jesus, the task of characterizing these figures or groups best begins with him.

29. Chatman, *Story and Discourse*, 125.
30. Cf. 3:15; 4:1–11; 26:36–46.
31. Cf. Chatman, *Story and Discourse*, 119–20, 124–26.
32. Forster, *Aspects of the Novel*, 103–18.
33. Cf. *Glossary of Literary Terms*, 185.
34. Jesus can, for example, change rather quickly from being "censorious" (23:13–36) to being "solicitous" (23:37) to being "deeply grieved" and "distressed" (26:37–38).

Jesus

The importance Matthew confers on Jesus conspicuously sets him apart from all other characters. Within the world of his story, Matthew establishes God's system of values as normative.[35] Correspondingly, he presents Jesus as God's supreme agent who is in complete accord with God's system of values. Other than God himself, therefore, Jesus is the one major character whom Matthew always puts in the right. The attitude Jesus takes toward characters and events determines to what extent the reader, too, gives them his or her approval. Hence, more than any other character or group of characters, Jesus influences the plot, or flow, of Matthew's story. For example, even when a babe in the infancy accounts the story revolves around him.

Jesus reveals through his words and deeds how he understands himself, his relationship to God, and his place in the history of salvation. He knows God to be his Father (11:25) and himself to be God's unique Son (11:27; 21:37–38a). As God's Son, he is aware of himself as being the decisive figure in the history of salvation (21:33–44), the one who is the "builder" of the church, the end-time people of God (16:18–19), and who is of ultimate significance for Israel[36] and the Gentiles alike (25:31–46).

How do other characters react to Jesus in Matthew's story? To get some indication of this, one might consider how various characters construe his identity. Though not a character, Matthew, as narrator, announces that he holds Jesus to be Christ, Son of David, Son of Abraham (1:1), and Emmanuel (1:23) and Son of God (2:15). For his part, Joseph, the husband of Mary, does as the angel has commanded and gives "Jesus" his name (1:21, 25). The Magi regard Jesus as the King of the Jews and worship him as such (2:2, 11). Conversely, Herod the Great and, later, Pilate take King of the Jews to mean that Jesus is an insurrectionist (2:6, 13; 27:37). John the Baptist thinks of Jesus as the Coming One, that is, the Messiah, who is to carry out at once the final judgment (3:11–12; 11:2–3). At Jesus' baptism and transfiguration, God affirms him to be his unique Son (3:17; 17:5). Satan, too, knows Jesus to be the Son of God, and tempts him as such (4:3, 6). Demons recognize Jesus as the Son of God and hence as their tormentor (8:29). The religious leaders look upon Jesus as being a deceiver and one who is in collusion with Satan (9:34; 12:24; 27:63). The Jewish crowds, although they twice name Jesus Son of David only to dismiss the idea in the first instance (12:23) and to explain it away in the second (21:9, 11), settle on taking him to be a prophet: John the Baptist, Elijah, Jeremiah, or some other prophet (16:14; 21:11, 46). Like one segment of the crowds, Herod Antipas, too, thinks of Jesus as being John the Baptist raised from the dead (14:2). By

35. See below, n. 118.
36. Cf 12:41–42; 15:24; 21:43.

contrast, the people of Nazareth cannot imagine that Jesus is anyone other than the son of the carpenter (13:55). Again, several of the minor characters address Jesus as the Son of David (9:27; 15:22; 20:30–31; 21:15). And in a different vein, the disciples confess Jesus to be the Son of God (14:33; 16:16), as do the Roman soldiers at the foot of the cross (27:54).

As a barometer of the way characters react to Jesus, what do such diverse views suggest? They suggest that Jesus is an extraordinary personage toward whom others are unable to remain neutral: he evokes fervid responses that run the gamut from ardent confession to abject repudiation. They also suggest that whereas transcendent beings, such as God, Satan, and demons, all know Jesus to be the Son of God, human characters diverge widely in their perceptions of him. Jesus' identity, therefore, is not immediately apparent to humans, which means that if the reader is to grasp the meaning of Matthew's story, he or she must be able to understand and evaluate the basis on which any given human character decides who Jesus is and therefore what he is about.

Which traits does Jesus possess in Matthew's story and how do they manifest themselves in his interaction with others? Because of the multiplicity of traits ascribed to Jesus, he is in Forster's terms a "round" character. Here, however, only those traits can be cited that appear to be crucial. (a) In relation to his mission, Jesus is "saving," "authoritative," and utterly "certain" that he is accomplishing God's purposes. The single most fundamental character trait ascribed to Jesus is the power to save, as the angel declares to Joseph: ". . . you shall call his name Jesus, for he will save his people from their sins" (1:21). Correlatively, with incomparable authority Jesus teaches, preaches, heals, calls disciples, and bests his opponents in debate.[37] And in the sure conviction that he is doing God's will, Jesus journeys to Jerusalem to suffer, die, and be raised (16:21). (b) In relation to God, Jesus is "perfect" (5:48), that is to say, he loves God wholly with heart, soul, and mind (22:37).[38] Jesus loves God with his whole heart, for he is blameless in his fealty to God (4:1–11). Jesus loves God with his whole soul, for he is prepared to surrender his life should God so will (26:36–46). And Jesus loves God with his whole mind, for he lays claim for himself neither to the prerogatives of worldly power[39] nor to the security of family, home, and possessions (8:20; 12:50). (c) In relation to himself, Jesus possesses "integrity." The operative principle in this connection is the affirmation that "by their fruits you will know them" (7:16, 20; 12:33). When Jesus is judged by this principle, no discrepancy is found between what he says and what he does. (d) In relation to his disciples, Jesus is "enabling" and "faithful."

37. Cf. 3:16; 7:29; 9:6; 11:27; 21:23–27 with 4:18–22, 23; 9:9, 35; 11:1.
38. Cf. Gerhardsson, "Hermeneutic Program," 129–50.
39. Cf. 20:25, 28; 21:5.

The disciples have forsaken all to be with Jesus (19:27–29), and Jesus promises them that to the consummation of the age, they can rest assured of his sustaining and abiding presence (18:20; 28:20). *(e)* In relation to the Jewish crowds and the minor characters, Jesus is "compassionate." The crowds in Jesus' eyes are like shepherdless sheep, harassed and helpless, and in his loving concern for them he would gather them to him (9:36; 14:14; 15:32). A number of minor characters approach Jesus for healing, and with rare exception he readily and mercifully grants them their requests (cf. 20:29–34). *(f)* In relation to the religious leaders, Jesus is "confrontational." In Jesus' view, the religious leaders are evil (12:34), and they take after the one with whom they have affinity, the devil or the Evil One (13:38–39). *(g)* And in relation to his death, Jesus is "self-giving." The essence of righteousness is love: toward God and toward the neighbor. Love toward the neighbor means serving others, not lording it over them. In his death, Jesus serves all others, for he gives his life to redeem the world (20:25–28).

Accordingly, Jesus, the protagonist, stands forth in Matthew's story as the supreme representative of God's system of values who understands himself to be God's unique Son and the decisive figure in the history of salvation; who evokes a multiplicity of perceptions from others concerning his identity as well as fervid responses that range from confession to repudiation; and who is in his interactions with others "saving," "authoritative," "enabling" and "faithful," "compassionate," "confrontational," and utterly "self-giving," even while proving himself to be a person of "integrity" whose "perfect fealty" is to God. How are such other persons as the disciples, the religious leaders, the crowds, and the many anonymous individuals to be characterized? To ascertain this, one will want to pay special attention to the attitudes that Matthew as narrator and Jesus take toward these characters and that the characters take toward themselves.

The Disciples

Though a group, the disciples may be treated as a single character. Like Jesus, they are "round," but whereas this is the case with Jesus because of the great number of traits he possesses, this is the case with the disciples because they possess not only numerous traits but also traits that conflict. Except for Judas's act of betrayal[40] and perhaps the climactic resurrection scene in Galilee (28:16–20), the disciples do not greatly influence the plot, or flow, of Matthew's story. This is not to deny, of course, that there are not also scenes and speeches involving the disciples that have crucial significance for the time that is envisaged following the death and resurrection of Jesus.[41]

40. Cf. 26:14–16, 20–25, 47–49.
41. Cf., e.g., chaps. 5–7; 10:16–42; 16:18–20; 17:24—18:35; chaps. 23–25; 26:26–29; 28:16–20.

Because the disciples possess conflicting traits, the reader is invited, depending on the attitude Matthew as narrator or Jesus takes toward them on any given occasion, to identify with them or to distance himself or herself from them. It is through such granting or withholding of approval on cue, therefore, that the reader becomes schooled in the values that govern the life of discipleship in Matthew's story.

Matthew divides the second part of his story (4:17—16:20) into two major sections (4:17—11:1; 11:2—16:20). Within the first section, he rehearses the call of the disciples and their ministry to Israel (4:17—11:1). In so doing, he likewise identifies the fundamental marks of discipleship. For example, the disciples, summoned by Jesus to come after him, are "followers" who give him their total allegiance and embrace the task of becoming fishers of men.[42] Having forsaken home, family, and goods, they become "brothers" of Jesus and of one another.[43] As disciples, they are "learners" (23:10), attending to Jesus' words, including all his discourses, and bearing witness to his deeds. They are likewise "sons of God," for Jesus teaches them to know God as Father and to do his will.[44] And because in summoning them Jesus invites them to live in the sphere of God's end-time Rule,[45] he furthermore graciously enables them to share in his "authority" (10:1) and instructs them in a "ministry" in Israel in which they, too, will preach the nearness of the Kingdom and heal every sickness and every infirmity (10:1, 5, 7). Conversely, through their association with Jesus, they also become "vulnerable" to attack from outside enemies.[46]

The various character traits associated with these marks—being "loyal," "loving," "attentive" and "observant," "obedient" and "trusting," "authoritative," "servantlike," and "vulnerable"—all cast the disciples in a positive light. Nevertheless, conflicting traits also surface in 4:17—11:1. The scribe whom Jesus turns away from following him is "presumptuous": he wrongly believes he can surmount the rigors of discipleship on the strength of his own resolve (8:19–20). The man who is already a disciple and whom Jesus commands to follow him at once is "irresolute": he fails to recognize that discipleship brooks no divided loyalty (8:21–22). And the disciples on the stormy sea fall prey to "little faith": not realizing that their faith will sustain them in the peril they face, they give in to cowardice (8:23–27).

In the section 11:2—16:20, the disciples are characterized in the main by being contrasted with Israel: while Israel is darkened and without understanding, the disciples are "enlightened." Thus, what the Father conceals

42. Cf. 4:19–20, 21–22; 8:22; 9:9; also 19:27.
43. Cf. 10:2–4; 12:49; 18:35; 23:8; 25:40; 28:10; also 19:27.
44. Cf. 5:45; 13:38; 6:9; 7:21.
45. Cf. 4:17, 23; 9:35; 10:7; 13:38.
46. Cf. 9:14; chap. 10; 12:1–2; 15:2; chaps. 24–25; 27:64; 28:11–15.

from the wise in Israel, he reveals through Jesus to "infants," that is, to the disciples (11:25–27). Whereas all segments of Israel repudiate Jesus, the disciples become his new family called to do the will of his heavenly Father (chaps. 11–12). To the Jewish crowds "it is not given" to know the mysteries of the Kingdom of Heaven, but to the disciples "it is given" (13:11). If the Jewish public and Herod Antipas mistakenly perceive Jesus to be a prophet of whatever note (16:13–14), the disciples rightly confess him to be the Messiah, the Son of the living God (16:16). And if the leaders of the Jews believe Jesus to be in collusion with Satan (12:24), provoke him to controversy,[47] and plot his death (12:14), the disciple Peter stands forth as the "rock" on which Jesus will build his church (16:18).

But again, conflicting with this trait of being enlightened are other, unfavorable traits. On two occasions the disciples, faced with a challenging situation, become "distraught": although Jesus has given them to share in his authority, they do not undertake to feed the crowds but despair of their resources (14:16–17; 15:33). Out on the water, the disciples lose the courage of faith and become exceedingly "fearful": when confronted with what they think is an apparition they cry out in terror (14:26), and Peter, having received permission to walk on the water, is suddenly overcome by doubt (14:30–31). And instead of availing themselves of their gifts of understanding, the disciples stand "perplexed" before a parable of Jesus and Peter asks that it be explained to them (15:15–16; cf. 16:5–12).

In the third part of Matthew's story (16:21—28:20), the characterization of the disciples develops principally through a direct comparison of their values with the values of Jesus. To be sure, the disciples also evince some of the same traits in this part that they did earlier. On a positive note, they continue to be "learners";[48] and they are "obedient" as well, as when they carry out Jesus' instructions for obtaining the donkey and the colt (21:2–7) or in making preparations for the celebration of the Passover (26:18–19). Negatively, the disciples likewise remain susceptible to bouts of "little faith," as when they are unable to heal the demoniac boy (17:14–20); and because they do not realize that faith to perform miracles is also theirs simply for the asking, they are unwarrantedly "surprised" when the fig tree Jesus curses suddenly withers (21:18–22).

Still, central to this part of Matthew's story is the stark contrast that exists between Jesus' view of his passion and the disciples' view. Jesus announces to the disciples that it is God's will that he suffer and be killed (16:21). Peter, however, takes strong issue with this and asserts that, to the contrary, God should forbid that this might ever happen to him (16:22). This sharp exchange constitutes a clash of two systems of values: that grounded in

47. Cf. chap. 12; 15:1–20; 16:1–4.
48. Cf. chaps. 18; 24–25.

"thinking the things of God," and that grounded in "thinking the things of humans" (16:23e). Since Jesus thinks the things of God, he is "self-giving" and construes his passion in terms of rendering to others self-sacrificial service (20:28). Since Peter and the disciples think the things of humans, they are "self-concerned," bent on saving their lives and avoiding suffering and death (16:25).

On the journey to Jerusalem, the disciples reflect in their behavior this latter system of values. To their credit, they do understand Jesus' predictions of his passion (26:2), and it is said, following the second one, that they are "saddened" by it (17:22–23). Nevertheless, they also show that they are "status-conscious" (19:13–15), "enamored of wealth" (19:23–26), "anxious about their future" (19:27), and "desirous of power and position" (20:20–24).

The upshot is that when Jesus actually enters upon his passion, the disciples, although they want to stand by him (26:41), are totally unable to cope with events and end up by failing him. At first they show that they are "imperceptive" to the true meaning of what is taking place: when the woman pours ointment on Jesus' head, they indignantly label as wasteful what is in reality the preparation of his body for burial (26:8, 12). Later, they show that they are also "self-deluded" and Judas shows that he is "deceitful." Thus, Judas, although he has already sold himself to the chief priests (26:14–16), asks Jesus whether he will be the one to betray him in such manner as to anticipate that Jesus' answer will be no (26:25). And the other disciples boldly express false confidence in their ability to remain loyal to Jesus: they all insist that if need be, they will die with him rather than deny him (26:30–35). In Gethsemane, too, yet another example of this same "self-delusion" occurs: Peter and the two sons of Zebedee, though confident that they possess the fortitude to face death with Jesus, cannot even muster the strength to watch with him but instead fall asleep (26:36–46). Indeed, indicative of how "futile" are the thoughts and actions of the disciples relative to Jesus' passion is the attempt by one of them upon Jesus' arrest to defend him by drawing a sword (26:51–53). But be that as it may, the sober result is that following the arrest of Jesus, all the disciples in one way or another desert him: (a) Most become "disloyal" to him by breaking their bond of allegiance and fleeing (26:31, 56); (b) Judas, who has already been "deceitful" (26:25) and "treacherous" (26:47–49), soon becomes "self-destructive" as well (27:3–10); and (c) Peter, by denying Jesus, becomes "apostate" (26:69–75). The disciples had wanted to stand by Jesus in his passion, but they could not. As Jesus had said, ". . . the spirit indeed is willing, but the flesh is weak" (26:41). In relation to the passion of Jesus, the disciples exhibit many traits that spring from a system of values that is not that of Jesus.

The narrator's last word on the eleven disciples, however, is not one of failure. On the mountain in Galilee, the risen Jesus reconciles them to himself. Although they can still fall victim to "little faith" (28:17), they nonetheless undertake the worldwide missionary task to which he commissions them on the "authority" he grants them and "confident" of his sustaining presence to the consummation of the age (28:16–20).

Perhaps the preceding characterization of the disciples can best be summarized by relating it to the following word Jesus speaks to the disciples in his missionary discourse: "It is sufficient for a disciple to be like his teacher . . ." (10:25). By inviting the reader to approve of some of the traits of the disciples and to disapprove of others, Matthew brings the reader to a realization of what this rubric means. Summoned by Jesus, the disciples become "followers" who live in the sphere of God's end-time Rule; "learners" and "sons of God"; "brothers" of Jesus and of one another; ones who share in Jesus' "authority" and "ministry" to Israel and are consequently "vulnerable" to attack; and ones who are, in contrast to Israel, the recipients of divine revelation and hence are "enlightened." On the one hand, therefore, the disciples are "like" their teacher.

On the other hand, the disciples are also "unlike" their teacher. The one or the other of them can be "irresolute," or they can be susceptible to bouts of "little faith," or they can become "distraught" or "fearful." When faced with the passion of Jesus, they even operate with a system of values that is oriented toward "self-concern" and "saving one's life" and is therefore diametrically opposed to that of Jesus. The result is that they show themselves, on the way to Jerusalem, to be "status-conscious," "enamored of wealth," "anxious about their future," and "desirous of power and position"; and, during the passion, to be "imperceptive," "self-deluded," "futile" in thought and action, and "disloyal." For his part, Judas becomes "deceitful," "treacherous," and "self-destructive"; and Peter becomes, through his denial of Jesus, "apostate." In the thought of Jesus, the disciples are "willing" in spirit but "weak" in flesh. Nonetheless, the final word on the disciples is that Jesus reconciles them to himself. Although they will continue to be beset by "little faith," they nevertheless undertake the worldwide mission with which Jesus entrusts them, "empowered" by him and "confident" of his sustaining and abiding presence.

The Religious Leaders[49]

The term "leaders" is itself used in Matthew's story to refer to groups of persons who occupy positions of authority in Israel (15:14; 23:16, 24). Literary-critically, therefore, this term can also aptly be used to denote all such groups of persons. Those who comprise the religious leaders are the Pharisees, the Sadducees, the chief priests, the elders, and the scribes. In

49. Cf. also Kingsbury, "Developing Conflict between Jesus and the Jewish Leaders."

one instance, mention is likewise made of the Herodians (22:16).[50] Because all of these groups are presented in Matthew's story as forming a united front opposed to Jesus,[51] they can be treated as a single character.

Except for Jesus himself, the religious leaders are the ones who influence most the development of the plot of Matthew's story. Their characterization is, in fact, shaped through their conflict with Jesus. But if Jesus is a "round" character, the religious leaders are a "flat" character. The many traits ascribed to them are in essence manifestations of a single "root trait," and they give no evidence of undergoing change in the course of the story. The attitudes that John the Baptist, Jesus, and Matthew as narrator adopt toward them consistently cause the reader to distance himself or herself from them. On this score, the same can also be said of such figures as Herod the Great, Archelaus, Herod Antipas, Pilate, the Roman soldiers who abuse and crucify Jesus (but note their "conversion" at 27:54), and the guard of soldiers ordered to stand watch over Jesus' tomb.

Despite this depiction of the various groups of leaders as a united front and not as the diverse or even conflicting parties or classes history knows them to have been, some few historical distinctions among them can nevertheless be observed. For example, the stereotyped phrase by which reference is made to the High Council, or Sanhedrin (26:59), is "the chief priests and the elders (of the people)."[52] Others who are also members of the Sanhedrin are the scribes;[53] and the high priest, who is the presiding officer, is Caiaphas (26:3, 57). Historically, until the fall of Jerusalem in A.D. 70 the Sanhedrin exercised broad powers in Palestine of a religious, political, and judicial nature.[54] Necessarily, however, it was obliged to defer to the authority of the respective prefects Rome appointed to Palestine.[55] In Matthew's story, the Roman prefect of note is of course Pilate, so that it is only with his approval and under the auspices of his office that the sentence of death the Sanhedrin gives Jesus can legally be carried out (26:65–66; chap. 27). In other respects, whereas the chief priests and the elders are associated more particularly with Jerusalem and the temple,[56] the scribes and the Pharisees are closely linked to the synagogue[57] and very

50. In 22:16, mention is made of the "Herodians" in conjunction with the disciples of the Pharisees, but how the reader is to think of them is far from certain (cf., e.g., Sandmel, "Herodians," 2:594–95; Gnilka, Evangelium nach Markus, 1:128–29).

51. Cf., e.g., Hummel, Auseinandersetzung, 12–22; Walker, Heilsgeschichte im ersten Evangelium, 11–33; Van Tilborg, Jewish Leaders, 1–6.

52. Cf. 21:23; 26:3, 47; 27:1, 3, 12, 20; 28:11–12.

53. Cf. 26:57; also 16:21; 27:41.

54. Cf. Reicke, New Testament Era, 142–52.

55. Cf. ibid., 138, 144.

56. Cf., e.g., 16:21; 21:23; 26:3, 47; 27:1, 3, 12, 20; 28:11–12; also 2:3–4; 20:18; 21:15; 26:14, 59.

57. Cf. 23:6, 34; also 6:2, 5; 10:17; 12:2, 9, 14.

frequently mentioned in connection with matters of the law[58] and of the tradition of the elders (cf., e.g., 15:1–2).

How do John the Baptist, Jesus, and Matthew as narrator view the religious leaders, and what do the latter disclose of themselves? Most immediately, the impression one gets is that the religious leaders exhibit numerous character traits in Matthew's story. Close scrutiny, however, reveals that these traits are in reality manifestations of a single "root trait." The first major appearance the religious leaders in the persons of the Pharisees and Sadducees make in Matthew's story is in the pericope on the ministry of John the Baptist. The first words John directs at them are the epithet with which he denounces them, namely, "brood of vipers" (3:7). At the heart of this epithet lies the notion that the religious leaders are "evil." It is because they are evil that they are, as John says, ripe for eschatological judgment (3:7–10) or, as Jesus says, headed for Gehenna (23:33). In yet another word, Jesus captures the meaning of this epithet even more pointedly: "Brood of vipers! How can you speak good, when you are evil?" (12:34).

The notion that "evilness" is the root trait, or fundamental quality, characterizing the religious leaders harmonizes well with the dualism that pervades Matthew's story. In Matthew's world of thought, the one who is "good" is God himself (19:17), and the one who is the "Evil One" is the devil (13:19, 38–39). As the supreme agent of God, Jesus raises up in the world "sons of the Kingdom" (13:38), whereas the devil raises up "sons of the Evil One" (13:38–39). As persons who are evil, the leaders have affinity with the devil (12:34) and their place is within his sphere of influence (cf. 12:26c). They "think evil in their hearts" (9:3–4), and Jesus discerns this (9:4; 22:18). On two occasions Jesus also excoriates them as the epitome of "an evil and adulterous generation," that is, as a generation that does the devil's will and is faithless to God (12:39, 45; 16:4). Opposed as they are to him, Jesus foresees that they will be no less opposed to the post-Easter emissaries he predicts he will send them (23:33–36).

Because the religious leaders are depicted as a flat character whose root trait is "evilness," the reader can surmise early in the story that Matthew's characterization of them will be uniformly, and even monotonously, negative. Made out to be inwardly "evil," the leaders manifest their evilness in a variety of other character traits. These other traits, in turn, are descriptive of the leaders both as "leaders" and as a character-group that interacts with such other characters as Jesus, the disciples, and the crowds.

As "leaders," the religious leaders evince their evilness most prominently by showing themselves to be "hypocritical." Hypocrisy in Matthew's

58. Cf., e.g., 23:2; also 5:20; [9:11]; 12:2; 19:3; 22:15, 17, 34–36; 23:16–22, 23–24.

story is the opposite of being "perfect." To be perfect is to be wholehearted, or single-hearted, in the devotion with which one serves God (5:48; Deut. 18:13). To be hypocritical is to be "divided" in one's fealty to God. Hypocrisy, then, is a form of inner incongruity, to wit: paying honor to God with the lips while the heart is far from him (15:7–8); making pronouncements about what is right while not practicing them (23:3c); and appearing outwardly to be righteous while being inwardly full of lawlessness (23:28).

The hypocrisy that typifies the religious leaders as "leaders" gives rise in its own right to two further character traits: being "lawless," and being "in error" (i.e., being "false teachers"). "Lawlessness" in Matthew's story is not doing the will of God,[59] which is epitomized as loving God with heart, soul, and mind and loving the neighbor as the self (22:37–40). Evidence that the leaders do not love God is adduced from their practice of piety: as they give alms, pray, and fast, they act not in worship of God but ostentatiously, out of eagerness to be seen by people (6:1–18; 23:5). Moreover, their lack of love for the neighbor reveals itself in the fact that they have been faithless in looking after Israel, the trust committed to their care (9:36). In line with this, they have also been willfully impervious to the truth that what God desires most of them in their treatment of others is "mercy" (9:13; 12:7).

Along with being lawless, being "in error" is likewise an expression of the hypocrisy that betokens the religious leaders (22:29). As errorists, the leaders are "false teachers." Esteeming themselves to be expert in matters of law, scripture, and religion, they are in reality unable to "read" scripture so as to discern its meaning.[60] For example, although they know from scripture where the Messiah is to be born (2:4–6) and that they are to expect the coming of Elijah (17:10–11), when Elijah does appear in the person of John the Baptist they refuse him repentance (17:12–13; 21:31–32) and presage thereby that they will also cause Jesus Messiah to suffer (17:12). Entrusted though they are with the task of teaching Israel, the teaching they deliver is "without authority" and, like leaven, "corrupting" (7:29; 16:11–12). A case in point is the Pharisaic "tradition of the elders" (15:2). Observing how it is applied, Jesus decries it as "teaching as doctrines the precepts of men" (15:9), and charges that because of it the very word of God is rendered void (15:6). Then, too, on the whole matter of the way the religious leaders relate to God's word in scripture, the stark irony is that while they are indeed instrumental in bringing this word to fulfillment, they do so as ones who falsify it[61] and who appeal to it with perverse intent;[62] who repudiate the Son whom God has promised in it to Israel (27:43); and who consequently

59. Cf., e.g., 12:50 with 13:41; also 7:21, 23; 23:27–28.
60. Cf. 9:13; 12:3–4, 5–7; 19:4–9; 21:16, 42; 22:31–32.
61. Cf. 15:3–13; 22:29.
62. Cf. 22:17–18, 35; 27:6–10.

bring divine judgment on both themselves (21:41) and the nation (21:43; 22:7).

As hypocrites who are both lawless and false teachers, the religious leaders are furthermore depicted as being "spiritually blind" ("blind guides"; 15:14). In their blindness, they can be observed either to give no leadership to the people (9:36), or ineluctably to lead them into a "pit" (15:13–14). It is in Jesus' speech of woes that illustrations abound as to what it means for the leaders to be blind guides.[63] Accorded the privilege and responsibility of providing access to God's Kingdom through the right teaching of his will, they in fact so teach as to gainsay Jesus and to bar entry to God's Kingdom (23:13). When they proselytize, they make of the convert twice as much a child of Gehenna as themselves, for they bind the convert to their practice of the law (23:15). In drawing punctilious distinctions between oaths that are binding and oaths that are not, they succeed only in showing themselves to be false teachers (23:16–22). While they go beyond what the law requires and tithe the most insignificant of the garden herbs, they neglect in the process those matters that constitute the very essence of the law (23:23–24). Although they scrupulously concern themselves with minor things, such as the cleansing of the outside of vessels, they overlook the circumstance that they ought to be concerned with major things, like the moral integrity of the inner person (23:25–26). Outwardly they appear to people to be righteous, that is, those who know and do God's will; but inwardly they are full of pretension and lawlessness, for they are blind to the will of God (23:27–28). And even though they seemingly honor the prophets, the fact of the matter is that they are no different from their fathers, who did not shrink from shedding the blood of the prophets (23:29–31).

Accordingly, the evilness that characterizes the religious leaders in Matthew's story in their capacity as "leaders" manifests itself in such other character traits as that they are "hypocritical," and by extension also "lawless" and "in error" ("false teachers"), and "spiritually blind" ("blind guides"). How does this same evilness manifest itself in the interaction of the leaders with Jesus, the disciples, and the crowds?

Through their interaction with Jesus, the religious leaders show that they are "implacably opposed" to him. As they see it, Jesus is not the Son of God who speaks and acts on the authority of God so as to call Israel to repentance and to life in the sphere of God's end-time Rule. Instead, they understand him to be a "deceiver" (false messiah) who acts in collusion with Satan and who threatens both to usurp their authority as Israel's rightful leaders and to subvert the nation through the overthrow of law,

---

63. Cf. 23:16, 17, 19, 24, 26. For a thorough treatment of the seven woes of Matthew 23, cf. Garland, *Matthew 23*.

tradition, and temple cult.[64] In their dealings with Jesus, their implacable opposition to him comes to the fore in any number of character traits they exhibit, such as the following: (a) They are "malicious," charging Jesus with blasphemy for forgiving sins (9:3–4), demanding of him a sign to prove that he is not in collusion with Satan (12:38; 16:1–4), and repeatedly putting him to the test in ways that, ironically, place them in the service of Satan, the fountainhead of all temptation.[65] (b) They are "legalistic," insisting on formal observance of the law and tradition even though this results in lovelessness in the face of human need or inattentiveness to the deeper intention of the law.[66] (c) They are "slanderous," defaming Jesus by attributing his exorcisms to the power of Beelzebul (9:32–34; 12:22–24). (d) They are "conspiratorial," plotting the death of Jesus.[67] (e) They are "fearful," determining to arrest Jesus, held by the public to be a prophet, in a manner that will not stir the crowds to action against them (21:46; 26:5). (f) They are "deceptive," scheming to entrap Jesus in argument so that he will be led to discredit himself by advocating either opposition to, or collaboration with, "Caesar" (22:15). (g) They are "cunning," enlisting the services of Judas, the crowds, and Pilate in bringing about the death of Jesus.[68] (h) They are "unjust," striving at Jesus' trial for false testimony by which to condemn him to death (26:59–62). (i) They are "blasphemous," turning the truth of Jesus' claim to be the Messiah Son of God into the lie that it is an offense against the majesty of God (26:63–66; 27:41–43). (j) They are "apprehensive of the future," concerned that not even the death of Jesus will succeed in purging Israel of the "fraud" he has perpetrated (27:62–66). (k) And they are "corrupt" and "mendacious," bribing the soldiers following the resurrection to spread the lie that Jesus' disciples came by night and stole his body (28:11–15).

Should the religious leaders evince their evilness in interaction with Jesus by showing themselves to be "implacably opposed" to him, they relate no differently to the disciples. From the standpoint of the leaders, the disciples, as followers of Jesus, are likewise enemies of Israel, for they, too, violate law and tradition.[69] Although on the whole the leaders have relatively little to do with the disciples, their opposition to them finds expression in character traits like these: (a) They are "accusatory," charging the disciples with breaking the sabbath law by working and with transgressing the tradition of the elders by eating with unwashed hands (12:1–2; 15:1–2). (b) They are "guileful" and "callous," purchasing the services of

64. Cf. 27:63–64; 9:34; 12:24; 7:28–29; 9:8; 15:12–14; 22:29; chap. 23; 12:2, 10; 9:11, 14; 15:1–2.
65. Cf. 4:1, 3; 16:1; 19:3; 22:18, 35.
66. Cf. 9:10–13; 12:1–8, 9–13; 15:1–20.
67. Cf. 12:14; 26:3–4; 27:1.
68. Cf. 26:4, 14–16; 27:2, 11–26; 27:20.
69. Cf. 9:14; 12:1–2; 15:1–2.

Judas to betray Jesus yet leaving Judas to his own devices in coming to terms with his burden of guilt (26:14–16; 27:3–4). *(c)* They are "calumnious," concocting the lie following the resurrection that the disciples were guilty of stealing the body of Jesus (27:64; 28:13). *(d)* And in the future they will be "hostile," inflicting verbal and physical abuse on the disciples and persecuting them even to the point of putting them to death.[70]

Finally, the religious leaders also attest to their evilness by the way they relate to the crowds. On this score, they demonstrate that they are "faithless" to their trust. In the leaders' view, the crowds, although they do not believe in Jesus, are nevertheless susceptible to the deceit he practices. They follow him (e.g., 4:25), are amazed at his teaching and search him out for healing,[71] glorify God over his works,[72] toy with but reject the idea that he might be the Son of David (12:22–23), and hold him to be a prophet (16:14; 21:11, 46). In the way they themselves deal with the crowds, the leaders reveal that they do not attend to the crowds as a trust committed to their care by exhibiting such character traits as the following: *(a)* They are culpably "remiss" as leaders, leaving the crowds "harassed and helpless, like sheep without a shepherd" (9:36). *(b)* They are "pitiless," obligating the crowds to observe a welter of precepts while neglecting to provide them with the necessary guidance (23:4). *(c)* They are "pretentious," drawing attention to themselves for purposes of gaining public acclaim and personal honor (23:5–12). *(d)* They are "fearful," unwilling to arrest Jesus in public lest this arouse the crowds, seeing in him as they do a prophet (21:11, 46; 26:5). *(e)* In their guile they are "manipulative," persuading the crowds to demand of Pilate that Jesus be put to death (26:4; 27:20).

In sum, the religious leaders in Matthew's story are fundamentally characterized as being "evil." This root trait, in turn, manifests itself in other character traits they exhibit both in their capacity as "leaders" and in their interaction with Jesus, the disciples, and the crowds. As "leaders," the religious leaders prove themselves to be "hypocritical," which also results in their being "lawless" and "in error" ("false teachers"), and they are "spiritually blind" ("blind guides"). In terms of the way they interact with Jesus, they show themselves to be "implacably opposed" to him, and they demonstrate this in that they are "malicious," "legalistic," "slanderous," "conspiratorial," "fearful," "deceptive," "cunning," "unjust," "blasphemous," "apprehensive of the future," "corrupt," and "mendacious." In their encounter with the disciples, the leaders reveal that they are likewise "implacably opposed" to them, and they give evidence of this in that they are "accusatory," "guileful," "callous," "calumnious," and potentially "hos-

70. Cf. 5:11–12; 10:17, 23; 23:32–36.
71. Cf. 5:1; 7:28–29; 21:23; 26:55; 4:23–25; 8:16; 12:15; 14:14; 15:30; 19:2.
72. Cf. 9:8, 33; 15:31.

tile." And in their dealings with the crowds, the leaders show that they are "faithless" to them as their trust, and they attest to this by the fact that they are culpably "remiss," "pitiless," "pretentious," "fearful," and "manipulative."

The Crowds

If the characterization of the religious leaders is wholly negative, the same cannot be said of the Jewish crowds. Like the leaders, the crowds, too, may be dealt with as a single, "flat" character. They are not rich in traits, and the ones they possess tend not to change until the end of Matthew's story, when they suddenly appear with Judas to arrest Jesus (26:47, 55). The characterization of the crowds develops along two lines: through their interaction with Jesus; and through their being contrasted with their leaders. Until Jesus' arrest, the reader's attitude toward the crowds is largely one of approval and sympathy.

Through their interaction with Jesus, the crowds show that they are "well-disposed" toward him. Jesus himself looks upon the crowds with compassion, for they are "harassed" and "helpless," being "leaderless" (9:36). They for their part follow him[73] and throng about him.[74] He teaches them,[75] and they are "amazed"[76] at his teaching. He heals their sick,[77] and they witness his miracles and become "frightened" (9:8) or "astonished" (9:33; 15:31). In two instances crowds become "hungry" while with Jesus, and he feeds them (14:15–21; 15:32–38). On occasion, however, a crowd can also become "obstructionist," as when the people ridicule the notion that the daughter of the ruler is not dead but sleeping (9:23–25a) or attempt to hush the two blind men who appeal to Jesus for healing (20:31).

Amicable though the crowds may be, they are nonetheless "without faith" in Jesus. True, they once raise the question of whether he is the Son of David (12:23), and they also hail him as such upon his entry into Jerusalem (21:9). But the grammatical form in which they put their question anticipates a negative answer (12:23), and when asked who this Jesus is whom they have hailed as the Son of David, they reply that he is the prophet from Nazareth (21:11). Indeed, "prophet" is exactly what the crowds take Jesus to be,[78] and this is in Matthew's story a misguided conception, for Jesus is in reality the Messiah Son of God (3:17; 16:16). In more sinister fashion, it is also the crowds whom Jesus censures as "this generation" that repudiates both himself and John (11:7, 16–19), and it is

73. Cf. 4:25; 8:1; 12:15; 14:13; 19:2; 20:29; 21:9.
74. Cf. 8:18; 12:46; 13:2; 17:14.
75. Cf. 11:7; 12:46; 15:10; 21:23; 23:1; 26:55.
76. Cf. 7:28; 22:33.
77. Cf. 4:23–25; 9:35; 11:5; 14:14; 15:30; 19:2.
78. Cf. 16:13–14; 21:11, 46.

the crowds who stand before his parables as those who are "blind, deaf, and without understanding" (13:1–2, 10–13).

Although the crowds are without faith in Jesus and see in him only a prophet, in being generally well-disposed toward him, they contrast sharply with their leaders. This contrast between crowds and leaders is highlighted in several instances, and the effect of this is to show the reader that if the crowds are not disciples of Jesus, neither are they his inveterate enemies. Thus, in the case of the paralytic, some of the scribes regard it as blasphemy that Jesus forgives sins, but the crowds witness the absolution and healing of the man and are awe-struck by this and glorify God (9:2–8). Following an exorcism by Jesus, the crowds marvel and say, "Never was anything like this seen in Israel," but the Pharisees retort, "He casts out demons by the prince of demons" (9:32–34). In response to another exorcism of Jesus, the crowds at least raise the question whether he might be the Son of David, but the Pharisees flatly assert once again that it is only with Satan's help that he casts out demons (12:22–24). In debate over the resurrection, at the same time Jesus reduces the Sadducees to silence, the crowds react to his teaching with astonishment (22:23–33, 34). And in two further instances, Jesus either delivers teaching to the crowds which the Pharisees find offensive (15:10–12) or utters woes in the presence of the crowds and his disciples against the scribes and Pharisees (chap. 23).

On balance, then, the Jewish crowds are "well-disposed" toward Jesus but "without faith" in him. In being without faith in Jesus, they contrast with the disciples. And in being well-disposed toward Jesus, they contrast with their leaders.

The Minor Characters

The minor characters are the persons who dot the pages of Matthew's story. Except for one like "Joseph" (1:18—2:23), they appear briefly in a scene and then vanish. Most of these persons do not so much as bear a name, passing before the reader merely as the "Magi" (2:1–12), "a leper" (8:2), "a centurion" (8:5), "the mother-in-law [of Peter]" (8:14), "two demoniacs" (8:28), the men who bring Jesus a paralytic (9:2), "a ruler" (9:18), "a woman" (9:20), "two blind men" (9:27), the townspeople of Nazareth (13:54), "the men of that place [Gennesaret]" (14:35), "a Canaanite woman" (15:22), "a man" (17:14), "a child" (18:2), "children" (19:13), "the young man" (19:22), "the mother of the sons of Zebedee" (20:20; 27:56), "two blind men" (20:30), "the children" in the temple (21:15), "a woman" (26:7), "[Pilate's] wife" (27:19), "the centurion" (27:54), "those who were with him [the centurion]" (27:54), and "many women" (27:55). Others are indeed introduced by name, but they, too, make sudden appearances only to vanish again just as quickly: "Joseph" (1:18—2:23), "Mary" (1:18; 13:55), "Barabbas" (27:15–23), "Simon [of Cyrene]" (27:32), "Mary Magdalene"

(27:56, 61; 28:1), "Mary the mother of James and Joseph" (27:56, 61; 28:1), and "Joseph [of Arimathea]" (27:57). Almost without exception, these persons are "stock" characters, that is to say, they possess one trait only. But in contradistinction to the disciples, the religious leaders, and the crowds, they cannot be treated as though they were all alike. The particular trait of any one or group of these persons is what determines to what extent the reader approves or disapproves of that person or group.

Those just listed are not the only persons to appear in Matthew's story. Others do so as well, but the purpose they serve is such that they can scarcely be said to exhibit traits.[79] Some, for instance, simply facilitate the action of a scene. Examples are "the herdsmen" (8:33), the "disciples of John" (11:2), "such a one" (26:18), "a servant girl" (26:69), "another [servant girl]" (26:71), and "the bystanders" (26:73). Others function as mere catalysts, creating opportunities for yet other characters to exhibit the traits they possess. Cases in point are the "dumb demoniac" in 9:32–34 or the "man with a withered hand" in 12:9–15. The healing of the demoniac provides the crowds and the religious leaders with an opportunity to show, respectively, that they are well-disposed or intensely hostile toward Jesus. And the restoration of the man's hand provides Jesus with an opportunity to show that he "does good" on the sabbath, whereas this prompts the religious leaders to show that they do evil, even plotting death. Additional persons who seem to function in Matthew's story along these lines are the "paralytic" (9:2), the "toll-collectors and sinners" (9:10), "the girl" (9:25), "a blind and dumb demoniac" (12:22), "the daughter [of the Canaanite woman]" (15:22, 28), "[Jesus'] mother and his brothers" (12:46), "the son [of a man]" (17:15, 17), and "the collectors of the half-shekel tax" (17:24). Finally, there are also those persons in Matthew's story who seem to meld completely with the setting of which they are a part. Examples of such are the brothers of Jesus ("James," "Joseph," "Simon," and "Judas"; 13:55), "[Jesus'] sisters" (13:56), and "Simon the leper" (26:6).

These aside, however, the principal way the reader discovers "what kinds of persons" the minor characters are is by observing them as they serve as "foils"[80] for other characters in the story, that is, as contrasts to other characters. The "Magi" (2:1) and the "centurion" (8:5) serve as foils for Israel: the faith of these Gentiles contrasts with the unbelief of Israel (2:1–12; 8:5–13). The "two blind men" (9:27), the "Canaanite woman" (15:22), the other "two blind men" (20:30), and the "children" in the temple

---

79. Such "persons" as these Chatman (*Story and Discourse*, 138–42) does not regard as bona fide "characters." Instead, he consigns them simply to the "setting" of the narrative.

80. Rhoads ("Narrative Criticism," 419) notes that in Mark the minor characters serve as "foils," and this observation is valid also with respect to Matthew.

(21:15) also serve as foils for Israel: these "no-accounts"[81] see and confess what Israel cannot, namely, that Jesus is its Davidic Messiah. Pilate's "wife" (27:19) serves as a foil for Pilate himself: her warning to Pilate not to have anything to do with that innocent man (Jesus) contrasts with Pilate's decision to accede to the Jewish demand that Jesus be put to death. "Barabbas" (27:15–26) serves as foil for Jesus: a notorious prisoner is set free, whereas an innocent man is delivered up to be crucified.

In most cases, however, the purpose of the minor characters is to function as foils for the disciples. The faith of many of them—such as the "leper" (8:2), the men who bring the paralytic to Jesus (9:2), the "ruler" (9:18), the "woman" with a hemorrhage (9:20), the "men [of Gennesaret]" (14:35), and the "man" whose son is an epileptic (17:14)—contrasts with the little faith the disciples display at points throughout Matthew's story (8:26; 14:31; 17:20). The humble station of the "child" in the one instance (18:2) and of the "children" in the other (19:13) contrasts with the disciples' concern for greatness and privilege (18:1; 19:3). The choice of the "young man" (19:22) to prefer wealth over discipleship contrasts with Jesus' word for the disciples to choose the attainment of the Kingdom over riches (19:23–30). And in the passion-narrative, several minor characters serve as foils for the disciples in the sense that they minister to Jesus in ways the disciples could have been expected to do but do not:[82] a "woman" (26:7) anoints Jesus, preparing him for burial; "Simon [of Cyrene]" (27:32) carries Jesus' cross; the "Roman soldiers" (27:54) make public confession of Jesus; "Joseph [of Arimathea]" (27:57–60) requests the body of Jesus and gives it proper burial; the "many women" (27:55–56) who had followed Jesus from Galilee do not desert him at the cross but stand at a distance watching; and after the sabbath, the "two Marys" (28:1) go as mourners to see Jesus' sepulcher. Perhaps "Joseph" (1:18—2:23) ought also to be seen as rendering service to Jesus in the infancy-narratives in like fashion as these minor characters do in the passion-narrative: through his acts of obedience to the commands of the angel during a similarly critical period, Joseph takes the pregnant Mary to be his wife, gives Jesus his name, saves him from death by fleeing to Egypt, and returns him to Israel but settles him in Nazareth outside the jurisdiction of Archelaus. With few exceptions, therefore, the minor characters are exemplary figures in Matthew's story and exhibit traits

81. The "blind," a gentile "woman," and "children" can be said to be "no-accounts" in the sense that they were, by reason of age, disability, or race and sex, what may be termed "marginal persons" within the framework of first-century Jewish society. Cf., e.g., Jeremias, *Jerusalem in the Time of Jesus*, 375; Schrage, "*Typhlos*," 272, 282–83, 287; Oepke, "*Pais*," 646, 649; idem, "*Gyne*," 777–87.

82. Rhoads and Michie (*Mark as Story*, 132–33) make this point relative to Mark, and it proves to be true of Matthew as well.

that reflect the system of values that both Jesus and Matthew as narrator advocate.

This completes our survey of the characters of Matthew's narrative. Jesus is the protagonist. The other major characters are the disciples, the religious leaders (and other authorities), and the Jewish crowds. Rounding out the list are numerous minor characters. We now need to look briefly at some of the important settings in Matthew's narrative.

Settings

The story of a narrative, observes Chatman, is made up not only of "characters" and "events," but also of "settings."[83] A "setting" is the place or time or social circumstances in which a character acts.[84] The purpose settings may serve varies considerably. In some instances, a setting simply makes action possible. In the case of the pericope on the question about fasting, for example, the setting is as minimal as the temporal adverb "then" (9:14). By contrast, in other instances the setting may be highly charged with meaning. For example, when Matthew reports as Jesus hangs upon the cross, "Now from the sixth hour there was darkness over all the land until the ninth hour" (27:45), he conveys a strong sense of impending disaster.

Within the context of Matthew's story, particular times and places are of no little significance. Thus, the conception, birth, and naming of Jesus mark the end of the time of prophecy and the beginning of the "time of fulfillment" (1:22–23). Indeed, the so-called "formula-quotations,"[85] which are peculiar to Matthew, highlight some ten occurrences associated with the life of Jesus as being special examples of the fulfillment of prophecy. And other key temporal references are, respectively, Jesus' announcements that God's Rule "has drawn near" (4:17) or "has come upon you" (12:28); his statements concerning the "hour" of his betrayal (26:45) or the "hour" or "day" that connotes the end or the final judgment;[86] and his frequent use of such idioms as "those [i.e., final] days"[87] or "the consummation of the age."[88]

As for place, "Bethlehem" is the lowly town in which prophecy dictates that the royal Messiah shall be born (2:4–6). "Egypt" is the land of refuge: just as Israel, who was God's son, found refuge in the person of Jacob in

83. Chatman, *Story and Discourse*, 138–45.
84. Abrams, *Glossary of Literary Terms*, 175.
85. Cf. 1:22–23; [2:5–6]; 2:15, 17–18, 23; 4:14–16; 8:17; 12:17–21; [13:14–15]; 13:35; 21:4–5; [26:56]; 27:9–10.
86. Cf. 24:36, 42, 44, 50; 25:13; 7:22; 10:15; 11:22, 24; 12:36.
87. Cf. 24:19, 21, 29, 38; also 3:1.
88. Cf. 13:39, 40, 49; 24:3; 28:20.

Egypt and was later called out, so Jesus Son of God finds refuge in Egypt and is later called out (2:13–15).[89] "Nazareth" is the village from which Jesus comes by virtue of his having grown up there,[90] and "Capernaum," which is "his own city" (9:1) and where he may have a "house,"[91] is where he resides during his ministry (4:13); nevertheless, both, along with "Chorazin" and "Bethsaida," become emblematic of Israel's repudiation of Jesus as its Messiah (11:20–24; 13:53–58). "Galilee" is the region in which Jesus discharges his ministry to Israel of teaching, preaching, and healing (4:23) and where he returns following his resurrection to commission his disciples to their worldwide missionary task (28:16–20; cf. 4:15).[92] Gentile cities or lands, such as the "country of the Gadarenes" (8:28) or "Tyre and Sidon" (15:21), lie beyond the purview of Jesus' own mission to the lost sheep of the house of Israel (15:24); Jesus' visit to them, however, portends the Gentile mission to come. And "Jerusalem," the "holy city"[93] and the "city of the great King" (5:35), is the city of repudiation[94] and of death[95] for Jesus, the place where his enemies are at home.[96]

Other locations, too, are of significance in Matthew. The "desert" is at once a place of end-time expectation, where John the Baptist prepares Israel for the coming of its Messiah (3:1–12), and a place of testing, where Satan would have Jesus break faith with God (4:1–4). It is also the place where Jesus would have the disciples realize that they already possess the requisite authority to feed the hungry crowds (14:16; 15:33). The "synagogue" is a local center of worship, teaching, and court proceedings under the authority of such religious leaders as the scribes and Pharisees.[97] Here Jesus confronts Israel with his message.[98] But here his opponents also try to ensnare him in his speech so as to bring accusation against him (12:9–10), and his disciples, as missionaries, will suffer severe persecution.[99] The "sea" is a place of great peril and destruction: in it humans and animals perish,[100] and although Jesus has mastery over it, it evokes feelings of

89. Cf. Bourke, "Literary Genus," 160–75; for a different view, cf. Brown, *Birth of the Messiah,* 213–19.

90. Cf. 2:23; 21:11; 26:71.

91. Cf. [8:14]; 9:1, 10, 28; 13:1, 36; 17:25.

92. As an example of how important the element of "setting" can be perceived to be in a narrative such as Matthew, Farmer (*Jesus and the Gospels,* 138–40) regards the passage 4:12–16, in which "Galilee" and other locations or areas figure prominently, as providing the "conceptual outline" for the whole of Jesus' ministry (4:12–20:16).

93. Cf. 4:5; 27:53.

94. Cf. 2:3; 23:37.

95. Cf. 16:21; 20:17–19.

96. Cf. 15:1; 16:21; 20:17–19.

97. Cf. 4:23; 9:35; 10:17; 12:9; 13:54; 23:1–7; 5:20; 6:2, 5.

98. Cf. 4:23; 9:35; 13:54.

99. Cf. 10:17; 23:34.

100. Cf. 8:32; 18:6; also 21:21.

cowardice, fear, and little faith in the disciples.[101] The "temple" is the house of God (21:13) which is under the control of the religious leaders, especially the chief priests,[102] and which is not serving its intended purpose as a place of worship (21:13). For the brief time Jesus teaches and heals there, he imparts God's benefactions to the people;[103] but once he leaves it, it is deserted (23:38) and ripe for destruction (24:1–2). In point of fact, Jesus himself supplants the temple as the "place" where God mediates salvation to people.[104] And the "mountain" is a site of end-time revelation:[105] here God declares Jesus to be his unique Son (9:7), and here Jesus Son of God, unlike Israel son of God of old, resists temptation and keeps faith with God (4:8–10). Here Jesus also performs such end-time acts as teaching the will of God (5:1–2); healing the people (15:29–31); foretelling the events that will lead up to the close of the age (24:3); disclosing through the act of prayer the unique relationship he has to God (14:23); and, following his resurrection, commissioning his disciples to their end-time ministry (28:16).

Settings, then, are temporal, geographical, or social in nature and serve to "set the character off."[106] Together with events and characters, settings make up the story of a narrative. Still, the story is only the one part of a narrative; the discourse is the other part, and it is this part that must now be discussed.

THE DISCOURSE OF THE NARRATIVE

If the "story" of a narrative such as Matthew is "what" is told (the life of Jesus from conception and birth to death and resurrection), the "discourse" is, in Chatman's terminology,[107] "how" this story is told, that is to say, the means the author uses in order to put the story across. The discourse of the Matthean narrative encompasses such matters as the "implied author" and the "narrator," the "point of view" espoused by the narrator or any character, and the "implied reader."[108] In addition, the kind and style of the language used to tell the story and the rhetorical techniques employed are also important elements of the discourse of Matthew. The latter will be dealt with in subsequent Chapters to the extent that they present themselves in the course of the investigation of the gospel story of Matthew itself. In what follows, it is the former that will receive attention.

101. Cf. 8:23–27; 14:24–33.
102. Cf. 21:15, 23, 45; 27:3–10.
103. Cf. 21:14–16; 26:55.
104. Cf. 1:21; 26:28; 27:51.
105. On the motif of the "mountain," cf. Donaldson, *Jesus on the Mountain*.
106. Chatman, *Story and Discourse*, 138.
107. Cf. ibid., 19–22.
108. On these matters, cf. ibid., chaps. 4–5.

The Implied Author and the Narrator

Literary theorists distinguish in analyzing a narrative among the "real author," the "implied author," and the "narrator."[109] The "real author" of Matthew is the historical person who created this narrative, the one scholars call the first evangelist. In the act of creating this narrative, the first evangelist also created a literary version of himself, a second self, which the reader comes to know through the process of reading the story of the narrative. This second self is the "implied author." The "narrator," in turn, is the voice, or invisible speaker, the reader hears as he or she moves through the story, the one who tells the reader the story. It is the narrator, for example, who intones the first words, "The book of the origin of Jesus Christ, Son of David, Son of Abraham" (1:1).

One of the reasons literary theorists distinguish between the "implied author" who stands behind the whole of a narrative and the "narrator" who tells the story is that a narrator can prove himself or herself to be "unreliable." The "unreliable narrator" is one found to be at odds with the implied author.[110] This occurs when the narrator does not espouse the same system of ideas, values, or beliefs that sustains and informs the story. In the case of Matthew, however, the reader has to do only with a "reliable narrator," one who is in full accord with the implied author. For this reason, the need to distinguish rigorously between the narrator and the implied author is not so pressing. In this study, at any rate, both narrator and implied author will be designated as "Matthew." In this way, a familiar nomenclature can be retained. By the same token, where it is desirable for the sake of the discussion to differentiate between Matthew as narrator and Matthew as implied author, this will be done. Along these same lines, the term "(first) evangelist" will also be reserved throughout the rest of this study to denote the real author of the First Gospel.

Correct though it is to recognize that the narrator of Matthew's story is none but the reliable voice of the implied author, one must nevertheless, if one is to understand the kind of narrator he is, take notice of the characteristics he exhibits.[111] One of these characteristics has already been mentioned, namely, that he is "reliable." Others are that he is "omnipresent" and "omniscient" as far as the world of his story is concerned; speaks in the "third person"; directs "comments" to the reader that provide inside information that is most often not available to the characters in the story; and indicates that the vantage point from which he involves himself in the story lies, temporally, between the resurrection and the Parousia.

---

109. Cf. Booth, *Rhetoric of Fiction*, 70–76; Chatman, *Story and Discourse*, 147–51; also Rhoads, "Narrative Criticism," 420–22.

110. Cf. Chatman, *Story and Discourse*, 226–28, 233–37.

111. The groundbreaking article by Petersen on "'Point of View' in Mark's Narrative" is also instructive for gaining insight into the narrator the reader encounters in Matthew.

As narrator, then, Matthew is "omnipresent" in relation to the world of his story. He is able to be in any place at any time in order to inform the reader of what is taking place. Not a character himself, he is the invisible speaker who is both above and beyond the story, since he is the one who tells it, and within the story, since there is no scene from which he is absent. Whether with Jesus in the desert (4:1) or with John in prison (11:2) or with the disciples in the boat (14:22, 24) or with Peter weeping bitterly by himself (26:75), Matthew is ever present.

Matthew as narrator is likewise "omniscient." There is nothing in the world of the story of which he does not have full knowledge. For example, he knows the thoughts the scribes express "to themselves" (9:3) or the words of the prayer Jesus utters in private in Gethsemane (26:39, 42). Similarly, he is aware of the feelings any given character experiences, as when Herod the Great becomes frightened (2:3), or Jesus has compassion on the crowds (9:36), or the religious leaders or the disciples become indignant (21:15; 26:8). And he is also privy to what characters sense, what they may hear (2:22; 4:12) or see (3:16; 9:11) on this or that occasion.

Despite Matthew's "omniscience" and "omnipresence" as narrator, however, there is one area in which he does not exercise these powers. This has to do with the way he deals with God. Unlike in the case of other characters, Matthew never permits the reader to imagine that he has "unmediated access" either to heaven, God's abode (5:34–35; 23:22), or to his "mind."[112] There are no scenes in Matthew's story whose settings are in heaven, and "privileged views" about what is transpiring in the "heart" of God are rare—if they can be said to be present at all.

The mode of narration Matthew employs in telling his story is that of the "third person" as opposed to the "first person."[113] In first-person narration, the narrator speaks as "I" and is himself or herself one of the characters in the story. In third-person narration, the narrator assumes the detached posture of an invisible "observer" of the action and refers to the characters either by "name" or as "he," "she," or "they." The pericope on the baptism reflects well Matthew's use of third-person narration: "Then *Jesus* came from Galilee to the Jordan to *John*, to be baptized by *him*. But *he* would have prevented *him*, saying . . . " (3:13–14).

In the course of relating his story, Matthew as narrator directs comments to the reader that provide him or her with inside information most often not available to the characters in the story. By means of such commentary, Matthew explains certain matters or, more significantly, interprets characters and events and renders judgment on them. By making the reader the

112. Cf. Kingsbury, "Figure of Jesus," 5. Even at 3:17 and 17:5, God does not speak "freely" but in words drawn from the OT.
113. Cf. Abrams, *Glossary of Literary Terms*, 143.

recipient of inside information, Matthew places him or her in the privileged position of being better informed than the characters in the story. For instance, through such narrative comments as are found in 1:1 and 2:15 (cf. 1:23), the reader knows far in advance of any human character that Jesus is Israel's Davidic Messiah, God's Son. Equally important, Matthew is also, through these comments, urging the reader to appropriate as "true" this understanding of Jesus. Other striking examples of narrative commentary in Matthew's story are the genealogy (1:1–17); the formula-quotations;[114] the explanation of terms (1:23; 27:33) or translation of foreign words (27:46); remarks that are addressed directly to the reader (24:15; 27:8; 28:15); and the many statements that apprise the reader of the thoughts (21:25–27), feelings (2:10, 22), perceptions (21:45; 22:18), and intentions (21:46) of characters.

The final characteristic of Matthew as narrator to be mentioned at this juncture is, in reality, a characteristic of Matthew as implied author. In three passages, the reader is addressed by a voice, but the nature of the comment in each case is such that it bursts the bounds of the story-world of Matthew. Clearly, in these passages the implied author disrupts the story in order to speak directly to the reader. In disrupting the story in this fashion, the implied author gives indication of the place in time he would assign himself. The first two passages are the comments found in 27:8 and 28:15: "Therefore that field [purchased with the money paid Judas] has been called the Field of Blood *to this day*"; and ". . . this story [that the disciples stole the body of Jesus] has been spread among the Jews *to this day*." And the third passage is the "aside" found in 24:15 in the eschatological discourse: "*Let the reader understand*." On the basis of these three passages, it is obvious that the place that Matthew, the implied author, assigns himself already lies at some distance from the event of the resurrection (28:1–15) and is situated in the time of the messianic woes and the church's mission to the nations (24:8, 14–15). From this particular place, Matthew as implied author looks back upon the whole of the story of the life and ministry of Jesus of Nazareth and also involves himself, through his voice as narrator, in every aspect of this story.

Point of View

Another facet of the "discourse" of Matthew, that is, of the way in which the first evangelist has chosen to put his story across, is that of "point of view."[115] Major aspects of point of view are the "evaluative" (often called the ideological), the "phraseological," the "spatial and temporal," and the "psychological."[116]

114. See above, n. 85.

115. Chatman, *Story and Discourse*, 151–58. Also Rhoads, "Narrative Criticism," 421–22.

116. Cf. Uspensky *(Poetics of Composition)* and Lanser *(Narrative Act*, 184–222). As far as Matthew's Gospel itself is concerned, an instructive study of "point of view" that draws on the work of Uspensky is that of Anderson ("Point of View in Matthew").

"Evaluative point of view" has to do with some conception of reality. It denotes a particular way of looking at things which also entails rendering some judgment on them in terms of the degree to which they are "good" or "bad," "right" or "wrong." To the extent divulged by a story, the narrator and the various characters all have their evaluative points of view. Typically, these evaluative points of view give rise to conflict.

Characteristic of a gospel story like Matthew is that the many conflicting evaluative points of view expressed by the various characters can fundamentally be reduced to two: the "true" and the "untrue."[117] No effort is made in Matthew to carve out room for grey areas. The measuring rod for distinguishing truth from untruth is, as the passage 16:23 indicates, "thinking the things of God" (as opposed to "thinking the things of humans"). Within the world of Matthew's story, therefore, the evaluative point of view that the implied author has chosen to make normative is that belonging to God.[118] What this means, in turn, is that the evaluative point of view that Matthew ascribes to himself as narrator or to any given character is to be adjudged true or false depending upon whether it aligns itself with, or contravenes, the evaluative point of view of God. Because Matthew as implied author reliably places his voice as narrator in the service of the evaluative point of view he has made normative (i.e., God's evaluative point of view), and because Jesus is the supreme agent of God, the reader can rest assured that the evaluative points of view of both Matthew as narrator and Jesus will be in complete alignment with the evaluative point of view of God. Accordingly, there is only one true way in which to view things in Matthew, and this is the way of God. God's way is also the way in which both Matthew as narrator and Jesus view things.

By contrast, as one moves, respectively, from the disciples to the Jewish crowds and to the religious leaders, the degree to which each group deviates from "thinking the things of God" and "thinks the things of humans" becomes ever greater. Whereas the disciples are blessed with the capacity

117. Cf. Lotman, "Point of View in a Text," 343.

118. In his article "'Point of View' in Mark's Narrative" (107–8), Norman Petersen was the first to make the crucial observation that, in Mark's Gospel, the evaluative point of view of the narrator is identical with that of the central character, Jesus. Sound as this observation is, I found in my own work on Mark's Gospel (cf. J. D. Kingsbury, *The Christology of Mark's Gospel* [Philadelphia: Fortress Press, 1983], 47–50) that one must take yet a second step and observe that not only does Mark as implied author align the evaluative point of view of the narrator with that of Jesus but, beyond this, he furthermore aligns the evaluative points of view of both the narrator and Jesus with the evaluative point of view of God. In Mark's gospel story, then, the evaluative point of view that has been made normative is that of God. In a subsequent article on Matthew's Gospel (Kingsbury, "Figure of Jesus," 4–7), I have argued that here, too, Matthew as implied author has established God's evaluative point of view as normative. Indeed, one could easily show that, in all four canonical Gospels, it is God's evaluative point of view that has been established by the implied author as normative.

to think the things of God, there are glaring instances where they think the things of humans. The Jewish crowds, though destined to think the things of humans,[119] nevertheless on occasion appear to think the things of God (cf. 9:33; 15:31). The religious leaders, however, seem never, except unwittingly, to think the things of God and always to think the things of humans.

"Phraseological point of view" concerns the "speech," or "diction," that typifies and distinguishes Matthew as narrator or any given character. For its part, the "speech" of Matthew or a character is a good indicator of the evaluative point of view that he or a character espouses. For example, the formula-quotations are all spoken by Matthew himself, and a key component in each is the citation of OT scripture. Because OT scripture counts as the word of God,[120] the result of the fact that the formula quotations make up an important part of Matthew's speech is that he thus becomes, as narrator, an exponent of God's evaluative point of view in assessing the salvation-historical significance of various events in the life of Jesus.[121] Again, the citation of OT scripture is also typical of Jesus' speech throughout Matthew's story. What this indicates, as is apparent from passages such as 15:4 and 22:31–32, is that Jesus, too, is a thoroughly reliable exponent of God's evaluative point of view. And to take a third example, the words "if you are the Son of God" are first associated in Matthew's story with Satan, who utters them in order to test Jesus (4:3, 6). Later, therefore, when Jesus hangs upon the cross and the passersby shout at him, ". . . if you are the Son of God, come down from the cross" (27:40), the reader recognizes from the phraseology of the passersby that they, like Satan previously, are testing Jesus and that they consequently have aligned themselves with Satan.

"Spatial and temporal point of view" pertains to the position in time and space from which characters or events are observed or described. As has been noted, the peculiar place Matthew as implied author assigns himself within the world of his story lies beyond the resurrection but short of the Parousia (24:15; 27:8; 28:15). From this place, Matthew oversees all time and space in his story-world and, through his voice as narrator, involves himself in them. Spatially, Matthew as narrator is omnipresent in relation to the story he tells, for he moves about freely to report the action, taking up positions outside or within any particular scene. Concomitantly, once Jesus makes his appearance in the story as an adult, Matthew as narrator "accompanies" him,[122] with few exceptions,[123] from baptism to death (3:13–27:56). Overwhelmingly, therefore, Jesus becomes the focal point of attention

---

119. Cf. 13:2, 10–13; 27:20, 25.
120. Cf. 1:22; 2:15; 15:4; 22:31.
121. See above, n. 85.
122. Cf. Anderson, "Point of View in Matthew," 14–17.
123. Cf. 14:3–12; 27:58, 69–75.

throughout the story, as others "come" to him, or "follow" him, or "bring" the sick to him.[124] Still, prior to Jesus' baptism and following his death, Matthew tracks a series of less prominent characters,[125] but always in the interest of conveying information to the reader about Jesus. By the same token, when Matthew as narrator closes his story with the Great Commission, he is again present with Jesus (28:16-20; cf. 28:9-10).

To turn to the temporal plane of point of view, Matthew as narrator first surveys in the genealogy the history of Israel (1:1-17), and then tells the story of the life of Jesus from conception and birth to death and resurrection (1:18—28:20). Because Matthew's is the voice of one who looks back on the life of Jesus, he recounts events in past time (cf., e.g., 2:1: "Now after Jesus *had been born* in Bethlehem of Judea in the days of Herod the king, behold, wise men from the East *came* to Jerusalem . . ."). But this notwithstanding, in some eighty instances Matthew shifts from past time and employs the historical present[126] (cf., e.g., 3:13: "Then Jesus *comes* from Galilee to the Jordan to John . . ."). Matthew's use of the historical present has the effect of eliminating any distance in time between himself as narrator and Jesus or other characters, so that he reports the action as Jesus or the characters experience it. Then, too, more often than not Matthew thus makes himself contemporary with the characters in his story in order to focus on the words Jesus is speaking on any occasion. The rhetorical effect such contemporaneity has is that it enables Jesus to address directly not only other characters in the story but also the reader. Temporally, therefore, Matthew as narrator fundamentally rehearses the story of Jesus' life in past time. By the same token, he frequently makes himself contemporary with Jesus or other characters through his use of the historical present for the dual purpose of making the action more vivid and especially of having Jesus speak directly not only to other characters but also to the reader.

"Psychological point of view" refers to knowledge on the part of Matthew as narrator or of a character about what some (other) character thinks, intends, feels, sees, or otherwise experiences. Omniscience of this kind is predicated both to Matthew and to Jesus. They provide the reader as a matter of course with inside views into the inner workings of others.[127] For example, Matthew as narrator knows that Jesus "marvels" at the centurion's faith (8:10), or that the Pharisees approach Jesus with the "intent of testing him" (19:3), or that the disciples become "very sorrowful" when Jesus predicts his suffering and death a second time (17:23). Similarly, Jesus, too,

124. This point is also made by Weaver, "Missionary Discourse in Matthew," 72-74.
125. Cf. 1:18—3:12; 27:57—28:8; 28:11-15.
126. On the manner in which Matthew employs the historical present, cf. Anderson, "Point of View in Matthew," 11-14; also Hawkins, *Horae Synopticae*, 148-59.
127. Cf. Anderson, "Point of View in Matthew," 17-22.

knows or sees that the Pharisees have "taken counsel against him, how to destroy him" (12:14), or that the disciples have become "indignant" at the woman who has poured expensive ointment on his head (26:8, 10), or that the men who have brought him a paralytic have "faith" that he can heal him (9:2). The reason the reader is provided with inside views of characters is to shape his or her attitude toward them. Through the inside views that Matthew as narrator gives of Jesus, he portrays him sympathetically.[128] Through the inside views that he and Jesus give of other characters, they portray them either sympathetically or unsympathetically. The upshot is that whereas the reader is led never to disapprove of Jesus, he or she is led in some scenes to view characters with approval but in others to view them with disapproval.

To recapitulate, the major aspects of point of view are the evaluative, the phraseological, the spatial and temporal, and the psychological. "Thinking the things of God" is the evaluative point of view that Matthew, the implied author, has established as normative for his story. The ones who are consistently in alignment with this point of view are Matthew as narrator and Jesus. Phraseologically, therefore, what Matthew as narrator says is "reliable," and what Jesus says is "truth," not "untruth." Spatially and temporally, Matthew as narrator, by "accompanying" Jesus through his ministry and by enabling him, through the use of the historical present, to confront directly not only other characters but also the reader, underscores the fact that Jesus is the supreme exponent of God's evaluative point of view. And psychologically, Matthew, again as narrator, by leading the reader, through the use of inside views, always to regard Jesus sympathetically and to regard other characters sympathetically or unsympathetically depending upon whether they draw close to Jesus or oppose him, furthermore enhances Jesus' stature as the supreme exponent of God's evaluative point of view.

The Implied Reader

Just as literary theorists like Chatman, in discussing the "discourse" of a narrative, distinguish among the real author, the implied author (the real author's "second self"), and the narrator (the "voice" that tells the story), so they also distinguish among the "real reader," the "implied reader," and the "narratee."[129] Applied to Matthew's Gospel, the term "real reader" denotes any flesh-and-blood person who has actually heard it or read it. This

---

128. Cf. esp. 9:36; 14:14; 20:34; 26:37.
129. Cf. Chatman, *Story and Discourse*, 147–51, 253–62; Prince, "Fictional 'Narratees,'" 100–106; Iser, *Act of Reading*, 27–38; Lanser, *Narrative Act*, 179–84. In speaking of types of "readers," one has already entered the area of reader-response criticism. For helpful summary articles on such criticism, cf. Tompkins, "Introduction to Reader-Response Criticism," ix–xxvi; Suleiman, "Varieties of Audience-Oriented Criticism," 3–45.

person may be the Christian of the first century for whom the Gospel was originally written (often called the "intended reader"), or anyone in the twentieth century who takes it to hand. By contrast, the term "implied reader" denotes no flesh-and-blood person of any century. Instead, it refers to an imaginary person who is to be envisaged, in perusing Matthew's story, as responding to the text at every point with whatever emotion, understanding, or knowledge the text ideally calls for. Or to put it differently, the implied reader is that imaginary person in whom the intention of the text is to be thought of as always reaching its fulfillment. And third, the term "narratee" denotes, most simply, whoever it is to whom the narrator (the "voice" that tells the story) is to be construed as addressing his many remarks. Thus, it is to the narratee that Matthew as narrator is speaking when in 1:1 he utters the words "The book of the origin of Jesus Christ, Son of David, Son of Abraham." But as correct technically as it may be to say this, the fact of the matter is that in this instance the narratee proves to be but a stand-in for the implied reader. One can simplify matters, therefore, and merely construe Matthew the narrator as addressing himself to the implied reader.

Accordingly, the important thing to keep in mind is that the implied reader is the one who is silently and invisibly present throughout Matthew's story to attend to every word. What is more, like the implied author, the implied reader, too, has a place or position of his or her own within the world of Matthew's story. This position lies, as the passages 24:15; 27:8; and 28:15 reveal, at some distance from the resurrection but short of the Parousia. It is, in fact, identical with the place of Matthew as implied author. From this vantage point in time, the implied reader likewise oversees the story of the life and ministry of Jesus of Nazareth as Matthew conveys this through his voice as narrator, and he or she can comprehend the whole of this story.

This insight, that the implied reader not only is present throughout Matthew to hear the entire story but also has a position of his or her own that lies between the resurrection and the Parousia, is of no little significance, especially for understanding the great discourses of Jesus (chaps. 5–7; 10; 13; 18; [23]; 24–25). Consider, for example, the missionary discourse in 9:35—10:42.[130] In 10:5–6, Jesus enjoins the disciples, "Go nowhere among the Gentiles, and enter no town of the Samaritans, but go rather to the lost sheep of the house of Israel." For the implied reader, this injunction comes as no surprise, because it dovetails neatly with the story of Jesus' ministry to Israel as recounted thus far (4:17—9:34; 4:17, 23; 9:35–36). In 10:17–18, however, Jesus suddenly tells the disciples about

130. For a recent comprehensive treatment of this discourse, cf. Weaver, "Missionary Discourse in Matthew," chap. 3.

persecutions that will befall them and that envisage not solely a mission to Israel, but also a mission aimed at Gentiles: "Beware of men; for . . . you will be dragged before governors and kings for my sake, to bear testimony before them and the Gentiles." For the implied reader, this sudden reference in chapter 10 to a gentile mission comes unexpectedly. From the perspective of the flow of Matthew's story, these words of Jesus in v. 18 do occasion surprise for the implied reader.

Still, from another perspective—the temporal position of the implied reader beyond the resurrection (24:15)—the movement in the text of chapter 10 from an exclusive mission to Israel (vv. 5–6) to a mission that includes Gentiles as well (v. 18) merely parallels the movement within the wider story of Jesus. This movement portrays Jesus, on the one hand, as being sent only to the lost sheep of the house of Israel (15:24) but, on the other hand, as initiating a universal mission to the Gentiles immediately after his resurrection (28:18–20). From his or her peculiar vantage point beyond the resurrection, the implied reader is fully able to comprehend, and to relate to each other, the particularism of 10:5–6 concerning Israel and the universalism of 10:18 concerning the Gentiles. Consequently, the same saying or event that occasions surprise for the implied reader when he or she approaches it in terms of the flow of Matthew's story is comprehensible and occasions no surprise when he or she views it in terms of a special position in the time following the resurrection. In similar fashion, other passages in other discourses of Jesus that likewise occasion surprise for the implied reader in light of the flow of Matthew's story—because they do not "fit" the earthly ministry of Jesus and are so clearly "out of place" (cf. 5:11–12; 7:15–23; 13:38; 18:19–20; 23:34)—are perfectly intelligible when viewed from the perspective of a special position beyond the resurrection in the time of the risen Jesus and of the universal mission (24:15).

One final remark about the implied reader needs to be made. Prior to this present section on "the implied reader," numerous references were made simply to "the reader." These references to "the reader" (except where the latter was defined as a person of the first century or of modern times) in reality envisaged "the implied reader." Accordingly, unless there is some reason to use the specific term "the implied reader," the practice will continue of speaking more simply of "the reader." Henceforth, therefore, "the reader" is to be understood as "the implied reader."

With these observations, the discussion of the implied reader may be brought to a close and, with it, also the larger discussion regarding the "discourse" of a narrative. If the "story," with its events, characters, and settings, constitutes the one part of a narrative, the "discourse," which has to do with how the story is told and concerns such matters as the implied author, the narrator, point of view, and the implied reader, constitutes the other part of narrative. To set the stage for an examination of the gospel story of Matthew itself, two issues must yet be dealt with that have thus far been withheld from consideration, namely, the structure of Matthew's Gospel and its view of the history of salvation.

THE STRUCTURE OF MATTHEW AND ITS VIEW OF THE HISTORY OF SALVATION

Matthew's story of the life of Jesus unfolds in three broad segments or parts.[131] To signal the beginning of each new part, Matthew employs a formula, or stereotyped phrase: "From that time on Jesus began to preach [to show his disciples] . . . " (4:17; 16:21). The thing to note is that these three parts comprising Matthew's story are not to be conceived of in static terms as large blocks of material separate from one another. Instead, one is to understand that each time the formula just cited occurs, it introduces a new phase in the ministry of Jesus. Every story, including Matthew's, takes many turns while being narrated. Some turns in the story are of primary significance, whereas others are of secondary, tertiary, or even lesser significance. For one to call special attention to the formula that appears in 4:17 and 16:21 is for one to advance the claim that these verses mark the points in Matthew's story where it takes its two most important turns. Specifically, the double use of this formula calls the reader's attention to the turn of the story from its beginning phase (1:1—4:16) to its middle phase (4:17—16:20), and from its middle phase to its end phase (16:21—28:20). So construed, this formula plays a dynamic role in guiding the reader through Matthew's story.

When this formula is taken as one's cue, it gives rise to this broad outline of the story of Matthew: (I) The Presentation of Jesus Messiah (1:1—4:16); (II) The Ministry of Jesus Messiah to Israel and Israel's Repudiation of Jesus (4:17—16:20); and (III) The Journey of Jesus Messiah to Jerusalem and His Suffering, Death, and Resurrection (16:21—28:20). As this outline suggests, Matthew tells the story of the life of Jesus of Nazareth first by presenting him to the implied reader and then by describing, respectively, his public ministry to Israel and his journey to Jerusalem where he suffers, dies, and is raised.

In considering the element of time in a narrative, Chatman distinguishes between "story-time" and "discourse-time."[132] "Discourse-time" has to do with the order in which the reader is actually told about the events that make up a story. For instance, it is the discourse-time of Matthew that dictates that the reader is not told of the death of John the Baptist until chapter 14, at which juncture John's death is presented as having already

---

131. On the structure of Matthew, cf. Kingsbury, *Matthew: Structure, Christology, Kingdom,* 1–25. For an excellent, thorough treatment of this topic, cf. Bauer, "Structure of Matthew's Gospel."

132. Chatman, *Story and Discourse,* 62–63.

taken place. By contrast, "story-time" merely refers to the chronological order in which all the events cited in a narrative occur. In Matthew's Gospel, story-time extends from creation on the one hand to consummation on the other (19:4, 8; 25:31–46), though the greater interest lies with the time that extends from Abraham to the consummation (1:1–17; 28:20). In any case, Chatman's story-time approximates what biblical scholars have customarily called the "history of salvation." In terms of this history, the point to be made is that Matthew, in telling of the life of Jesus, is careful to situate it within the broad context of God's dealings with his people. Inasmuch as the time involved stretches from Abraham to the end of the age, Matthew divides this time into distinct epochs and periods.

The two epochs Matthew marks off in the history of salvation are the age of prophecy, or the "time of Israel (OT)," and the eschatological age of fulfillment, which is the "time of Jesus (earthly—exalted)."[133] To stress the passing of the first and the arrival of the second, Matthew makes liberal use of formula quotations to call attention to the fulfillment in the life of Jesus of some aspect of OT prophecy.[134]

For its part, the age of fulfillment, or the "time of Jesus (earthly—exalted)," runs from Jesus' birth (1:16, 22–23) to his return in majesty and splendor at the consummation (25:31–46). Within this epoch, Matthew differentiates among several periods through his use of the expressions "the Kingdom of Heaven is at hand" and "the gospel of the Kingdom." In particular, Matthew employs these expressions to divide the "time of Jesus (earthly—exalted)" into the ministries to Israel of John (3:1–2), of Jesus (4:17), and of the pre-Easter disciples (10:7) and the ministry to the nations of the post-Easter disciples, or church (14:14; 26:13).

Accordingly, Matthew both knits together, and differentiates among, the ministries of John, Jesus, the pre-Easter disciples, and the post-Easter church. Nevertheless, it is the ministry of Jesus that is decisive in this sequence. John is the forerunner of Jesus (17:10–13), and the pre-Easter and post-Easter disciples carry out their ministries only on the commission of Jesus (10:5; 28:18–20). This is why the "time of fulfillment" is indeed the "time of Jesus (earthly—exalted)."

This survey of both the topical outline of Matthew's life of Jesus and the salvation-historical context within which it has been situated raises the question of the fundamental message of Matthew's story. The key passages 1:23 and 28:20, which stand in a reciprocal relationship to each other, highlight this message. At 1:23, Matthew quotes Isaiah in saying of Jesus: in "Emmanuel . . . God [is] with us." And at 28:20 the risen Jesus himself

---

133. On Matthew's understanding of salvation-history and the scholarly discussion of this topic, cf. Kingsbury, *Matthew: Structure, Christology, Kingdom*, 25–37.
134. See above, n. 85.

declares to the disciples: "I am with you always, to the close of the age." Strategically located at the beginning and the end of Matthew's story, these two passages "enclose" it. In combination, they reveal the message of Matthew's story: *In the person of Jesus Messiah, his Son, God has drawn near to abide to the end of time with his people, the church, thus inaugurating the eschatological age of salvation.*

Embedded in this message is a claim and a call to commitment. As a word of prophecy, 1:23 shows that in the birth of "Emmanuel," that is, Jesus Son of God, the hope of Israel has at last come to fulfillment. Hence, the affirmation this passage makes is that Jesus is of decisive significance for the salvation of Israel. In 28:18–20, the risen Son of God commissions his followers to "make disciples of all nations." Hence, the affirmation this passage makes is that Jesus is of decisive significance for the salvation of the Gentiles. Together, therefore, these passages set forth the bold claim that the story of Matthew raises on behalf of Jesus: for the salvation of both Jew and Gentile, Jesus Son of God is of decisive significance. Then, too, because the story of Matthew ends with Jesus' enjoining the disciples, and with them the reader, to engage in mission, it consequently ends by issuing the disciples and the reader the call to commit themselves without reserve to the carrying out of this mission.

This completes our consideration of a literary-critical approach to Matthew. We now turn to an investigation of the gospel story itself. We shall treat, respectively, the figure of Jesus, his ministry to Israel, his journey to Jerusalem and passion, his use of "the Son of man," his speeches, his antagonists, his disciples, and the community of Christians for whom this gospel story was written.

2

The Presentation of Jesus
(1:1—4:16)

The plot of Matthew's story revolves around Jesus, and integral to this plot is the element of conflict. By and large, two conflicts dominate: that between Jesus and Israel, especially the religious leaders; and that between Jesus and the disciples. Whereas the first conflict turns out tragically for Israel, the second ends in reconciliation for the disciples. In this and the next two Chapters (3 and 4), the object is to treat Jesus' conflict with Israel by tracing the story-line of Jesus. In Chapter 7, the focus will be on the story-line of the religious leaders. In Chapter 8, Jesus' conflict with the disciples will be discussed and their story-line traced.

In the previous Chapter we saw that Matthew's story divides itself into three parts (beginning, middle, and end) and that 1:1—4:16 constitutes the first part. There is a scholarly tradition, however, that holds that 1:1—2:23 forms the first part. As proof of this, reference is often made to the break in time between the years of Jesus' infancy (1:1—2:23) and the appearance of John and Jesus as adults (3:1—4:16). To trace properly the flow of Matthew's story, it is necessary to recognize that 1:1—4:16 does in fact constitute a major segment.

Four factors indicate the unity of 1:1—4:16.[1] The first and most important is that the climactic statement regarding the identity of Jesus, which is the motif that dominates the beginning of Matthew's story (cf. 1:1), does not occur until the baptism (3:13–17). In the baptismal pericope, God himself enters the world of Matthew's story and declares Jesus to be his beloved Son (3:17). In making this declaration, God expresses to Jesus, and to such transcendent beings as Satan as well (4:3, 6), his evaluative point of view concerning Jesus' identity, that is to say, how he "thinks" about Jesus.

To be sure, prior to the baptism Matthew as narrator has already touched

---

1. Cf. Kingsbury, *Matthew: Structure, Christology, Kingdom*, 7–17; also the lengthier study by Bauer, "Structure of Matthew's Gospel," 159–79.

on the truth that Jesus is the Son of God. The thing to observe, however, is the way he does this. He does it by directing private comments to the reader not communicated to any human character within the story (1:22–23; 2:15). The upshot is that God's baptismal declaration at 3:17 reveals itself to be climactic within the context of 1:1—4:16 because this is the place where God's understanding of Jesus as his Son ceases to be of the nature of private information available only to the reader and becomes instead an element within the story that henceforth influences the shape of events.[2]

A second factor that calls attention to the unity of 1:1—4:16 is the formula quotations in 2:23 and 4:12–16. It is generally held that the travels of Jesus prior to his public ministry come to an end when Joseph brings Mary and the infant Jesus from Egypt and settles in Nazareth (2:23). A glance at these formula-quotations, however, shows that not until Jesus has taken up residence in Capernaum, which becomes "his own city" (9:1), do his early travels end. To stress this point, the passage 4:12–14 has been so worded as to link up flawlessly with the previous passage 2:22–23. These passages read as follows:

. . . he [Joseph, with Mary and the infant Jesus] *went and dwelt in a city called Nazareth*, that what was spoken by the prophets might be fulfilled. . . .

. . . he [Jesus] *left Nazareth and went and dwelt in Capernaum* by the sea, in the regions of Zebulun and Naphtali, that what was spoken by the prophet Isaiah might be fulfilled. . . .

A third factor attesting to the unity of 1:1—4:16 is the presence in the Greek text at 3:1 of the particle *de* ("now," "then"). The surrounding context reveals that this particle frequently appears in the opening line of a pericope in order to connect that pericope with preceding narrative (cf., e.g., 1:18; 2:1, 13, 19; 4:12). By employing *de* at 3:1, Matthew shows that the interpreter is not to posit a fundamental break in the text between chapters 2 and 3 but is, on the contrary, to regard the materials of the two chapters as belonging together.

A final factor that betokens the unity of 1:1—4:16 is that all the pericopes making up this larger section narrate events that are *preliminary* to Jesus' ministry to Israel. In the temptation scenes (4:1–11), Jesus faces the devil in private encounter. At the baptism, Jesus is, as will become apparent, the only human character in Matthew's story to see the Spirit descend upon him and to hear God's baptismal declaration (3:16–17). And as John the Baptist discharges his ministry, his sole aim is to ready Israel for the time when Jesus will come and commence his public activity (3:11–12; 4:17).

---

2. To illustrate this, notice how the words Satan speaks in 4:3, 6 ("If you are the Son of God . . .") pick up directly on the declaration God makes in the baptismal pericope ("This is my beloved Son . . .").

Accordingly, these events, too, and not just those attending Jesus' infancy, can be seen as preliminary to the beginning of Jesus' public ministry in Israel (4:17). To repeat, the whole of 1:1—4:16, and not merely chapters 1–2, form the first part of Matthew's story.

THE DAVIDIC MESSIAH-KING

The Genealogy

Jesus is God's supreme agent in Matthew's story, and the purpose of the genealogy with which Matthew begins is to advance this claim. The genealogy asserts God's direct control of Israel's history and sets forth in the listing of Jesus' forebears an initial evaluative point of view concerning his identity. Through the use of the expression *biblos geneseōs* ("book of the origin") in the introduction of the genealogy (1:1), Matthew echoes such OT passages as Gen. 2:4; 5:1 (LXX).[3] These passages are themselves introductions to genealogies, and these genealogies bear witness to the governance of human history by God (Gen. 2:4—4:26; 5:1—6:8). Add to this observation the interpretive clues provided by the key verse 1:17, and the message of the genealogy is plain: the whole of Israel's history has been so guided by God that the promises made to Abraham and to King David which ostensibly had come to naught in the Babylonian captivity have attained their fulfillment in the coming of the heir of Abraham and David, namely, the Messiah. Consequently, Jesus is, as Matthew says in 1:1, "Christ" ("Messiah"), "Son of David," and "Son of Abraham."

Through this string of names and titles placed at the head of his story, Matthew sounds the theme of the "identity of Jesus" and makes of each designation a vehicle for becoming acquainted with him. To these, other designations will shortly be added. The question is: How does each designation enrich the reader's understanding of Jesus?

As 1:16 of the genealogy indicates, "Jesus" is the personal name of the protagonist of Matthew's story. Although Joseph is the one who gives Jesus his name (1:25), he does so on instructions from the angel of the Lord (1:20). Ultimately, therefore, God himself is the source of Jesus' name. As to meaning, "Jesus" denotes that "God [is] salvation," and the angel touches on this as he tells Joseph that Jesus "will *save* his people from their sins" (1:21). Accordingly, the force of the name "Jesus" is that in the one thus called, God is active to save. Hence, of all the traits Matthew ascribes to Jesus in the course of his story, the one most fundamental is that he is "saving."

Despite the fact that "Jesus" is a personal name and occurs no fewer than 150 times in Matthew's story, it is striking that human characters never

3. Cf. Johnson, *Biblical Genealogies*, 149, 186.

make use of it when addressing Jesus himself. Indeed, only five times does "Jesus" occur conversationally among characters in Matthew.[4] Overwhelmingly, Matthew reserves the name "Jesus" for his own use. Why does he do so? He does so in order that he might thereby establish the closest possible association between himself as narrator and Jesus. To what end? To the end that his evaluative point of view as narrator (i.e., his conception of reality) might coincide with that of Jesus.

But how does Matthew's use of the name "Jesus" result in an identification of his evaluative point of view with that of Jesus? In itself, the name "Jesus" alludes to the truth that God is active in Jesus to save. Consequently, the name itself attests to Jesus as being God's supreme agent who espouses God's evaluative point of view in accomplishing the mission God has set for him (1:21). When, therefore, Matthew reserves the use of Jesus' name virtually for himself so as to associate himself as closely as possible with Jesus, he effectively gives the reader to understand that both he, as narrator, and Jesus will reliably advocate God's evaluative point of view, his conception of reality, as this is explicated in the gospel story.

Apart from the genealogy (1:1–25), Jesus' name identifies him, in relation to his origins, as the one who is born in "Bethlehem of Judea" (2:1, 5–6) but is raised in "Nazareth of Galilee."[5] To the villagers of Nazareth, he is the "son of the carpenter," his mother is "Mary," and he has both "sisters" and "brothers" ("James," "Joseph," "Simon," and "Judas"; 13:55–56). As an adult, Jesus moves from Nazareth to "Capernaum" (4:13), which becomes "his own city" (9:1) and where he seemingly has a "house."[6] In Jerusalem to the south, he can be recognized as one who hails "from Galilee" (26:69, 73; 21:11).

If the genealogy is that of "Jesus," the protagonist of the story, Matthew nonetheless refers to him in 1:1 by means of the full name "Jesus Christ." In this verse, the Greek term *christos* ("Anointed One," "Christ," "Messiah") is a personal name ("Jesus *Christ*") that is likewise a title ("Jesus [who is] *Messiah*"). Among the major titles ascribed to Jesus in Matthew's story, *christos* is the most general. This explains why one must always look to the context, immediate or wider, in order to know how to construe it. Thus, if in 1:1 *christos* is interpreted in terms of "Son of David" and "Son of Abraham," elsewhere it also points to Jesus as the "Coming One" (11:2–3) or as the "King of the Jews" (2:2, 4) or as the "Son of God."[7] Ask, therefore, what the title *christos* says of Jesus in Matthew's story, and the answer is that it rather summarily characterizes him as God's Anointed, the King and Shepherd of Israel (2:2, 4, 6). As the one foretold by the prophets (2:6), he has

4. Cf. 21:11; 26:69, 71; 27:17, 22; also 27:37.
5. Cf. 2:23; 21:11; 26:71.
6. Cf. 9:10, 28; [12:46]; 13:1, 36; 17:25.
7. Cf. 16:16, 20; 26:63, 68.

ardently been awaited by Israel (11:2–3). By his coming, he brings the long history of Israel, begun in Abraham, to its fulfillment (1:1–17). As to origin and pedigree, he is miraculously conceived by the Spirit and adopted into the line of David (1:18–25). As to his ministry, it will issue at the last in salvation or condemnation for people (3:11–12; 11:2–6).

Matthew affirms in 1:1 not only that Jesus is the Christ, or Messiah, but also that he is "Son of David" and "Son of Abraham." In what sense is Jesus the "Son of Abraham"? He is the Son of Abraham both because it is in him that the entire history of Israel, which had its beginning in Abraham, attains its goal (1:17) and because he is the one through whom God will extend to the nations his blessing of salvation (8:11; 28:18–20).

To affirm that Jesus is the Son of Abraham seems to pose no problem in Matthew's story. But the same cannot be said as regards the title "Son of David."[8] In fact, Matthew goes to some lengths in chapter 1 to show not only "that" but also "how" Jesus can legitimately be designated in v. 1 as the "Son of David." In recounting the final link of the genealogy (1:16), Matthew permits it to be "broken." Instead of stating, in line with the pattern he has established, ". . . and Jacob fathered Joseph, and Joseph fathered Jesus," he states, ". . . and Jacob fathered *Joseph the husband of Mary, of whom Jesus was born [begotten]*" (1:16). The problem Matthew thus incorporates into the genealogy is this: How can Jesus legitimately be designated the Son of David (1:1) when Joseph son of David (1:20) is not his father and Mary, his mother, is not said to be from the line of David? Matthew's answer to this problem is found in 1:18–25: Jesus can legitimately be designated the Son of David because Joseph son of David obeys the instructions he receives from the angel of the Lord and gives Jesus his name (1:20–21, 25). In other words, Jesus, born of Mary but not fathered by Joseph, is legitimately Son of David because Joseph son of David adopts him into his line.

Later in his story, Matthew portrays Jesus as acting in his capacity as the Son of David and hence fulfilling in his ministry the end-time expectations associated with David (21:9, 15). As the Son of David, Jesus enters Jerusalem and "takes possession" of it, yet shows himself in so doing to be not a warrior king, but the humble King of peace (21:4–5). In the main, however, Jesus performs acts of healing as the Son of David. Those directly or indirectly linked with these acts are people who count for nothing in Israel's society: the "blind"[9] and such "disenfranchised persons"[10] as a gentile woman (15:21–28) and children (21:15). Just as the title "Son of Abraham" characterizes Jesus as the one in whom the Gentiles will find

8. Cf. Kingsbury, "Son of David," 591–602.
9. Cf. 9:27–31; 12:22; 20:29–34; 21:14.
10. See above, p. 27 n. 81.

blessing, so the title "Son of David" characterizes Jesus as the one in whom Israel will find blessing. Because these blind and disenfranchised persons "see" and "confess" that Jesus is Israel's Davidic Messiah, they play a not insignificant role in the conflict Jesus has with Israel. In that "Son of David" constitutes for them their evaluative point of view concerning Jesus' identity, they call attention to the guilt that is Israel's for not receiving Jesus as its Davidic Messiah.

To conclude, Matthew employs the genealogy to assert that God has guided the whole of Israel's history so that it might culminate in the birth of "Jesus," the protagonist of his story, who is "Messiah," "Son of David," and "Son of Abraham." This is the initial evaluative point of view concerning Jesus' identity that Matthew advances, and in the rest of 1:1—4:16 he augments it considerably.

The Magi and the Flight to Egypt

Following the birth of Jesus in Bethlehem, Matthew reports that Magi from the East arrive in Jerusalem and inquire after him (2:1). "Where," they ask, "is he who is born King of the Jews?" (2:2). "King of the Jews" is consequently the evaluative point of view of the Magi concerning Jesus' identity. And because the Magi have come to offer Jesus their sincere worship (2:2, 11), Matthew urges the reader to accept this title, too, as correctly applying to Jesus. As Matthew will later show, Jesus is indeed the King of the Jews, yet not as one who restores to Israel its national splendor or foments rebellion against Rome, but as one who saves others by willingly submitting to suffering and death (27:27–31).

In contrast to the Magi, Herod the Great and all Jerusalem react with fear to the news that the Messiah, the King of the Jews, has been born (2:2–4). Moreover, Herod himself proves to be prototypical of others with whom Jesus will become embroiled in conflict in the course of his ministry, namely, Pilate and the religious leaders. As the Messiah, the King of the Jews, Jesus looms in Herod's eyes as a threat to assume the throne of Israel. This is why Herod plots to have Jesus killed (2:8, 13). According to Herod's evaluative point of view, Jesus is an insurrectionist. Similarly, Pilate also deals with Jesus on the presumption that the Messiah, the King of the Jews, is one who lays political claim to the throne of Israel (27:11–14). Since Pilate accedes to the charge that Jesus is the King of the Jews, he permits Jesus to be crucified (27:37). According to Pilate's evaluative point of view, too, Jesus is an insurrectionist.

The manner in which Herod reacts to the perceived threat the infant Jesus poses anticipates the manner in which the religious leaders will later respond to the adult Jesus. Both Herod and they reveal themselves to be "spiritually blind" (2:3; 27:63); "fearful" (2:3; 21:46); "conspiratorial" (2:7;

12:14); "guileful" and "mendacious";[11] "murderous" (2:13; 12:14); "wrathful" (2:16; cf. 21:15); and "apprehensive of the future" (2:16; 27:62–64).[12] In Matthew's story, Herod is the precursor of the religious leaders, and his opposition to Jesus foreshadows theirs.

God himself foils the plot of King Herod. He directs the Magi through a dream not to return to Herod (1:12) and dispatches an angel to Joseph to instruct him, again in a dream, to flee to Egypt and to remain there until Herod dies (2:13–14). In obeying at once this command from God and the other commands that follow, Joseph's righteousness (1:19) casts Herod's wickedness in ever sharper relief. After Herod's death, the angel of the Lord again comes to Joseph in a dream and orders him to return to Israel (2:19–21). Then, warned by God through still another dream, Joseph settles in Nazareth (2:22–23).

THE SON OF GOD

The Figure and Ministry of John

To prepare the way for the ministry of Jesus, John the Baptist appears in his appointed role of "forerunner" (3:3; 11:10). As forerunner, John is "Elijah" in the sense that he fulfills the end-time expectations associated with this prophet (11:14; 17:10–13). For example, Malachi had prophesied that before the terrible day of the Lord came, Elijah would be sent to ready Israel for the judgment this day would bring (Mal. 4:5–6). In John's ministry, this prophecy becomes reality, but in altered fashion: John is the forerunner not of God, but of Jesus Messiah; and he prepares the way not for the final judgment as such, but for the ministry of Jesus (11:10, 14; 17:10–13).

While the ministry of John precedes that of Jesus, the term "forerunner" connotes more than mere temporal precedence. As Jesus' forerunner, John foreshadows in his person and work the person and work of Jesus. Both John and Jesus are the agents of God sent by God (11:10; 10:40). Both belong to the time of fulfillment (3:3; 1:23). Both have the same message to proclaim (3:2; 4:17). Both enter into conflict with Israel: in the case of the crowds, a favorable reception ultimately gives way to repudiation;[13] in the case of the leaders, the opposition is implacable from the outset (3:7–10; 9:3). Both John and Jesus are "delivered up" to their enemies (4:12; 10:4). And both are made to die violently and shamefully (14:3–12; 27:37). To know of John is to know in advance of Jesus.

11. Cf. 2:8; 26:4; 28:13–14.
12. Cf. also Fiore, "Characterization in Matthew," 5.
13. Cf. 3:5–6; 4:24–25; 11:16–19.

The mission of John is to "restore all things" (17:11). To accomplish this, he proclaims to Israel from the desert of Judea, "Repent, for the Kingdom of Heaven is at hand!" (3:1–2). At the heart of this summons lies the notion that Israel has lost its way. What is required is that Israel turn from evil, place its trust in God, and obey him. Urgency is also of the essence, for God has already set in motion the events that will issue in judgment. Indeed, the Coming One is soon to appear, and when he does he will, with incomparable authority, carry out the final judgment to salvation or condemnation (3:11–12).

The crowds in Israel give ear to John's proclamation. Matthew records: "Then went out to him Jerusalem and all Judea and all the region about the Jordan" (3:5). Submitting to John's baptism, the crowds confess their sins and show themselves to be a repentant people ready for the arrival of the Coming One and the final judgment (3:6, 11–12).

Along with the crowds, the religious leaders also go out to John for baptism (3:7). For them, however, John has only scathing words (3:7–10). He describes them as a "brood of vipers," which is to say that he likens them to venomous snakes that are evil to the core. He likewise challenges them to demonstrate by their deeds that they have not rejected his summons to repentance, warning them that they cannot rely on descendancy from Abraham to persevere in the approaching judgment.

John, then, is the divinely sent forerunner who readies Israel for the imminent arrival of Jesus. But this notwithstanding, John's conception of Jesus' ministry, though it is correct, is also insufficient. To John's way of thinking, Jesus is the Coming One (= Messiah; 11:2–3) who will appear in order to carry out the final judgment to salvation or condemnation (3:11–12). "Even now," John exclaims, "the ax is laid to the root of the trees; every tree therefore that does not bear good fruit is cut down and thrown into the fire!" (3:10). According to John's evaluative point of view, Jesus is the Coming One whose arrival on the scene of history portends the end-time judgment.

This evaluative point of view of John concerning the person and ministry of Jesus explains why John, in prison, sends disciples to Jesus to ask whether he is in fact the Coming One or whether they are to await another (11:2–3). John has heard of the "works of [Jesus] Messiah," but they have not issued in the final judgment (11:2; 3:11–12). In giving reply to John's query, Jesus refers to his ministry of word and deed in such manner as to show that it fulfills OT expectation and consequently does not point away from him as being the Messiah, or Coming One, but toward him (11:4–5). Moreover, from other parts of Matthew's story the reader, if not John, knows that there will in truth be a coming of Jesus that will result in final judgment (13:35–43; 25:31–46). But however that may be, for the time being Jesus' reply to John also serves as a word of caution to him not to take offense at him, that is, not to lose trust that he is in fact the Coming One John thinks him to be and the one whose ministry will indeed achieve its divinely appointed purposes.

The Baptism of Jesus

The crown of the first part of Matthew's story, which treats of Jesus' identity (1:1—4:16), is the baptismal scene. Here God, himself participating as "actor" in the story, empowers Jesus for messianic ministry and solemnly declares "who Jesus is." Apart from the introduction (3:13), the unit falls neatly into two sections: the dialogue between John and Jesus (3:14–15) and the two revelatory events that follow (3:16–17).

No sooner has John foretold the imminent arrival of the Coming One than Jesus appears at the Jordan River to be baptized by John (3:13). John would prevent this, objecting that he has need to be baptized by Jesus (3:14). Jesus overrules John, however, urging that God would have them be wholly obedient and do all that he requires of them ("it is fitting for us to fulfill all righteousness"; 3:15).[14] Accordingly, the reason Jesus insists on being baptized at the Jordan is that it is God's will that John should baptize him and that he should submit to such baptism. Then, too, although Jesus does not undergo baptism because he, like Israel, has need to repent of sin, the fact remains that in being baptized by John, he voluntarily identifies himself with sinful humankind (1:21; 26:28).

Matthew does not describe the baptism of Jesus itself. The focus is on the two revelatory events that follow (3:16–17). After Jesus' baptism, Matthew remarks that "immediately he went up from the water" (3:16). If in the preceding scene Jesus and John stood alone in private conversation (3:14–15), now Jesus removes himself also from John to step unaccompanied into the presence of God (3:16a). No one other than Jesus himself, therefore, sees the Spirit descend upon him (3:16: "he saw"), and only he, along with such transcendent beings as Satan (4:3, 6), hears the voice from heaven (3:17).

Retrospectively, later developments in Matthew's story corroborate this observation. Had the crowds heard the voice from heaven, it is inexplicable why one segment of the public does not at least entertain the idea that Jesus is the Son of God.[15] And had John heard the voice from heaven, it is odd that his question of 11:2–3 contains no hint of this. On the contrary, it reflects the selfsame view of Jesus that John had expressed prior to the baptism, namely, that Jesus is the Coming One (3:11–12). To repeat, Jesus alone of the human characters in Matthew's story sees the Spirit descend in 3:16 and hears the voice speak in 3:17.

14. Cf. Schweizer, *Good News*, 53–56.
15. Cf. 12:23; 16:13–14; also 13:55; 14:1–2.

The first revelatory event is one of sight: "And behold, the heavens were opened and he [Jesus] saw the Spirit of God descending like a dove, and alighting on him" (3:16). The purpose of the opening of the heavens is both to permit the Spirit to descend and to signal that divine revelation is about to take place (Ezek. 1:1). The descent of the Spirit upon Jesus denotes the divine act whereby God empowers him to accomplish the messianic ministry he is shortly to begin (4:17). Such empowerment, of course, is not to be construed as Jesus' initial endowment with the Spirit, for he was conceived by the Spirit. Instead, it specifies in what way Jesus proves to be the mightier One John had said he would be (3:11). It also serves as the reference point for understanding the "authority" with which Jesus discharges his public ministry.[16] Empowered by God's Spirit, Jesus speaks as the mouthpiece of God (7:28–29) and acts as the instrument of God (12:28).

The second revelatory event is one of sound: "And behold, a voice from heaven said, 'This is my beloved Son, in whom I take delight!' " (3:17). Important as is the first revelatory event, this one is more important still, for Matthew has accorded it the position of stress.

The voice from heaven is the voice of God.[17] The words God speaks are drawn from Ps. 2:7; Isa. 42:1; and Gen. 22:2. In Isa. 42:1, the servant in whom God delights is the one God has "chosen" for ministry. In Gen. 22:2, Abraham's beloved son Isaac is his "only" son. And in Psalm 2, God is described as solemnly addressing the words "My son are you" to the king-designate from the house of David, his anointed ("messiah"), who on the day of his coronation assumes the throne of Judah. Together, these several emphases combine in 3:17 to form a solemn affirmation in which God declares that Jesus, the Anointed One (Messiah-King) from the line of David, is his only, or unique, Son whom he has chosen for eschatological ministry.

This declaration of 3:17 is one that God makes within the world of Matthew's story. God, we noted, speaks it over Jesus (3:17) but also in the hearing of transcendent beings, such as Satan (4:3, 6). In affirming that Jesus is his royal Son, God states "who Jesus is" according to his evaluative point of view, that is, how he "thinks" about Jesus (16:23e). Because Matthew so constructs his story that God's evaluative point of view is normative, the reader knows that in hearing God enunciate his understanding of Jesus, he or she has heard the normative understanding of Jesus, the one in terms of which all other understandings are to be judged. In Matthew's story, God himself dictates that Jesus is preeminently the Son of God.

We observed at the outset of this Chapter that God's empowerment of Jesus with his Spirit and especially his declaration from heaven bring the

---

16. Cf. 7:29; 11:27; 21:23–27.
17. Cf., e.g., 17:5; Gen. 15:4; Deut. 4:36; Dan. 4:31.

entire first part of Matthew's story (1:1—4:16) to its culmination. This is the case on two counts. For one thing, God's designation for Jesus ("my Son") both overlaps in meaning the other designations we have encountered thus far ("Messiah" ["Coming One"], "Son of Abraham," "Son of David," and "King of the Jews") and transcends them. And for another, although there are indications prior to the baptism that Jesus is the Son of God, including narrative comments made directly to the reader (1:22–23; 2:15), the passage 3:17 is the first place where this truth, uttered by God as "actor," assumes the form of an event that occurs within the story itself.

In what way does God's designation of Jesus as "my Son" in 3:17 both overlap in meaning the other designations encountered thus far and transcend them? The expression "my Son" stems from Ps. 2:7. In Psalm 2, the one from the house of David (= "son of David") whom God decrees is "my son" is likewise said to be God's "king" (2:6) and God's anointed (LXX: *christos* ["messiah"]; 2:2). In other words, Psalm 2 reflects in prophetic, rudimentary form the highly developed portrait of Jesus one finds in the first part of Matthew's story. The Jesus whom God declares in 3:17 to be "his royal Son" is none other than the Jesus whom Matthew, as narrator, has presented as "Messiah," "Son of David," and "Son of Abraham" (1:1) and whom the Magi have reverently called "King of the Jews" (2:2) and John the "Coming One" (= "Messiah"; 3:11; 11:2–3). In short, God's designation of Jesus in 3:17 overlaps these other designations in meaning because the Jesus who God says is "my Son" is, in fact, the Davidic Messiah-King, the descendant of Abraham.

By the same token, God's designation of Jesus as "my Son" also transcends these other designations in meaning. It does so because Matthew imbues it with a quality the others do not possess in like measure. This quality is that it attests to the unique filial relationship that exists between God and Jesus: Jesus is conceived by God's Spirit (1:18, 20) and empowered by God's Spirit (3:16) so that he is Emmanuel, or "God with us" (1:23); as such, he is the one in whom God reveals himself to humankind (11:27) and who is God's supreme agent of salvation.[18] While it is the case that through the call to discipleship others enter into fellowship with God and hence become "sons of God,"[19] Jesus alone is "the Son of God." For this reason, he speaks of God as "my Father"[20] or, with an eye to the disciples, as "your Father,"[21] but never as "our Father." The Lord's Prayer is no exception to this, because "our Father" (6:9) are words the disciples as a group are to utter in their approach to God. To reiterate, by virtue of the unique filial

18. Cf. 1:21; 4:17, 23; 11:27; 26:28; 27:54; 28:5, 18b.
19. Cf. 4:18–22; 5:9, 45; 9:9; 13:38.
20. Cf., e.g., 7:21; 10:32–33; 12:50; 16:17; 26:39.
21. Cf., e.g., 5:16, 45, 48.

relationship he has to God, the Jesus of Matthew's story is preeminently the Son of God.

True as it surely is that God's declaration of Jesus as his Son in 3:17 constitutes the climax of the first part of Matthew's story, this is not to say that there are not indications prior to the baptism that Jesus is God's Son. On the contrary, there are numerous such indications, of which the following are but a selection: (a) In 1:16 of the genealogy, Matthew casts the verb "to be born [begotten]" in the passive voice (the "divine passive") to alert the reader to the fact that "Jesus is born [begotten]" by an act of God. (b) In 1:18–25, Matthew points out that Mary's conception of Jesus is not through Joseph, who makes no attempt to have relations with her during her pregnancy, but "by the Holy Spirit." (c) In the "aside" of 1:23, Matthew tells the reader that Mary is a virgin when she gives birth to her son and that her son is Emmanuel, or "God with us" (i.e., the Son of God). (d) Throughout 2:7–23, Matthew, by consistently designating Jesus as "the child" and repeatedly employing the expression "the child and [with] his mother," effectively prevents the reader from thinking of Jesus as the son of Joseph and instead reminds him or her that because the virgin Mary has given birth to a son who was conceived apart from Joseph son of David by the Holy Spirit, this son of Mary is at the same time the Son of God. (e) In the "aside" of 2:15, Matthew quotes an OT passage to the reader and applies it in such fashion that God is made to refer to Jesus as "my Son." (f) And by placing the baptismal pericope in juxtaposition to the pericope on the ministry of John, Matthew gives the reader to understand that the "Coming One" of whom John prophesies is Jesus precisely as the Son of God whom God empowers with his Spirit (3:11, 13–17).

Accordingly, it is apparent that prior to the baptism, Matthew gives ample indication in his story that Jesus is the Son of God. Nevertheless, this recognition in no wise mitigates the contention that it is in God's declaration of Jesus as his Son in 3:17 that one reaches the climax not only of the baptismal pericope itself, but also of the entire first part of Matthew's story (1:1—4:16). In this part, Matthew presents Jesus to the reader. The evaluative point of view concerning Jesus' identity which Matthew sets forth is that Jesus, the Messiah-King from the line of David and of Abraham, is uniquely the Son of God. The crucial element in this evaluative point of view—that Jesus is the Son of God—Matthew as narrator does not state in the opening verse of his story. Perhaps the reason for this silence in 1:1 is that what immediately follows is a genealogy that begins with Abraham (1:2). By beginning as it does with Abraham and not with Adam and God (Luke 3:34, 38), this genealogy can bear no direct witness to the divine sonship of Jesus. But be that as it may, Matthew's procedure prior to the baptism is to allude to the truth of Jesus' divine sonship with circumlocu-

tions (1:16, 18, 20), with metaphors,[22] or with a term ("son") that is susceptible to dual meaning,[23] and, in the "asides" he gives to the reader (1:23;
2:15), even to permit it to be stated explicitly in words of prophecy. Still, all
such hints or statements of this truth are merely anticipatory of that climactic moment following the baptism when God himself enters the world of
Matthew's story as "actor" and proclaims over Jesus (3:17) and in the
hearing of such transcendent beings as Satan (4:3, 6) that Jesus is his unique
Son.

The Temptation of Jesus

By the end of the baptismal pericope, the Jesus of Matthew's story stands
before the reader preeminently as the Son of God who has been empowered with the Spirit of God. So identified, Jesus is led by the Spirit into
the desert to engage the devil, or Satan, in conflict in the place of his abode
(4:1–11). The form this conflict takes is that three times Satan puts Jesus to
the test.[24] Ultimately, the substance of each test has to do with Jesus'
devotion, or obedience, to God. The intent of Satan in each test is to entice
Jesus to break faith with God, his Father, and thus disavow his divine
sonship. Should Satan succeed at this, he succeeds in effect in destroying
Jesus. In testing Jesus, Satan cunningly adopts God's evaluative point of
view according to which Jesus is his Son (4:3, 6).

Satan's testing of Jesus is also antitypical to the testing Israel faced in its
desert wanderings from Egypt to Canaan (Deut. 6:10–19; 8:1–10). Israel,
too, was designated by God as "his son" (Exod. 4:22–23). Nevertheless,
when Israel son of God was put to the test, it failed.

Approaching Jesus three times in Matthew's story, Satan urges him to
place concern for self above allegiance to God. In the first test, Satan
suggests that Jesus miraculously still his hunger. But were Jesus to do so,
he would be forcing, solely for his own benefit, a change in the circumstances into which God has brought him (4:2–4). In the second test, Satan
suggests that Jesus cast himself down from the pinnacle of the temple. But
were Jesus to do so, he would make himself guilty of endeavoring to coerce
God into serving him by wondrously preserving Jesus' life from destruction (4:5–7). In the third test, Satan suggests that Jesus, to secure control
over the substance of the nations of the world, fall down and worship him.
But were Jesus to do so, he would be placing lust for the wealth of the
world above fealty to God (4:8–10). The outcome of the three tests is that
Jesus withstands the enticements of Satan and therefore vanquishes him

22. Cf. 2:8–9, 11, 13–14, 20–21; 3:11.
23. Cf. 1:20, 23, 25: the "son" of Mary is at the same time the "son" of God ("God with us").
24. For a discussion of the pericope on the temptation, cf. Gerhardsson, *Testing of God's Son*.

(4:11a). Unlike Israel son of God, Jesus Son of God is perfect in his devotion, or obedience, to God, his Father.

Jesus' conflict with Satan is the first major conflict of his career, since he was but an infant when Herod threatened his life. Occurring as it does prior to Jesus' public ministry, it possesses fundamental significance for both his ministry and the rest of the history of salvation. In Matthew's scheme of things, the world is the scene where two kingdoms, or spheres of power, are locked in cosmic battle (13:36–43).

On the one hand, there is the Kingdom of Heaven, which has by God's design become a present, though hidden, reality in Jesus Son of God. Through the ministries of Jesus and of his pre-Easter and post-Easter disciples, Jesus summons first Israel and then also the Gentiles to repentance and to discipleship, sonship, brotherhood, and life in the sphere where God, through Jesus, rules. Such summoning to life in the sphere of God's Rule will continue until Jesus' return in splendor for judgment at the consummation of the age.

On the other hand, there is the kingdom of Satan (12:26). In this sphere of power Satan himself rules, and he has at his command both angels (25:41) and demons (10:8, 12:24), or unclean spirits (10:1). In both Israel and the world, Satan is at work to bring humans under his control (13:24–30, 38–39). The mark of those who serve him is that they are evil (13:49) and lawless (13:41), for they live contrary to the will of God.

By withstanding the testing of Satan following his baptism, Jesus Son of God demonstrates that he is stronger than Satan. In the long term, therefore, Satan, the reader knows, is doomed (25:41). But short of the consummation, Satan continues to wield power in the world (13:36–43). Throughout the ministry of Jesus, he enlists Israel and, at times, disciples of Jesus in his cause. Israel, in fact, has become "this evil generation."[25]

Especially do the leaders of the Jews have affinity with Satan. Satan is the "Tempter" who puts Jesus to the test (4:3), and they, too, put Jesus to the test.[26] Satan is the "Evil One" par excellence,[27] and they, too, are evil.[28] Satan is the personal "Enemy" of Jesus (13:25, 39), and they, too, are the enemies of Jesus, bent on destroying him (12:14; 26:3–4).

Also standing under the influence of Satan are the Jewish crowds. True, they trail after Jesus (4:25), are astonished at his teaching and miracles and praise God for the latter,[29] and hold him to be a prophet (16:14; 21:46). Still, they never receive him for the one he is, Israel's Davidic Messiah and God's

---

25. Cf. 11:16; 12:39, 41, 42, 45; 16:4; 23:36.
26. Cf. 16:1; 19:3; 22:18, 35.
27. Cf. 13:19, 38.
28. Cf. 12:34–35, 39, 45.
29. Cf. 7:28; 9:33; 15:31.

Son. Instead, they repudiate him,[30] and as he hangs upon the cross, they put him to the test (27:40). To the crowds, too, Jesus ascribes the epithet "this [evil] generation" (11:16).

Nor do the disciples escape the machinations of Satan. Peter "stands in" for Satan as he rejects the notion that Jesus should submit, in obedience to God, to suffering and death (16:21–23). In addition, those who follow Jesus are continually in danger of becoming servants of "lawlessness" and "evil," of which Satan is the root source.[31] To meet this danger, Jesus instructs the disciples in the Lord's Prayer to petition God, " . . . but deliver us from the Evil One" (6:13).

In a word, then, following God's baptismal declaration Jesus Son of God proves, in conflict with Satan, that he is perfect in obedience to God and superior in strength to Satan. Although Satan, the transcendent fountainhead of evil, continues to vie with Jesus Son of God in this age for the allegiance of humans, at the consummation he, his angels, and all those who give him their fealty will be consigned by Jesus to perdition.

The Relocation of Jesus

To bring the first part of his story to an end, Matthew tells of Jesus' return to Galilee and the completion of his "preliminary" travels. If Joseph settled in Nazareth after the return from Egypt (2:22–23), Jesus now leaves Nazareth and moves to Capernaum (4:12–13), which becomes "his own city" (9:1). He is thus poised to begin his public ministry.

SUMMARY

Matthew employs the first part of his story (1:1—4:16) to present Jesus, the protagonist, to the reader. Through the device of the genealogy, Matthew advances an initial evaluative point of view concerning Jesus' identity, namely, that God has so guided Israelite history that it might reach its culmination in the birth of Jesus, the Messiah-King from the line of David and Abraham (1:1–17).

Preeminently, however, Jesus is the Son of God. In 1:1, Matthew makes no mention of this, perhaps because the genealogy begins not with God and with Adam (Luke 3:38), but with Abraham (1:2). Still, although Abraham, not God, is the first link in the genealogy, the "origin" of Jesus is nonetheless to be traced to God. Conceived in Mary by the divinely wrought act of God's Holy Spirit, Jesus is without human father (1:16, 18, 20). As Matthew says in an "aside" to the reader, Jesus is "God with us," that is, the Son of God (1:23; cf. 2:15). What "Son of God" connotes is the

---

30. Cf. 11:16–19; 27:25.
31. Cf. 5:37; 7:16–20; 13:49; 15:19; 18:32; 20:15; 25:26; 7:21–23; 24:12.

unique filial relationship Jesus has with God, his Father (3:16–17; 11:27). In Jesus Son of God, one encounters God (11:27).

After Jesus has been born, Herod the Great threatens his life (chap. 2). In his conflict with Jesus, Herod is the precursor of both Pilate and the leaders of the Jews.

To prepare for the ministry of Jesus, John the Baptist undertakes his ministry to Israel (3:1–12). As the forerunner of Jesus, he typifies in his person and work the person and work of Jesus. The division in Israel that John occasions foreshadows the division Jesus, too, will at first encounter: the favorable response of the people will contrast with the obduracy of the religious leaders.

The climax of the first part of Matthew's story occurs in the baptismal pericope (3:13–17). In the revelatory events that follow Jesus' baptism, God empowers Jesus with his Spirit and declares over him and in the hearing of the world of transcendent beings that Jesus is his unique Son whom he has chosen for messianic ministry (3:16–17; 4:3, 6). Here God himself enters the world of Matthew's story as "actor" and enunciates that evaluative point of view concerning Jesus' identity which is normative for all other evaluative points of view.

Declared by God to be his Son, Jesus enters into cosmic conflict with Satan (4:1–11). Withstanding the testing of Satan, Jesus Son of God proves himself to be perfect in obedience to God and superior in power to Satan. Although Satan will contend with Jesus for the allegiance of humans until the end of time, Jesus' triumph over Satan assures the reader that the Son of God and the Kingdom of God will ultimately prevail.

On hearing news that John the Baptist has been "delivered up" and taken into custody, Jesus returns to Galilee and completes his preliminary travels by moving from Nazareth to Capernaum (4:12–16). All is now right for him to embark on his ministry to Israel.

3

The Ministry of Jesus to Israel and Israel's Repudiation of Jesus (4:17—16:20)

In the first part of his story Matthew presents Jesus to the reader. In the second part (4:17—16:20) he tells of Jesus' ministry to Israel (4:17—11:1) and of Israel's repudiation of him (11:2—16:20). In describing the repudiation of Jesus, Matthew also deals with the wonderment and speculation about his identity that his public activity elicits.

THE MINISTRY OF JESUS TO ISRAEL

The ministry of Jesus Messiah, the Son of God, to Israel (4:17—11:1) is one of teaching, preaching, and healing. To alert the reader to this, Matthew punctuates the narrative with three summary-passages (4:23; 9:35; 11:1). In line with these passages, Jesus launches his ministry by proclaiming, "Repent, for the Kingdom of Heaven is at hand!" (4:17). Through this message, Jesus proffers salvation to Israel. He, like John the Baptist before him (3:2), looks on Israel as a people that has lost its way. The crowds are "harassed" and "helpless," like sheep left to fend for themselves (9:36). The leaders have become evil (12:34–35), unable to discern the will of God. Jesus summons both crowds and leaders to turn about and to live in the sphere of God's Rule by becoming his followers and, through him, sons of God (5:45; 13:38) and brothers of himself and of one another (12:48–50; 23:8).

Jesus' next act is to call four fishermen to become his disciples, thus surrounding himself with eye- and ear-witnesses (4:18–22). Followed by these disciples and attracting huge crowds (4:23–25), he ascends a mountain and there programmatically teaches the will of God (5:1—7:29). Descending from the mountain, he wanders in the area of Capernaum and travels across the Sea of Galilee and back (8:1—9:34). While so doing, he performs ten mighty acts of deliverance and educates his followers in the nature and cost of discipleship. At the height of his activity, he commissions the Twelve to a ministry of their own in Israel, one of preaching and healing though not of teaching (9:35—10:42). Their ministry to Israel is an extension of his (10:5b–6; 15:24).

Because Jesus, through his ministry of teaching, preaching, and healing, proffers salvation to Israel, the element of conflict does not dominate the plot of Matthew's story in 4:17—11:1. But this notwithstanding, the reader at first encounters intimations of conflict between Jesus and the religious leaders and then becomes witness to their first disputes.

Thus, in the section 4:17—8:34 the reader is led merely to anticipate conflict. Scenes or statements occur that tell of persecution after the manner of the prophets (5:10–12); of the scribes and Pharisees as practicing a righteousness that falls short of what is necessary for gaining entrance into the Kingdom of Heaven (5:20); of the "hypocrites" in the synagogues as performing their acts of piety so as to enhance their personal prestige in the public eye (6:1–18); of the teaching of the scribes as being without authority and therefore unlike that of Jesus (7:29); of the sons of the Kingdom as being cast into the darkness outside while Gentiles sit at table in the future Kingdom with Abraham, Isaac, and Jacob (8:11–12); and of a scribe as being turned away by Jesus because he would arrogate to himself the authority to become Jesus' disciple (8:19–20).

In chapter 9, the conflict between Jesus and the religious leaders that the reader has been led to anticipate suddenly materializes. This conflict, however, is carefully orchestrated so that Jesus is not himself directly attacked for something he himself does. On the contrary, the various charges brought against him or the disciples are all "indirect" in character, to wit: some scribes, watching Jesus forgive a paralytic his sins, declare "within themselves" that Jesus is guilty of committing blasphemy (9:3–4); the Pharisees, in seeing Jesus sit at table with toll-collectors and sinners, approach the disciples and complain to them about Jesus (9:10–11); the disciples of John, siding on one occasion with the Pharisees, take exception to the fact that Jesus' disciples are not observing the custom of fasting and question Jesus about this (9:14); and the Pharisees, after witnessing the exorcism of a demon by Jesus, cast aspersions on Jesus' feat by claiming that he could do this only because he is in collusion with demonic forces (9:32–34).

In chapter 10, Jesus summons the disciples and delivers to them his missionary discourse. By the end of this discourse, the reader can sense that the trend of Matthew's story is toward irreconcilable conflict between Jesus and the religious leaders. In ominous words, Jesus describes the bitter conflict the disciples will face as they go out to preach and heal in Israel (10:16–39). On hearing this, the reader no longer doubts that the time is fast approaching when the religious leaders will confront Jesus personally and attack him directly.

The Preaching of Jesus

Jesus presents himself to Israel by "preaching" (4:17), and the message he proclaims is "the gospel of the Kingdom" (4:23; 9:35). In the time following Easter, the disciples, too, will proclaim "the gospel of the Kingdom" (24:14). By drawing this parallel between Jesus and the post-Easter disciples, Matthew shows that throughout the entire "time of Jesus," from his life on earth to his Parousia in splendor, the gospel of the Kingdom has been, is being, and will be proclaimed. Through such proclamation, Jews and Gentiles alike will be summoned to decision. The question is whether they will repent, become followers of Jesus, and enter the sphere of God's gracious Rule, or whether they will refuse such entrance and live in the sphere where Satan rules (13:37–39).

What the phrase "the gospel of the Kingdom" means comes to light in Matthew's use of the terms "gospel" and "Kingdom." To get at the meaning of the term "gospel," a glance at the passage 26:6–13 is helpful. It reveals that the gospel is "news" that is inextricably bound up with Jesus—what he has said or done or what has happened to him—and that it begs to be proclaimed to the world. On balance, then, the term "gospel" in the phrase "the gospel of the Kingdom" may be defined as the news about the Kingdom (which saves or condemns) which is revealed in and through Jesus Messiah, the Son of God, and is announced first to Israel and then to the Gentiles.

What is the meaning of the term "Kingdom"?[1] To begin with, the absolute designation "the Kingdom" is simply an abbreviation of the fuller expression "the Kingdom of Heaven." Although statistically Matthew prefers the latter to "the Kingdom of God," the two expressions are to all intents and purposes synonymous. Because the genitive "(of) Heaven" is subjective in nuance and a metonym for "God," the purpose of the expression "the Kingdom of Heaven" is to assert the truth that "God rules (reigns)." Hence, "the Rule of God," or "the Reign of God," is a proper paraphrase of it.

Matthew presents John the Baptist, Jesus, and the earthly disciples as all announcing in Israel that "the Kingdom of Heaven is at hand (ēggiken)" (3:2; 4:17; 10:7). The Greek verb ēggiken denotes a "coming near," or "approaching," that is spatial or temporal in character. Hence, for John, Jesus, and the disciples to announce that the Kingdom of Heaven is at hand is for them to announce that God has drawn near with his end-time Rule.

How does Matthew conceive of God as having drawn near? God draws near in the person of Jesus, who is the Messiah Son of God. In words

---

1. On Matthew's view of "the Kingdom of Heaven [God]," cf. Kingsbury, *Matthew: Structure, Christology, Kingdom*, 128–60; Kretzer, *Herrschaft der Himmel*. For a review of scholarly research on Jesus' view of the Kingdom, cf. Chilton, "Introduction," 1–26.

drawn from the OT, Matthew puts it this way at 1:23: in the son (conceived by the Spirit) and born of the virgin, God has at the last drawn near to dwell with people. And in 12:28, Jesus himself declares: "But if by the Spirit of God I cast out demons, then the Kingdom of God has come upon you!"

From the remarks just made, it is apparent that the focus of the term "gospel" in the phrase "the gospel of the Kingdom" is on Jesus Messiah, the Son of God. Similarly, the focus of the term "Kingdom" is on God. Still, because Jesus is the one in whom God draws near with his end-time Rule, the term "Kingdom" may properly be said to have a double focus. But be that as it may, the way in which Matthew would have the reader define the phrase "the gospel of the Kingdom" is clear: it is the news (which saves or condemns) that is revealed in and through Jesus Messiah, the Son of God, and is proclaimed first to Israel and then to the Gentiles to the effect that in him God has drawn near with his end-time Rule to humankind, thus inaugurating the age of salvation.

The emphasis thus far has been on God's Kingdom as a present reality. As Matthew describes it, however, the Kingdom is also both a hidden reality and a reality yet to be consummated. The circumstance that the Kingdom is a hidden reality is attested to by the reaction Jesus' activity elicits from the crowds and the religious leaders. Although the crowds follow Jesus (4:25) and even acclaim him for his ministry of word and deed,[2] they do not perceive him to be the bearer of God's Kingdom. On the contrary, they see in him only a prophet,[3] and he in turn censures them as "this [evil] generation" that repudiates both him and John the Baptist, his forerunner (11:16–19). For their part, the religious leaders, too, witness Jesus' ministry, but far from discerning in him the presence of God, they take him to be an errorist, or false messiah (27:63), who owes his astonishing authority to the prince of demons (9:34; 12:24). God's Kingdom is present in Jesus, but as a hidden reality.

God's Kingdom is furthermore a reality that will be consummated only in the future. Not until the end of the age, when the exalted Jesus shall have returned with his angels in power and great glory to preside over the final judgment, will the Rule of God encompass the world and be acknowledged by all people everywhere (13:36–43; 25:31–46).

The Teaching of Jesus

In his ministry, Jesus Messiah, the Son of God, summons Israel to repentance and to entrance into the sphere of God's end-time Rule. Fundamentally, the teaching of Jesus envisages human conduct as it comports itself amid life in this sphere. By citing "teaching" ahead of preaching and

2. Cf. 7:28; 9:8, 33; 15:30–31.
3. Cf. 16:13–14; 21:11, 46.

healing in the summary-passages (4:23; 9:35; 11:1), Matthew gives it the position of stress and invites the reader to attach special importance to it.

Surprisingly, Jesus' teaching occasions less conflict in Matthew's story than one would expect. The reason is that the religious leaders are the recipients of none of the great discourses of Jesus,[4] and even Jesus' speech of woes is not delivered to the scribes and Pharisees but to the disciples and the crowds (chap. 23). It is in certain of the debates Jesus has with the religious leaders that his teaching generates conflict.

Almost always at issue in these debates is the correct interpretation of, or the proper adherence to, the Mosaic law or the Pharisaic tradition of the elders. Cases in point are those debates that deal with the practice of having table fellowship with toll-collectors and sinners (9:10–13); the nonobservance of the custom of fasting (9:14–15); alleged violations of the sabbath law (12:1–8, 9–14); the disparagement of the tradition of the elders sparked by the charge of noncompliance with the ritual obligation of washing the hands before eating (15:1–20); the dispute over the question of divorce (19:3–9); the problem of the legality of paying taxes to Caesar (22:15–22); the argument (with the Sadducees) over the reality of the resurrection (22:23–33); and the questions relating to the greatest commandment of the law (22:34–40) and to the Davidic sonship of the Messiah (22:41–46). These issues constitute an index of the "flash points" that motivate the religious leaders not only to oppose Jesus but also to conspire to take his life (12:14; 26:3–4). In their eyes, Jesus is a threat to the continued existence of Jewish society, for he places himself above law and tradition. In Jesus' perspective, the debates concerning law and tradition are all to be resolved by the proper application of one basic principle, or better, of a single attitude of the heart, namely, utter devotion to God and radical love of the neighbor (5:48; 22:37–40).

Taken as a group, the debates Jesus has with the religious leaders are a glaring indication that the distance between him and them is unbridgeable. A more subtle indication of this distance is the manner in which Matthew makes use of the synonymous terms "rabbi" and "teacher." When the true disciples and those minor characters who exhibit faith call upon Jesus, they do so as "Lord," acknowledging thereby that he is one of exalted station who exercises divine authority.[5] By contrast, when the religious leaders, a stranger, or the traitor Judas address Jesus, it is as "rabbi" or "teacher."[6] On one occasion Jesus himself refers to himself as "teacher," but he points out in this connection that it is as "the Messiah" that he is teacher (23:8–10).

4. Cf. chaps. 5–7; 10; 13; 18; 24–25.

5. Cf., e.g., 8:2, 6, 8, 21, 25; 9:28; 14:28, 30; 15:22, 25, 27; 16:22; 17:4, 15; 18:21; 20:30, 31, 33; 26:22.

6. Cf. 8:19; [9:11]; 12:38; [17:24]; 19:16; 22:16, 24, 36; 26:25, 49. Also Bornkamm, "End-Expectation and Church," 41–43.

And on one occasion Jesus instructs the disciples to refer to him as "teacher," but this is in regard to a conversation they are to have with a stranger in which "teacher" expresses the way this man will view Jesus (26:17–19). The thing to notice in all this is that the designations "rabbi" and "teacher" attribute to the person so addressed human respect but nothing more. Hence, in addressing Jesus as "teacher," the religious leaders accord Jesus the honor they would accord any teacher, but that is the extent of it. To their mind Jesus' station is not that of the Messiah Son of God, his authority is not divine, and they in no sense follow him or have faith in him.

In substance, Jesus' teaching is the exposition of the will of God in terms of its original intention (19:4, 8). Three examples in particular illustrate this. In debate with the Pharisees and scribes from Jerusalem, Jesus introduces his quotation of the law not with the words "For Moses said . . . ," but with the words "For God said . . ." (15:4). Again, in debate with the Pharisees on divorce Jesus flatly declares that the will of Moses is to be looked upon as having been transcended by the will of God (19:4, 7–9). Last, in debate with the Sadducees over the question of the resurrection, Jesus refutes their argument with the telling question, ". . . have you not read what was said to you by God . . ." (22:31). Plainly, Jesus advances the claim in his teaching that he is the supreme arbiter of the will of God.

Intrinsic to this claim of Jesus is yet another claim that is no less weighty, namely, that what he teaches is of permanent validity. As far as the activity of preaching goes, Jesus does this, but so do John and the pre-Easter and post-Easter disciples. But when it comes to teaching, Jesus alone is the one who undertakes this. Never is it even intimated that John or the pre-Easter disciples teach, and when the exalted Jesus commissions the post-Easter disciples to go to the nations, it is no accident that what they are given to teach is "all that *I* have commanded you" (28:20). As Jesus says in his eschatological discourse, "Heaven and earth shall pass away, but my words shall not pass away" (24:35).

Part and parcel of Jesus' teaching of the will of God is his teaching of the law of Moses. For purposes of clarification, the term "law" (*nomos*), when used by itself in Matthew's story,[7] does not refer merely to the so-called Ten Commandments but, more broadly, to the five books of Moses, or the Pentateuch. Similarly, the expression "the law and the prophets" denotes quite simply the whole of the OT as it is known to Matthew, the implied author, and functions as scripture.[8]

To determine Jesus' attitude toward the law of Moses in Matthew's story, the place to begin is with the programmatic statements Jesus makes in the

---

7. Cf. 5:18; 12:5; 15:6; 22:36; 23:23.
8. Cf. 5:17; 7:12; 11:13; 22:40.

Sermon on the Mount concerning the law and the prophets (5:17–20).[9] As Jesus sees it, the law and the prophets serve two purposes: they function ethically as a norm of human behavior;[10] and they function salvation-historically in that they prophesy the time of fulfillment (11:13). In the passage 5:17–20, Jesus attests to both these purposes. He asserts in 5:17 that, salvation-historically, he has come not to annul the law or the prophets, but to fulfill them, that is to say, to bring them to completion. In what way does Jesus bring about such fulfillment, or completion? He does so by being who he is (the Messiah Son of God) and through what he both says and does. Here in the Sermon on the Mount, the focus is, as the introduction stipulates (5:2), on the words, or teaching, of Jesus. Hence, a primary way in which the law and the prophets, when viewed as functioning ethically as the norm of human behavior, receive their final revelation is in the teaching of Jesus.

Following verse 17 in the passage 5:17–20, Jesus no longer speaks of law and prophets but solely of the law. The law is, as was mentioned, the law of Moses. But again, it is the law of Moses as it is being taught by Jesus. In the final analysis, therefore, what Jesus says about the law applies to it as something being authoritatively reinterpreted by his teaching. It is not the Mosaic law in and of itself that has normative and abiding character for disciples, but the Mosaic law as it has passed through the crucible of Jesus' teaching.[11]

To continue with 5:17–20, Jesus affirms that until heaven and earth pass away at the consummation of the age, the law will retain its validity so that all the things of the law might be done (5:18). Exactly how one is to construe all the things of the law as being done comes to light, as will soon be seen, in Jesus' teaching of love as that which lies at the heart of the whole of the law (and the prophets) (22:37–40). With this in mind, not even the most insignificant commandment is to be broken by what a disciple does or by what a disciple teaches (5:19). Indeed, so serious is the breaking and keeping of commandments that it will affect a disciple's "ranking" in the consummated Kingdom of Heaven (5:19). In sum, the righteousness the disciples are to evince in their lives is a conduct that shows itself to be superior to ("greater" than) that which typifies the scribes and Pharisees (5:20).

9. More recent investigations of Matt. 5:17–20 and, in general, of Jesus' attitude toward the law are those of Banks ("Matthew's Understanding," 226–42), Sand (*Gesetz und Propheten*), Meier (*Law and History,* esp. 41–171), Gerhardsson ("Hermeneutic Program," 129–50), Luz ("Erfüllung des Gesetzes," 398–435), Broer (*Gesetz und Radikalisierung,* 11–74), Guelich (*Sermon on the Mount,* esp. 134–74), Martin ("Christ and the Law," 53–70), Strecker (*Bergpredigt,* 55–64), and Betz ("Hermeneutical Principles," 37–53).

10. That the law and the prophets (i.e., the scriptures) do function in this manner is plainly indicated in 7:12 and 22:40.

11. Cf. 5:18, 21–48; 22:37–40; 24:35; 28:20.

In the portion of the Sermon on the Mount following 5:17–20, Jesus expounds on the "greater righteousness" that the disciples, as those who live under his aegis in the sphere of God's end-time Rule, are to practice. It is radical in nature and has to do with conduct toward God and toward the neighbor. As conduct toward God, it comes to expression in such fundamental acts of piety as almsgiving, prayer, and fasting when they are done not for public show, but in the spirit of true worship (6:1–18). As conduct toward the neighbor, the greater righteousness is epitomized in the antitheses (5:21–48), those authoritative sayings of Jesus that appear as variations of the formula, "You have heard that it was said to the men of old . . . but I say to you . . . " As the antitheses prescribe, the disciple is not only not to kill, but not even to become enraged (5:21–26); not only not to commit adultery, but not even to lust (5:27–30); not merely to comply with the law in obtaining a divorce, but not to divorce at all (5:31–32);[12] not merely to obey the law and not swear falsely, but not to swear at all (5:33–37); not merely to adhere to the law in securing retribution, but to offer no resistance at all to one who would harm or exploit the disciple (5:38–42); and not merely to love the neighbor while hating the enemy, but not to hate the enemy at all but instead to love him (5:43–48).

Is there a center to Jesus' radical teaching concerning the life of the greater righteousness, the law, and, in general, the will of God? The answer is yes, and this center is "love." In the pericope on the Great Commandment (22:34–40),[13] Jesus declares that the first and greatest commandment is that "You shall love the Lord your God with all your heart, and with all your soul, and with all your mind" (22:37–38; Deut. 6:5). Wholly to love God as Jesus here enjoins is (a) to give to him one's total allegiance; (b) to serve him even to the point of surrendering one's life if necessary; and (c) so to administer one's substance (position and property) that it attests to one's complete devotion to him. And the second commandment, which is like the first, is, Jesus asserts, that "You shall love your neighbor as yourself" (22:39; Lev. 19:18). By finding in these two commandments the ground, or the intention, of all the precepts of the law and, indeed, of the entire will of God as set forth in the whole of the OT scriptures (cf. 22:40), Jesus advances no less a claim than that keeping the law or doing the will of God is always, in essence, an exercise in love.

That "love" is the deepest intention of the will of God as taught by Jesus is also apparent from other passages in Matthew's story. In the verse that concludes the antitheses in the Sermon on the Mount, Jesus mandates that disciples be "perfect" (teleios), that is, give demonstration of their love of

---

12. For a survey and critique of various ways in which this antithesis on divorce has been interpreted, cf. Vawter ("Divorce Clauses," 155–67), Meier (Law and History, 140–50), and Martin ("Christ and the Law," 55 n. 12).

13. Cf. Gerhardsson, "Hermeneutic Program," 129–50.

God by rendering to God wholehearted devotion (5:48; Deut. 18:13). At the end of the Sermon on the Mount, Jesus enjoins love of neighbor by citing the golden rule: "So whatever you wish that men would do to you, do so to them" (7:12). In the pericope on the rich young man, Jesus proffers the man eternal life by summoning him to discipleship, at the core of which is, again, love of neighbor (19:16–21). In his speech of woes against the scribes and Pharisees, Jesus designates "mercy" (i.e., love), along with justice and faithfulness, as comprising the weightier matters of the law (23:23). In the pericopes on plucking grain on the sabbath and on healing the withered hand, Jesus twice suppresses the sabbath law in favor of the law of love (12:7, 12). And in the pericope on the call of Matthew, Jesus has table fellowship with toll-collectors and sinners, thereby showing that mercy, or love, takes precedence over Pharisaic rules regarding ritual uncleanness (9:10–13).

A word is yet in order about Jesus' attitude toward the Pharisaic tradition of the elders. This tradition was, historically, oral in form. It consisted of a vast number of regulations, regarded as obligatory for the individual Jew, the purpose of which was to make the law of Moses applicable to new times and new circumstances. As was indicated in passing above, Jesus appears to take a dim view of this tradition as giving expression to the will of God. In 16:11–12, he warns the disciples to beware of the teaching of the Pharisees and Sadducees, for it is, like leaven, corrupting. In chapter 23, it is with bitter sarcasm that he attacks Pharisaic theology and practice.[14] In 15:3–6, he declares that on the matter of "Corban" (in this instance, dedicating to God and thus craftily keeping for oneself the "gift" that otherwise should have been set aside for the support of one's parents), the tradition of the elders nullifies the word of God itself. In 15:20, Jesus sets aside the stipulated ritual of the tradition of the elders of not eating with unwashed hands. And in 9:10–13, Jesus ignores Pharisaic regulation that would impute ritual uncleanness to him for eating with toll-collectors and sinners in order to symbolize hereby the forgiveness of sins he grants them and the future fellowship they will enjoy with him in the consummated Kingdom of Heaven. But if all these words and deeds of Jesus suggest a wholesale rejection on his part of the tradition of the elders, it cannot be denied that at 23:2–3 he gives the crowds and the disciples to understand that "the scribes and the Pharisees sit on Moses' seat, so practice and observe whatever they tell you"; and that in 23:23 he seems to speak approvingly of the Pharisaic rule concerning the tithing of mint and dill and cummin ("but these things one ought to have done"). To date, no scholarly proposal for resolving these apparent contradictions has proved entirely satisfactory. Nonethe-

---

14. On the exposition of chap. 23, cf. Garland, *Intention of Matthew 23*; Lategan, "Structure and Reference in Mt 23," 74–87.

less, one thing is certain: in the world of Matthew's story, the norm for judging whether the observance of any aspect of the tradition of the elders fosters the doing of the will of God is whether such observance expresses wholehearted devotion to God or radical love of the neighbor.

In brief, then, Jesus' teaching in Matthew's story sets forth the will of God in terms of its original intention. For disciples, this teaching has both normative and abiding character.

The Healing of Jesus

Along with teaching and preaching, "healing," too, is singled out in the summary-passages as being typical of Jesus' ministry to Israel (4:23; 9:35). Also through healing Jesus summons Israel to repentance and to entrance into the sphere of God's end-time Rule (11:20–24; 12:28).

Jesus heals, just as he likewise preaches and teaches, in his capacity as the Messiah Son of God (4:17, 23–25).[15] Still, Jesus Son of God is at the same time the servant of God (12:18), and the Greek verb *therapeuein* can mean to "serve" as well as to "heal." Indeed, it is to cast Jesus' activity of healing in the mold of "serving" that Matthew informs the reader in a formula-quotation that Jesus, through healing, fulfills the words of the Servant Song of Isaiah: "He took our infirmities and bore our diseases" (8:16–17; Isa. 53:4). In healing, Jesus Son of God assumes the role of the servant of God and ministers to Israel by restoring persons to health or freeing them from their afflictions (11:5). Through serving in this fashion, Jesus "saves" (9:22).

The miracles themselves Jesus performs are termed "deeds of power" (*dynameis*, plural of *dynamis*).[16] The use of the term *dynamis* ("power") is itself revealing. *Dynamis* is associated with God (22:29) and can even be used, as Jesus does in the words of the psalmist, as a metaphor for "God" (26:64). Contrariwise, "power" in the sense of *dynamis* is not something that is predicated to Satan, demons, or the opponents of Jesus. On one occasion it is said of false prophets that they will perform deeds of power, but these are followers of Jesus who will do their miraculous, but lawless, works in his name and at the latter day be condemned by him (7:21–23). Otherwise, when the prediction is made that false messiahs and false prophets will arise and perform miracles, their acts are not termed deeds of power but "signs and wonders" (24:24). Jesus and the disciples, in turn, are never reported as doing "wonders" (*terata*), and the "sign" (*sēmeion*) is characterized as a miraculous feat that the religious leaders demand of Jesus as they tempt him to prove he is not in collusion with Satan (12:24, 38; 16:1). The sign Jesus does give them, a word prophesying his death and resurrection (12:39–40; 27:63), is not what they have in mind. When the death and

15. Cf. 8:29; 11:2–6; also 11:27; 14:22–33.
16. Important studies of the miracle stories in Matthew are those of Held ("Matthew as Interpreter," 165–299) and of Gerhardsson (*Mighty Acts*).

resurrection occur, the leaders refuse to acknowledge them (27:62–64). But be that as it may, the logic of Matthew's world of thought is plain as regards Jesus' miracles: God, the source of "power," has empowered his Son Jesus with the Spirit; in consequence of this, the miracles Jesus performs are "deeds of power" and not false "signs and wonders."

Jesus' activity of healing is the source of intense conflict between him and the religious leaders. It also creates division between the leaders and the crowds. The crowds witness Jesus' healings and glorify God because of them (9:8; 15:31) or exclaim that "Never was anything like this seen in Israel!" (9:33). The leaders witness Jesus' healings and charge him with exorcising demons on the authority of the prince of demons (9:34; 12:24) or accuse him of breaking the sabbath law (12:9–14). In point of fact, it is following Jesus' healing on the sabbath that Matthew recounts for the first time that the Pharisees go out and take counsel against him, how to destroy him (12:9–14).

Whether extolled by the crowds or denounced by the leaders, Jesus' healings still do not move Israel to repentance and to recognition of him as its Messiah (11:20–24, 25). On this score, the healing ministry that Jesus carries out specifically as the Son of David assumes significance.[17] In the pericopes portraying this ministry, those who appeal to, or hail, Jesus as the Son of David are blind men,[18] a gentile woman (15:22), and children (21:15). These are minor characters in Matthew's story, disenfranchised and without power in Jewish society.[19] For them to approach or acclaim Jesus as Israel's Davidic Messiah is for them to "see" and to "confess" the truth with which the crowds only toy[20] and which the religious leaders will not even so much as entertain.[21] Accordingly, discernible in Jesus' healing as the Son of David is a polemical strain: such healing underlines the guilt that is Israel's for repudiating its Messiah.

The miracles Jesus performs in Matthew's story divide themselves rather neatly into two groups: (a) therapeutic miracles (miracles of healing), in which the sick are returned to health or the possessed are freed of demons (cf. esp. chaps. 8–9); and (b) nontherapeutic miracles, which have to do with exercising power over the forces of nature.[22] In the summary-passages devoted to Jesus' healing, it is exclusively the therapeutic miracles to which

17. Cf. 9:27–31; 12:22–23; 15:21–28; 20:29–34; 21:14–15.
18. Cf. 9:27–31; 20:29–34; also 12:22–23.
19. See above, p. 27 n. 81.
20. The question the crowds raise in 12:23 as to whether Jesus is the Son of David antici-pates a negative answer, and in 21:9–11 the irony is that the crowds who hail Jesus as the Son of David understand him to be no more than a prophet.
21. Cf. 9:34 with 9:33; 12:24 with 12:23.
22. Cf. 8:23–27; 14:13–21, 22–33; 15:32–39; 17:24–27; 21:18–22.

Matthew makes reference.[23] This has the effect of highlighting their prominence as a part of Jesus' ministry. Moreover, it is also these miracles that create the stir in public: astonishment among the crowds[24] but disapprobation among the leaders (9:34; 12:24). In short, an essential mark of the therapeutic miracles is that they picture Jesus as being active in the full view of Israel.

As a group, the therapeutic miracles are remarkably uniform in structure and thematic.[25] The focus is squarely on Jesus and the suppliants, and the liberal use of direct speech lends immediacy to the encounter. For their part, the suppliants appeal to Jesus in great faith and with prayerlike petitions on behalf of themselves or of others for healing. Jesus, in turn, grants their requests of faith, doing so in a manner that corresponds to what was asked of him and that demonstrates the compassion, the will to heal, and the unparalleled authority that are his.

The nontherapeutic miracles are less uniform in structure and differ in thematic.[26] Here the focus is on Jesus and the disciples, and the characteristic feature is that Jesus reveals, in the midst of situations in which the disciples exhibit "little faith," his awesome authority. Then, too, the way in which Jesus reveals his authority is by exercising power over the forces of nature: he calms wind and wave (8:23–27), twice feeds the multitudes (14:13–21; 15:32–39), walks on water and rescues Peter from drowning (14:22–33), and curses a fig tree (21:18–22).[27] The reason Jesus gives the disciples these startling revelations is to bring them to realize that such authority as he exercises he makes available to them through the avenue of faith.[28] In the later situation of their worldwide mission, failure on the part of the disciples to avail themselves of the authority Jesus would impart to them will be to run the risk of failing at their tasks (28:18–20; chaps. 24–25).

To recapitulate, through healing Jesus summons the people of Israel to repentance and to the Kingdom, and he "serves" them by curing illnesses and releasing persons from their afflictions. Also, in exercising power over the forces of nature, he enables the disciples to catch a glimpse of the divine authority he is ever ready to share with them.

The Ministry of the Disciples to Israel

Thus far, Jesus has been calling Israel, through his ministry of teaching, preaching, and healing, to repentance and to entrance into the sphere of God's end-time Rule. In extension of his ministry, Jesus now commissions

23. Cf., e.g., 4:24; [11:5]; 15:30–31; 21:14.
24. Cf. 9:8, 33; 12:23; 15:31.
25. Cf. Held, "Matthew as Interpreter," 241–46.
26. Cf. Gerhardsson, *Mighty Acts,* 52–67.
27. Cf. further 17:14–20, 24–27.
28. Cf. 8:25–26; 14:15–16; 15:33; 17:19–20; 21:18–22.

the disciples to a ministry of their own in Israel (9:35–10:42).[29] Except for the activity of teaching, which Jesus reserves for himself, the disciples are to do exactly as he has done. Like him, they are to restrict their activity to Israel: "Go nowhere among the Gentiles," he commands them, "but go rather to the lost sheep of the house of Israel" (10:5–6; 15:24). Like him, they are to summon Israel to the Kingdom by proclaiming, "The Kingdom of Heaven is at hand!" (10:7; 4:17). And like him, they are to "heal every disease and every infirmity" among the people (10:1; 9:35; 4:23).

In giving the disciples instructions for their ministry to Israel, Jesus dwells for the most part on the fierce conflict they can expect to encounter (10:16–42). As they go out, they will be like sheep in the midst of wolves (10:16). Just as it has been said of Jesus that he acts in collusion with Satan (9:34; 12:24), so the same will be said of them (10:25). Indeed, in carrying out their mission, they must even be prepared, should this be necessary, to surrender their lives.[30] This strong emphasis on conflict in Jesus' missionary discourse is in keeping with its purpose: it is intended not only to foretell the repudiation by Israel that the disciples can expect to endure but also to foreshadow the repudiation that Jesus himself is about to endure (11:2—16:20).

Although Matthew introduces Jesus' missionary discourse with the narrative comment "These twelve Jesus *sent out*, charging them" (10:5a), he never reports that the disciples actually embark upon, or return from, this ministry for which they have been instructed (cf. 10:42—11:1). The reason Matthew makes no mention of the disciples' departure or return is not difficult to discern: the disciples are obligated to continue missionary work aimed at Israel until Jesus' Parousia at the end of the age (10:23).[31] Accordingly, by stating at the outset of the discourse that Jesus "sent out" the Twelve and yet remaining silent at the conclusion about any actual departure of the disciples, Matthew achieves two objectives: on the one hand, he leads the reader to assume that the disciples did undertake, in extension of Jesus' ministry, a ministry to Israel (10:5); and on the other hand, he spares himself the need to take note of any return of the disciples from ministry and hence avoids contradicting the notion that their missionary work in Israel will not have ended until Jesus shall have returned at the Parousia (10:23). Without question, this tactic by Matthew of referring to the disciples' "being sent" while at the same time remaining silent about their ever having gone out or returning, leaves an aura of unresolved tension surrounding the missionary discourse. Nonetheless, what Matthew has also

29. For a recent study of Jesus' missionary discourse, cf. Weaver, "Missionary Discourse in Matthew."

30. Cf. 10:17–18, 28, 38–39.

31. This point is effectively made by Brown in two articles: "Two-fold Representation of the Mission," 23; "Mission to Israel in Matthew's Central Section," 85–87.

achieved thereby is crucial for him: the continuance to the end of the age of the disciples' mission to Israel.

ISRAEL'S REPUDIATION OF JESUS

The motif that dominates Matthew's story throughout 4:17—11:1 is Jesus' ministry to Israel of teaching, preaching, and healing (4:23; 9:35; 11:1). Through this ministry, Jesus summons Israel to repentance and to life in the sphere of God's end-time Rule (4:17; 5:45). In 11:2—16:20, which comprises the latter half of the second part of Matthew's story (4:17—16:20), Israel's response to Jesus' ministry becomes the dominant motif. This response is one of repudiation; yet even as Israel repudiates Jesus, it wonders and speculates about his identity. The matter of Jesus' identity, then, surfaces as the second motif of importance in 11:2—16:20.

The pericopes that alert the reader to the centrality of these twin motifs are John the Baptist's question and Jesus' answer (11:2-6) and Jesus' rejection at Nazareth (13:53-58). These two pericopes stand out for two reasons: they are strategically located as far as the latter half of the second part of Matthew's story is concerned (11:2—16:20); and each one contains both a question having to do with Jesus' identity (11:3; 13:55) and a prominent reference to "taking offense" at him (11:6; 13:57).

The Repudiation of Jesus

As a result of Jesus' widespread activity of teaching, preaching, and healing, his fame spreads throughout Palestine and even Syria.[32] The crowds stream to him and follow him,[33] and the religious leaders place him under surveillance.[34] Still, the spread of Jesus' fame and the thronging to him of all manner of people are no indication that Israel has accepted him. Quite the contrary, Israel repudiates him (11:2—12:50), as the reader has well been forewarned.[35]

Thus, John the Baptist, perplexed because Jesus has not carried out the final judgment as he had anticipated (3:10-12), questions whether Jesus is in fact the Coming One (Messiah) he and his disciples have awaited (11:2-6). The Jewish crowds, decried by Jesus as "this [evil] generation," reject both John and Jesus: John, because they believe him to be possessed of a demon; and Jesus, because they take him to be a glutton and a drunkard, a friend of toll-collectors and sinners (11:16-19). The cities of Chorazin, Bethsaida, and Capernaum, in which Jesus has done most of his miracles, refuse to be moved to repentance (11:20-24). How is the reader to

32. Cf. 4:23-25; 9:26, 31, 33, 35; 11:2, 4; 13:54; 14:1.
33. Cf. 4:24-25; 8:1, 10; 9:33; 12:15; 13:2; 14:13; 15:30-31.
34. Cf. 9:3, 11, 34.
35. Cf. 2:3; 3:7-12; 9:3, 11, 14, 34; 10:5-42.

understand that Jesus should meet with such rejection? In private prayer, Jesus explains his rejection by invoking the will of his Father (11:25–26).

Next, the religious leaders clash with Jesus, and the level of tension in Matthew's story increases perceptibly. Two incidents occur, each for the first time. In one incident, the leaders (Pharisees), in charging the disciples with breaking the law by plucking grain on the sabbath and hence working, do what they heretofore have not done: they engage Jesus himself in direct debate (12:1–8). And in the second incident, the leaders not only engage Jesus himself in debate, but the charges they level against him are also for an action they anticipate he himself is about to take: Jesus is set to heal on the sabbath and therefore to make himself guilty in their eyes of breaking the law (12:9–14). Doubly challenged by the leaders, Jesus defends both the disciples and himself by contending that mercy, or love, takes precedence over casuistry (12:7, 12). In terms of the plot of Matthew's story, the latter, frontal attack against Jesus because of a deed he himself will perform (12:9–13) marks the place where the conflict between Jesus and the religious leaders reaches a new level of intensity. For the first time in the story, Matthew remarks to the reader, " . . . the Pharisees went out and took counsel against him, how to destroy him" (12:14). Given this narrative comment, the reader knows that the leaders' repudiation of Jesus has now become irreversible.

Aware that the danger he faces has suddenly become mortal, Jesus temporarily withdraws (12:15). This, however, does not result in any reduction in the level of tension in the story. In the scene that immediately follows, the religious leaders for a second time accuse Jesus in their thoughts of exorcising demons on authority of the prince of demons, and Jesus, knowing their thoughts, excoriates them as being evil (12:22–37). This skirmish, in turn, only incites another. The leaders next demand of Jesus that he perform a sign[36] so as to prove to them that he is not the agent of Satan but the agent of God (12:38–45). Jesus does give them a sign, but one they cannot immediately test, namely, the announcement of his death and resurrection (12:39–40; 27:63). And last, like the others in Israel, even the family of Jesus deserts him, which leaves the disciples as the only ones who still adhere to him (12:46–50).

Repudiated by all segments of Israel, Jesus responds by declaring that Israel has become hard of heart (13:13–15). Moreover, he gives public demonstration of this by addressing the crowds in parables, that is, in speech they cannot comprehend (13:2–3, 10–13). By contrast, he pro-

36. On the meaning of the request for a "sign," cf. Linton, "Demand for a Sign from Heaven," 112–29.

nounces the disciples "blessed" (13:16–17) and instructs them in the mysteries of the Kingdom of Heaven (13:11, 36, 51).

Nor does Jesus fare any better in his home town of Nazareth. When the people hear him teach in the synagogue, his words astonish them but they take offense at him (13:54, 57). Even more ominously, news reaches Jesus that Herod Antipas has beheaded John the Baptist, his "forerunner" (14:1–13a; 11:10). This once again prompts Jesus to withdraw: embarking on a series of journeys, he travels to deserted places, back and forth across the sea, and into gentile lands.[37] Against this background of travel, Matthew brings the second part of his story to a close (4:17—16:20). The notion that Jesus, sensing mortal danger, takes evasive action[38] serves the larger motif that Israel has responded to his ministry (4:17—11:1) by repudiating him (11:2—16:20).

Conflicting Views About the Identity of Jesus

Entwined with the motif of repudiation in 11:2—16:20 is also, we recall, the motif of wonderment and speculation in Israel about the identity of Jesus. This motif that centers on Jesus' identity serves the plot device of conflict in Matthew's story because Israel shows itself to be ignorant of who Jesus is. Not only this, but Israel's ignorance is also made to contrast with the knowledge of Jesus' identity of the disciples, the only group in Israel still holding to Jesus.

The questioning begins with John the Baptist. Sitting in prison and wondering about Jesus' identity because he has not inaugurated the final judgment, John inquires of Jesus through his disciples, "Are you the Coming One, or do we await another?" (11:2–3). The religious crowds, amazed at a healing Jesus performs, ask even as they anticipate a negative reply, "This can't be the Son of David, can it?" (12:22–23). The townspeople of Nazareth, astonished at the teaching of Jesus, question one another at the same time they take offense at him, "Isn't this the son of the carpenter?" (13:55). Herod Antipas, having heard news of Jesus, speculates about him: "This is John the Baptist, he has been raised from the dead, and therefore these powers are at work in him" (14:1–2). In stark contrast to all these, the disciples, having been caught in a storm at sea and having watched Jesus walk on water, rescue Peter from drowning, and calm the wind, worship him and confess, "Truly, you are the Son of God!" (14:24–33). Retrospectively, the disciples, in making this confession, are giving answer to the earlier question they had raised in an equally perilous situation at sea: "What sort of man is this, that even wind and sea obey him?" (8:27).

From all these conflicting thoughts about Jesus' identity, Matthew fash-

37. Cf. 14:13, 22, 34; 15:21, 29 (33), 39; 16:4c–5, 13.
38. Cf. 12:14–15; 14:13—16:20; also 2:12, 13, 14, 22; 4:12.

ions two evaluative points of view which he juxtaposes to each other in the pericope with which he brings the entire second part of his story to its culmination, Peter's confession near Caesarea Philippi (16:13–20). The one evaluative point of view is that of the various segments making up the Jewish public. The disciples, asked by Jesus who people imagine him to be, reply, "Some say John the Baptist, others say Elijah, and others Jeremiah or one of the prophets" (16:13–14). In other words, the evaluative point of view concerning Jesus' identity which the Jewish public takes is that he is a prophet of some stature or other (21:11, 26, 46). This evaluative point of view is, the reader knows, false, on three counts: (a) Jesus cannot be John the Baptist, Elijah, Jeremiah, or one of the prophets because John, himself "Elijah," is the forerunner of Jesus (11:10, 14), and the task of Jeremiah and the prophets is to "foretell" of Jesus.[39] (b) The answer that Jesus is a prophet elicits no blessing from him. (c) And, what is most important, to think of Jesus as a prophet does not tally with God's "thinking" about Jesus (3:17; 16:23e).

The second, contrasting evaluative point of view is that of Peter, who speaks on behalf of the disciples. In response to Jesus' question as to who the disciples understand him to be, Peter asserts, "You are the Messiah, the Son of the living God!" (16:16). This evaluative point of view is correct, for two of the same reasons the other one is false: (a) it elicits from Jesus a "blessing" (16:17); and (b) it tallies with the way God "thinks" about Jesus.[40] Accordingly, to bring the second part of his story to its culmination, Matthew shows that whereas the public in Israel does not receive Jesus and wrongly conceives of him as being a prophet, Peter, as spokesman for the disciples, confesses Jesus aright to be the Son of God and so reveals that the disciples' evaluative point of view concerning Jesus' identity is in alignment with that of God.

Climactic as Peter's confession is, it nonetheless meets with a command from Jesus that the disciples tell no one that he is the Messiah, that is, the Messiah Son of God (cf. 16:20 with 16:16). Why this prohibition? Because although the disciples correctly understand who Jesus is, they do not as yet know that central to Jesus' divine sonship is death on the cross. Hence, they are in no position at this point to go and make disciples of all nations. Then, too, because Jesus forbids the disciples to make known their realization that he is the Son of God, this continues to remain a secret as far as the Jewish public is concerned. On balance, however, the second part of Matthew's story ends on this note: Israel is ignorant of Jesus' identity but the disciples know who he is.

39. Cf. 2:17; 11:13; 13:17; 27:9.
40. Cf. 3:17; 16:17, 23e.

SUMMARY

In the second part of his story (4:17—16:20), Matthew tells of Jesus' ministry to Israel (4:17—11:1) and of Israel's response to him (11:2—16:20). Jesus' ministry to Israel consists in the main of teaching, preaching, and healing (4:23; 9:35; 11:1). Through this ministry, Jesus summons Israel to repentance and to life in the sphere of God's end-time Rule.[41] In extension of his own activity, Jesus also commissions the disciples to a ministry in Israel modeled on his own, one of preaching and healing though not of teaching (9:35—10:42). Despite warning signs and the occurrence of the first debates, during which some scribes charge "within themselves" that Jesus is guilty of blasphemy (9:3), the element of conflict does not control this segment of Matthew's story (4:17—11:1).

In the latter half of this part of Matthew's story, however, things change noticeably (11:2—16:20). To all intents and purposes, Jesus' efforts in Israel are without success. Israel's response to his ministry is one of repudiation. Indeed, the tension between Jesus and the religious leaders steadily mounts until it reaches the point of irreconcilable hostility. The leaders directly attack Jesus himself over matters pertaining to the Mosaic law, and they conspire on how to take his life (12:1–8, 9–14).

Despite its repudiation of Jesus, Israel nonetheless wonders and speculates about his identity (11:2—16:20). Whereas the religious leaders dismiss him outright as an agent of Satan (9:34; 12:24), the Jewish crowds look upon him as a prophet of one type or another (16:13–14). In contrast to both the crowds and the leaders, the disciples are led to confess Jesus aright to be the Messiah Son of God (16:16; 14:33). Their evaluative point of view thus coincides with that of God himself (3:17). Still, despite the correctness of the disciples' confession, Jesus commands them to silence as regards his identity (16:20). The reason is that although they know who he is, they do not as yet know that the central task lying before him is death on a cross. But this notwithstanding, the distance between the disciples on the one hand and Israel on the other is readily apparent: Israel is ignorant as to who Jesus is, but the disciples rightly perceive him to be the Son of God.

41. Cf. 4:17; 11:20–24; 12:28, 41.

4

The Journey of Jesus to Jerusalem and His Suffering, Death, and Resurrection (16:21—28:20)

Matthew devotes the third part of his story to Jesus' journey to Jerusalem and to his suffering, death, and resurrection (16:21—28:20). Here the conflict between Jesus and Israel (especially the religious leaders), which was foreshadowed in the first part of the story and which, in the second part, burst into the open (chap. 9) and then crystallized into irreconcilable hostility (chap. 12), runs its course to resolution in the passion and resurrection of Jesus (chaps. 26–28). The verse with which this third part begins, 16:21, prepares the reader already for the resolution of Jesus' conflict with Israel in at least two respects: (a) It underscores the fact that there are three principals involved in Jesus' passion, namely, God (*dei*: "it is necessary"), Jesus, and the religious leaders. And (b) it reminds the reader that while all three desire the death of Jesus, the objective the leaders pursue is destructive (12:14), whereas that intended by God and Jesus is to save (1:21). Secondarily, Jesus also enters into conflict in this part of Matthew's story with the disciples, for he must overcome their false sense of values and lead them to appropriate his evaluative point of view concerning servanthood.

To lend this third part of his story cohesion, particularly up to the point where Jesus enters Jerusalem in chapter 21, Matthew employs two literary devices. The one device is that of the "journey." In 16:21, Matthew reports that it is God's will that Jesus go to Jerusalem. As far as the travels of Jesus are concerned, 16:21 stands out as a watershed. Already prior to 16:21, Jesus has begun those travels that will ultimately bring him to Jerusalem (12:15; 14:13). But these travels prior to 16:21 are of a decidedly different nature from those that follow it. Prior to 16:21, Jesus' travels have, as was observed in Chapter 3, the character of "withdrawal in the face of danger," whether it be a conspiracy on the part of the religious leaders to kill him (12:14–15) or Herod's beheading of John the Baptist (14:13a). From 16:21 on,

Jesus' travels assume the character of a "divinely ordained journey to Jerusalem." To be sure, not until 19:1 does Jesus actually leave Galilee and head for Jerusalem. But this notwithstanding, the force of 16:21 is that it alerts the reader to the circumstance that the entire section of 16:21—20:34, including the portion that consists of Jesus' continued wandering in Galilee (16:21—19:1), is to be understood as part and parcel of Jesus' "journey to Jerusalem."

The second literary device Matthew employs to lend cohesion to this third part of his story is the passion-prediction. There are three such predictions (16:21; 17:22–23; 20:17–19), and these, in turn, are supplemented by a verse in the passion account itself which calls them to mind (26:2). These three passion-predictions are the counterpart to the major summary-passages found in the second part of Matthew's story (4:23; 9:35; 11:1). The function they serve is at least twofold. On the one hand, they invite the reader to view the whole of Jesus' life story following 16:21 from the single, overriding perspective of his passion and resurrection. On the other hand, they also invite the reader to construe the interaction of Jesus with the disciples throughout 16:21—28:20 as controlled by Jesus' concern to inculcate in them his understanding of discipleship as servanthood (16:24–25; 20:25–28).

THE JOURNEY OF JESUS TO JERUSALEM AND HIS ACTIVITY IN THE TEMPLE

The Journey of Jesus to Jerusalem

Jesus' first passion-prediction begins the third part of Matthew's story (16:21). As we recall from Chapter 3, although Peter's confession on behalf of the disciples that Jesus is the Messiah Son of God is correct (16:16), Jesus commands the disciples to silence concerning it (16:20). The reason for this, we saw, is that although the disciples know who Jesus is, they do not as yet know about the central purpose of his ministry. To apprise them of this, the first thing Jesus does in the third part of the story is to tell them that he is divinely appointed to go to Jerusalem and there to suffer, die, and be raised (16:21). In response to this new word, Peter rebukes Jesus, rejecting out of hand the notion that such a fate should ever befall him (16:22). This act of Peter is stark evidence of the conflict that henceforth colors Jesus' relationship with the disciples owing to the fact that they contest his evaluative point of view concerning his mission and therefore also concerning discipleship. Jesus reacts to Peter's remonstrance by reprimanding him: he censures Peter for placing himself in the service not of God, but of Satan (16:23). Then, addressing all the disciples, Jesus asserts programmatically that the corollary to suffering sonship is suffering discipleship (16:24).

Jesus' words to the disciples are followed by his transfiguration in the sight of Peter, James, and John (17:1–9) and his ensuing conversation with them about the suffering of John the Baptist as foreshadowing the suffering he must soon endure (17:10–13). Taking the three disciples with him, Jesus ascends a high mountain. Atop this mountain he is suddenly transfigured before them (17:2), and from a bright cloud they hear a voice exclaim, "This is my beloved Son, in whom I take delight; hear him!" (17:5). The voice is that of God, and for the second time God bursts into the world of Matthew's story as "actor" and expresses his evaluative point of view concerning Jesus' identity. Whereas the announcement ("This is my beloved Son, in whom I take delight") repeats the baptismal declaration (3:17), the injunction ("hear him!") is new. Within the context of Matthew's story, the purpose of the announcement is to confirm to the three the truth of the confession Peter made on behalf of all the disciples near Caesarea Philippi that Jesus is God's Son.[1] The purpose of the injunction is to exhort the three to receive and not to reject, as Peter did, the new word Jesus delivered to the disciples: that he, whom they rightly perceive to be the Messiah Son of God, has been ordained by God to submit to suffering and death in Jerusalem.[2] As Jesus and the three descend from the mountain, Jesus commands them to silence concerning their experience (17:9). The importance of this command is dual. With respect to the plot of Matthew's story, Jesus' command informs the reader that not until the resurrection will the disciples comprehend that death is the essence of the ministry of Jesus Son of God. And with respect to the truth of the divine sonship of Jesus, Jesus' command serves, like the one following Peter's confession as well, to suppress knowledge of this truth so that the experience of the three disciples atop the mountain does not result in its public disclosure.

Jesus and the three descend from the mountain to the crowd and the other disciples below, and Jesus teaches the disciples of the power of faith (17:14–20). Still in Galilee, he predicts his passion to the disciples for a second time (17:22–23). This prediction reminds the reader of the leitmotif of the third part of Matthew's story and conveys a sense of heightened tension. Then, on the heels of an exchange with Peter over the voluntary payment of the "half-shekel tax" (17:24–27), Jesus delivers his so-called ecclesiological discourse (chap. 18). His message to the disciples is that loving concern for the neighbor and the spirit of forgiveness are to be the hallmarks of the community of believers in whose midst he, the Son of God, will ever be present.[3]

Leaving Galilee at last, Jesus moves toward Jerusalem, traveling into the regions of Judea across the Jordan (19:1). Huge crowds follow him, and he

1. Cf. 17:5 with 16:16; 14:33.
2. Cf. 17:5 with 16:21–23.
3. Cf. 18:6, 10, 20, 21–22.

"serves" them by healing the sick (19:2). In debate with his opponents, he takes a radical stand against divorce,[4] instructing the disciples in the process (19:3–12). In addition, he also acts in all of the following ways: He counters the status-consciousness of the disciples by blessing the children (19:13–15). He summons the rich young man, who declines, to follow after him (19:16–22). He warns the disciples against the perils of wealth while also giving them a vision of the end-time rewards of discipleship (19:23–30). And he challenges the disciples through his narration of the parable of the laborers in the vineyard to be as unstintingly generous in their behavior toward one another as God is toward them (20:1–16).

About to go up to Jerusalem, Jesus takes the disciples aside and, for the third time, predicts his passion (20:17–19). Again the leitmotif of 16:21—28:20 sounds, and again the reader is reminded that the decisive struggle between Jesus and the religious leaders is inexorably approaching. To combat the disciples' desire for power and privilege, Jesus holds up himself, the man who willingly gives his life for others, as the example of servanthood they are to emulate in their lives together (20:20–28). Then, having passed through Jericho in the company of the disciples and a great crowd, Jesus heals two blind men who appeal to him in faith as Israel's Davidic Messiah (20:29–34). The "sight" of these blind men discloses the "blindness" of Israel's sight.

The Entry of Jesus into Jerusalem

From the outskirts of Jericho, Jesus journeys up to Jerusalem, arriving at the Mount of Olives (21:1). He dispatches two disciples to obtain the "messianic mounts" he foresees are awaiting his use, the donkey and her colt (21:2–6). Riding the animals, Jesus enters Jerusalem with great ceremony (21:7–9). He "takes possession" of the city as Israel's Davidic Messiah-King, but in humility and peace and without display of military might.[5] The crowds, spreading garments and tree branches on the way (21:8), pay him the homage that befits a king (2 Kings 9:13), and with their antiphonal shouts of "Hosanna," they hail him with petitions of salvation (Ps. 118:25–26).

If Jesus' entry into Jerusalem is thus enshrouded in the fulfillment of OT prophecy, it is at the same time an event that is ironic to the core. On the one hand, the Jewish crowds, and therefore Israel, do receive Jesus into Jerusalem as the Son of David (21:9). On the other hand, when upon Jesus' entry the crowds are asked by the inhabitants of Jerusalem who this Jesus is, they reply that he is "the prophet from Nazareth of Galilee" (21:10–11). Exactly as the disciples had said when questioned by Jesus near Caesarea

4. See above, p. 66 n. 12.
5. Cf. 21:5, 9; Zech. 9:9.

Philippi, the evaluative point of view of the Jewish public concerning Jesus' identity is that he is no more than a prophet (16:13–14; 21:46). In hailing Jesus as the Son of David, the Jewish crowds have spoken the truth, but they have done so unwittingly, seeing in him but a prophet.

Jesus' first act in Jerusalem marks the beginning of the penultimate stage of his conflict with the religious leaders and also shapes the setting for the remainder of his stay in the city prior to his passion: he cleanses the temple and briefly occupies it, and his presence there provokes the religious leaders, led by the chief priests, to engage him in direct confrontation. Until the destruction of Jerusalem in A.D. 70, the temple was not only the religious and cultic center of Judaism but also, as sanctioned by the Romans, the seat of domestic government for Judea and, at times, other parts of Palestine as well.[6] The Sanhedrin, or High Council, under the leadership of the high priest, met in plenary session in a hall in the temple area, and exercised, in addition to purely religious powers, legislative and judicial powers. Consequently, for Jesus to raise the claim through his cleansing of the temple that the temple has, under the custody of the religious leaders, become a "den of robbers" and that his purification of it from the desecration of merchants is its restoration to rightful use as Israel's house of prayer and worship, is for him to mount a massive assault on the authority and integrity of the religious leaders (21:12–13). This act on Jesus' part paves the way for the sharp debates with the religious leaders that follow.

As a token of these debates, Jesus heals, in conjunction with his cleansing the temple, the blind and lame who come to him, persons otherwise forbidden entrance to the temple (21:14–17; 2 Sam. 5:8). This prompts children who are also present in the temple to acclaim Jesus with shouts of "Hosanna to the Son of David!" (21:15). Witnessing the healings and hearing the shouts, the chief priests and the scribes, incited to indignation, call Jesus to task for his acceptance of the acclamation of children. Jesus silences them with the retort that if they could properly read scripture, they would know that the children's acclamation of him as the Son of David constitutes the fulfillment of prophecy. With this, Jesus leaves the temple and Jerusalem and spends the night in Bethany. For the reader, however, the irony of this scene is apparent: just as the Jewish crowds hailed Jesus as the Son of David upon his entry into Jerusalem but could not perceive the truth of their words, so now the religious leaders have heard the children hail Jesus as the Son of David but cannot perceive the truth of their words. The children, who are weak and not powerful in the Jewish society of Matthew's story, "see" and "confess" what Israel cannot, namely, that Jesus is its Davidic Messiah.

But correct though it surely is to look upon Jesus as being the Son of

6. Cf. Reicke, *New Testament Era*, 141–49.

David, Matthew shows later in his story that, of itself, this evaluative point of view is insufficient. This is the thrust of the pericope on the question about David's son (22:41–46). In debate with the Pharisees, Jesus confounds them with a problem of antinomy. The question he puts to them is: How is it possible for the Messiah to be both the "son" of David and the "lord" of David when these two views are ostensibly contradictory? Although Jesus leaves the answer to be inferred, the reader can well supply it: the Messiah is the "son" of David because he stands in the line of David (1:1, 6, 25). At the same time, the Messiah is also the "lord" of David because he is, as God's evaluative point of view concerning him dictates (3:17; 17:5), the Son of God and therefore of higher station and authority than David.

The Activity of Jesus in the Temple

Matthew continues to place Jesus, during his stay in Jerusalem prior to his delivery of the eschatological discourse and his ensuing passion, in the temple, where he teaches, debates, and speaks in parables (21:12—23:39). The tension between Jesus and the religious leaders increases to the breaking point, as the circle of the leaders who debate Jesus grows ever wider and as Jesus addresses his three parables against Israel to those identified with the Sanhedrin.

Thus, the circle of the religious leaders who approach Jesus in the temple to debate him widens to the point where it includes representatives of all the groups. The upshot is that Jesus is put to the test, respectively, by the chief priests and the scribes (21:15); by the chief priests and the elders of the people (21:23); by the disciples of the Pharisees together with the Herodians (22:15–16); by the Sadducees (22:23); and by a lawyer from the Pharisees (22:34–35). Nevertheless, Jesus himself closes the entire series by himself challenging the Pharisees (22:41). The result of these confrontations is that Jesus reduces all his opponents to silence. As Matthew comments at the conclusion of the final debate: "And no one was able to answer him a word, nor from that day did any one dare to ask him any more questions" (22:46).

Unable to best Jesus in debate, the religious leaders leave the scene of the temple. Alone with the crowds and the disciples, Jesus seizes the offensive and himself attacks the scribes and Pharisees in his scathing speech of woes (chap. 23). Following this speech, verbal exchanges between Jesus and the religious leaders are no more possible, and the leaders concentrate on destroying Jesus, not through debate, but through death on the cross.

During his stay in the temple, Jesus also, as was noted, speaks in parables. The three parables he narrates bespeak judgment on Israel owing to its repudiation of John the Baptist (21:28–32), of himself (21:33–46), and of his messengers (22:1–10). Of particular importance to the plot of Matthew's story is the second of these parables, that of the wicked husbandmen (21:33–46).[7]

Jesus addresses this parable to "the chief priests and the elders of the people," that is, to Jewish officialdom associated with the Sanhedrin (cf. 21:33 with 21:23). In it, Jesus sketches, with the aid of metaphors, God's dealings with Israel in the history of salvation. He identifies God with the owner of the vineyard, the religious leaders with the wicked tenant farmers, and himself with the son of the owner whom the tenant farmers kill but who is also vindicated. In making these identifications, Jesus boldly asserts that he is the Son of God whom the religious leaders will kill but whom God will vindicate through resurrection, and that his death and resurrection are the decisive events in the whole of salvation history. Then, too, as Jesus speaks of the son, or of himself, he presents the owner of the vineyard, or God, as referring to him as "my son" ("They will respect my son"; 21:37). This reference to "my son" calls to mind, of course, the words the heavenly voice uttered at the baptism and the transfiguration ("this is *my* beloved *Son*"; 3:17; 17:5). Accordingly, it is with phraseology attributable to God himself that Jesus asserts in this parable that God looks upon him as his Son. In the narration of this parable, therefore, the aim of Jesus is to make God's evaluative point of view concerning his identity his own and to confront the religious leaders with it.

This aim of Jesus is not lost on the religious leaders. They understand the metaphors he has used and the claim he has raised that he is, in the sight of both God and himself, the Son of God whom they will kill (21:45). Their response is to want to arrest him, but the reputation he enjoys in public of being a prophet causes them to hold off (21:46). Still, by wanting to arrest Jesus, the religious leaders show that they repudiate the message of his parable. In repudiating the parable's message, however, they likewise show that their understanding is, in reality, "obdurate understanding":[8] having grasped Jesus' message with their minds, they cannot accept it with their hearts, and so reject it. Ironically, in rejecting Jesus' message, the religious leaders are unwittingly rejecting the evaluative point of view of God concerning Jesus' identity.[9] The upshot is that even though they are told the secret that Jesus is the Son of God, they are unable to comprehend its truth. In the final analysis, therefore, although the secret of Jesus' divine sonship has been uttered in public, it nevertheless continues unbroken as far as the Jewish public is concerned.

---

7. On the role of this parable within the context of Matthew's gospel story, cf. Kingsbury, "Parable of the Wicked Husbandmen and the Secret of Jesus' Divine Sonship," 643–55. For a tradition-critical treatment of this parable, cf. Snodgrass, *Parable of the Wicked Tenants*.

8. Regarding the expression "obdurate understanding," cf. Pesch (*Markusevangelium*, 2:223) and Boucher (*Mysterious Parable*, 60, 84).

9. Cf. 21:37 with 17:5; 3:17.

As Matthew began his rehearsal of Jesus' ministry at 4:17, he depicted Jesus as becoming successively involved with three major groups, each of which functions as a character in his story: the *disciples* (4:18–22); the *crowds*, together with the disciples (4:25; 5:1–2); and the religious *leaders* (9:2–13). As an indication that only the climax of his story (i.e., the passion of Jesus) still remains to be narrated, Matthew now depicts Jesus' involvement with each of these same three groups as being successively terminated in a reverse order to the initial one, that is to say, in an order that is chiastic in nature. For example, by reducing the religious *leaders* in open debate to silence, Jesus forces their withdrawal from the scene (22:46). With the leaders gone, Jesus publicly addresses the *crowds* in the temple, together with the disciples (23:1). And leaving the temple, Jesus delivers his eschatological discourse to the *disciples* alone (24:1–3). Through the use of this chiastic pattern, Matthew signals the reader that the culmination of his story is at hand.

THE BETRAYAL, CONDEMNATION, CRUCIFIXION, AND RESURRECTION OF JESUS

As the culmination of Matthew's story, the passion account also constitutes the decisive stage in Jesus' conflict with Israel (chaps. 26–28).[10] Here the resolution of this conflict works itself out in dramatic detail.

At the beginning of the passion account, Jesus says to the disciples, "You know that after two days the Passover is coming, and the Son of man will be delivered up [betrayed] to be crucified" (26:1–2). These words remind both the disciples and the reader of the three passion-predictions Jesus has already given (16:21; 17:22–23; 20:18–19). In these predictions, especially the first one, Jesus made it known that he, God, and the religious leaders will be the three principals involved in his passion. Conversely, this also means that while such characters as the disciples (including Judas and Peter), the crowds, Pilate, the Roman soldiers, Joseph of Arimathea, and the women will likewise have their necessary roles to play, by comparison they will be minor.

All three principals, it was said, desire the death of Jesus, though for different reasons. Through the unfolding of Matthew's story, these reasons have become increasingly clear. God has ordained the death of Jesus because it is to be the crucial event in the whole of the history of salvation.[11] Jesus freely submits to suffering and death because he is, on the one hand, perfect in his devotion to God and, on the other hand, perfect in his service to humankind.[12] No helpless victim, Jesus knows and predicts his fate,

---

10. For a more detailed treatment of the passion account in Matthew, cf. Matera, *Passion Narratives and Gospel Theologies*, chaps. 4–6; Senior, *Passion of Jesus.*

11. Cf. 1:21; 20:28; 21:33–44; 22:1–10; also 26:28; 27:51.

12. Cf. 4:1–11; 5:48; 20:28; 22:37–40; also 26:26–29, 39, 42.

guides events both by what he does and by what he leaves undone so that
they will issue in his death, and yet will die as one completely innocent of
wrongdoing who will find in death the last and greatest test of his fealty to
God. By contrast, the religious leaders desire the death of Jesus because
they understand him to be a "deceiver," or false messiah (27:63). They
rightly perceive that he stands as a mortal threat to their authority and
therefore to the religion and society based on that authority (15:13; 21:43).
According to their evaluative point of view, Jesus blasphemously arrogates
to himself the prerogative of God to forgive sins; derives his astonishing
authority from having entered into collusion with Satan; places himself
above law and tradition; dismisses with antagonism the legitimate request
that he prove he does indeed act on authorization of God; impugns their
ethics and undermines their authority as interpreters of scripture and the
leaders of God's people Israel; and threatens Israel's very existence by
forming his own community of disciples who do as he does and violate law
and tradition.

The position other characters will take toward Jesus as he faces death is
likewise not unpredictable. Although the crowds hold Jesus to be a
prophet, they have never pledged him their allegiance (11:16–24), and at
the last they will join in solidarity with their leaders against him. The
disciples, although they have pledged Jesus their allegiance, have not
appropriated the notion that suffering sonship entails suffering discipleship, and this will result in their being ill-prepared, even unable, to cope
with the events surrounding his passion. Since Pilate and the Roman
soldiers have not yet appeared in the story, it can simply be said that,
except for those soldiers who acclaim Jesus at the foot of the cross, Pilate
and the Romans will prove themselves complicit in the crime perpetrated
against Jesus.

To pick up the flow of Matthew's passion account following Jesus' re-
capitulation of his passion-predictions (26:2), the initial scenes are calcu-
lated to establish, respectively, the culpability of the religious leaders for
Jesus' death, the unreadiness of the disciples to master the events that lie
before them, and the inability of Judas to foresee the true nature of the act
he is committing in agreeing to betray Jesus for gain.

In the one scene, then, the chief priests and the elders stand forth as the
ones most immediately responsible for the death of Jesus (26:3–5). Gathering in the palace of the high priest, they take counsel together how to have
Jesus arrested by cunning and killed (26:3–4). To avoid a disturbance
among the people, they decide not to try to take Jesus during the celebration of the Passover feast (26:5), a decision they will not keep (26:47).

In the next scene, the disciples, who are with Jesus in the house of Simon
the leper at Bethany, show themselves unable to comprehend the true
significance of events taking place (26:6–13). By indignantly dismissing as a

waste of money the woman's anointing Jesus with expensive ointment, they misconstrue what in reality constitutes the preparation of Jesus for burial (26:8, 12).

In the third scene, Judas reveals that he is totally oblivious to the deeper significance of his act of betraying Jesus. In hiring himself out to the chief priests, he places himself in the service of their desire to kill Jesus (26:14–16). In so doing, he has no idea that, ironically, he is thereby also fulfilling scripture and facilitating with his deceit God's plan of salvation (26:15; Zech. 11:12).

In sharp contrast to the religious leaders, the disciples, and Judas, Jesus demonstrates, by guiding and predicting events, that he is acutely aware that God is, in him and his destiny, bringing to fulfillment the divine plan of salvation. For example, Jesus displays his mastery of the situation by telling the disciples, as he sends them to make arrangements for eating the Passover meal, exactly where to go and with whom to speak (26:17–19). Later, as he reclines with the disciples at meal, he predicts that one of them will betray him, and he indicates to Judas that he knows it is he (26:20–25). In full knowledge of the significance of his death, he makes the meal itself the occasion on which he explains this to the disciples: in the bread they eat, which is his body, they have fellowship with him; in the cup they drink, which is his blood, they share in the atonement for sins which he will accomplish for all; and in the promise he gives them that he will no more drink wine until he is united with them in the Father's Kingdom, they have assurance that they will share future bliss with him (26:26–29).

Following the meal and under way to the Mount of Olives, Jesus makes three further predictions, all of which relate to the disciples: they all will desert him; Peter will deny him; but such failure notwithstanding, he will meet them in Galilee after his resurrection (and consequently reconcile them to himself) (26:30–35). On arrival at the Mount of Olives and the place called Gethsemane, Jesus attests in prayer to his perfect obedience to the Father: he goes to his death not as one who desires for himself the glory of martyrdom, but because he would do his Father's will (26:36–46). In thus wanting what God wants, Jesus freely subjects himself to what his enemies also want: his death. Then, in awareness that his hour of betrayal is at hand, Jesus goes to meet Judas and the hostile crowd with him. Although he could, if he wanted, call upon his Father and receive for his defense more than twelve legions of angels, he forgoes this and submits, in order to fulfill the scriptures, to betrayal by Judas, to arrest by his opponents, and to abandonment by the other disciples (26:47–56). Moreover, later, at the very time he will stand before the Sanhedrin and confess who he is, Peter will fulfill prophecy and deny him before others (26:58, 69–75).

The climactic event in this part of the passion account is Jesus' appearance before the Sanhedrin (26:57–68). In putting Jesus on trial, the religious leaders believe that they will finally achieve the resolution of their conflict with Jesus which they have long desired (12:14). During the proceedings, Jesus once again faces, as constituent groups belonging to the Sanhedrin, the chief priests and the elders (26:57, 59), those to whom he had previously addressed the parable of the wicked husbandmen (21:23). As long as the testimony brought against him is false, Jesus remains silent (26:59–62). Abruptly, however, the high priest places Jesus under oath to tell the Sanhedrin whether he is the Messiah, the Son of God (26:63).

In terms of the plot of Matthew's story, this unexpected query raises the problem as to the source from which the high priest has even gotten the idea to question Jesus about being the Son of God. This source is Jesus himself and his narration of the parable of the wicked husbandmen. As the presiding officer of the Sanhedrin, the high priest has knowledge of the claim to divine sonship which Jesus made in telling his parable to the chief priests and the elders. At the trial, therefore, the high priest seizes on Jesus' own claim, converts it from allegorical speech into literal speech, and hurls it back at Jesus as a weapon by which to destroy him. Because from Jesus' standpoint false testimony at the trial has suddenly given way to a query that expresses the truth, he breaks his silence and replies in the affirmative, "[So] you have said!" (26:64; cf. 27:43).[13] In consequence of Jesus' reply, the Sanhedrin, at the instigation of the high priest, condemns Jesus to death for having committed blasphemy against God (26:65–66).

And therein lies the irony of Jesus' fate. As far as Jesus himself is concerned, the irony is that the "crime" for which he is made to die is committing blasphemy against God, and yet what he has done is dare to think about himself as God revealed at the baptism and transfiguration that he does in truth "think" about him (3:17; 17:5; 21:37). As far as the high priest and the Sanhedrin are concerned, the irony is that in condemning Jesus to death for blaspheming God, they are alleging that they know the "thinking" of God. Yet even while alleging this, they are effectively disavowing God's "thinking" and demonstrating that they have in no wise penetrated the secret that Jesus is indeed the Son of God. In resolving their conflict with Jesus as they have, the religious leaders have achieved the opposite of what they intended: they have not only not pleased God, but they have also condemned to death the Son he has sent them and called forth his wrath on themselves and their nation (21:43–44; 22:7).

The Crucifixion of Jesus

Having sentenced Jesus to death, the chief priests and the elders deliver him to Pilate, the Roman governor (27:1–2).[14] Before describing Jesus'

---

13. Cf. Catchpole, "Answer of Jesus to Caiphas," 213–16.
14. For a penetrating study of Matthew 27, cf. Witherup, "Cross of Jesus."

hearing before Pilate, Matthew digresses in order to relate the death of Judas (27:3–10). In so doing, he virtually summarizes the passion account to this point by stressing such factors as the guilt of both Judas and the religious leaders, the innocence of Jesus, and the circumstance that, ironically, the passion of Jesus serves the salvation-historical purposes of God.

Judas himself attests to both his own guilt and the innocence of Jesus when, in returning the pieces of silver to the chief priests and the elders in the temple, he declares, "I have sinned in betraying innocent blood" (27:4). Also, in going out and hanging himself, Judas likewise brings to fulfillment the woe Jesus had pronounced in foretelling that one of the Twelve would betray him: ". . . but woe to that man by whom the Son of man is betrayed! It would have been better for that man if he had not been born" (26:24). As for the guilt of the religious leaders, the chief priests are made to acknowledge this in words they themselves utter: "It is not lawful to put them [the pieces of silver] into the treasury, since they are blood money" (27:6). And concerning the irony that God is at work in the passion of Jesus to accomplish his purposes, Matthew notes that the religious leaders, in using the blood money Judas had thrown down in the temple to purchase a potter's field for the burial of strangers, unwittingly fulfill OT prophecy (27:6–10).

Faced with the Jewish conspiracy against Jesus, Pilate makes himself complicit by acceding to the demand that Jesus be crucified (27:11–26). The role Pilate plays in the passion account is thus not unlike that of Judas, for by abetting the Jewish conspiracy, Pilate is at the same time, ironically, facilitating God's plan of salvation.

At Jesus' hearing, Pilate makes Jesus' identity the issue. He asks Jesus whether he is the "King of the Jews," and Jesus replies in the affirmative (27:11). To Pilate, Jesus' reply means, based on his evaluative point of view, that Jesus is an insurrectionist (27:37). But in spite of this, Pilate indicates by the way he conducts Jesus' hearing that he believes him to be innocent of this charge (27:11–24). Nevertheless, once Pilate can be satisfied that he has absolved himself of any guilt associated with Jesus' death and that the Jews have taken full responsibility for it, he consents to the legal plea that Jesus be crucified and delivers him to the soldiers (27:24–27).

The soldiers, in turn, take Jesus to the praetorium, and there make mockery of him as the King of the Jews (27:27–31). By this act, they unwittingly show in what way Jesus truly is the King of the Jews. He is so, not as one who restores to Israel its national splendor and not as one who foments rebellion against Rome, but as the one who saves others by willingly giving himself over to suffering and death.

Matthew presents Jesus' crucifixion as a testing (27:32–56; cf. 27:40).[15] At Golgotha and on the cross, Jesus does not permit concern for self to put

---

15. Cf. Gerhardsson, "Gottes Sohn," 96–103.

him at odds with God's appointed plan that he relinquish his life (27:33–50). Quite the opposite, Jesus demonstrates in all he is subjected to that his love for God is perfect, or single-hearted: what God wills, Jesus wills (26:42). Thus, Jesus loves God with his whole heart: just as his obedience to God led him to suffer hunger in the desert, so now it leads him to suffer thirst on the cross (27:33–34; cf. 4:3–4).[16] Jesus also loves God with his whole mind: out of obedience to God, he endures the total loss of all he possesses (his clothes) and even of the prerogative to have his body disposed of as he would wish (27:35–37).[17] And Jesus loves God with his whole soul, or life. Earlier he had said to his disciples: "For whoever would save his life will lose it" (16:25). On the cross, Jesus exemplifies his own counsel by resisting the temptation to do as the passers-by, the religious leaders, and the two robbers call on him to do, namely, to save himself by using his power to descend from the cross (27:39–44). Nor does Jesus endeavor to escape death by appealing to Elijah for miraculous deliverance, as some standing at the foot of the cross mistakenly think he does (27:47–49). On the contrary, as Jesus nears the moment he himself has chosen for his death (27:50), he faces his abandonment by God (". . . why have you forsaken me?"; 27:46) by crying out to God in trust ("My God, my God . . ."; 27:46). Nor is God to disappoint the "trust unto death" that Jesus places in him: on the third day, he is to raise Jesus from the dead.

At Jesus' death, Matthew tells of the occurrence of supernatural portents (27:51–54). Seeing these portents, the Roman soldiers guarding Jesus cry out in acclamation, "Truly this man was the Son of God!" (27:54). As characters who appear on the scene only briefly, it is not for the soldiers but for the reader to grasp the full import of their words. In this regard, three things stand out.

First, this acclamation of the Roman soldiers constitutes a vindication of Jesus' claim to be the Son of God (21:37; 26:63–64). In condemning Jesus to death at his trial and in blaspheming and mocking him as he hangs upon the cross, the Sanhedrin in the one instance and the passers-by and the religious leaders in the other repudiate Jesus' claim to be the Son of God (26:63–66; 27:39–43). Against the backdrop of this repudiation, the soldiers' acclamation becomes a counter-assertion, elicited by God himself through the supernatural portents he has caused to occur, that, on the contrary, Jesus "truly" was the "Son of God" (27:51–54).

Second, the verb in this acclamation is in the past tense ("was"; 27:54). In that the Roman soldiers say that Jesus was the Son of God, their acclamation calls attention to the fact that the cross marks the end of Jesus' earthly ministry. In the eyes of the religious leaders, the significance of this end is

16. Cf. Gerhardsson, "Du Judéo-christianisme a Jésus," 29.
17. Cf. ibid., 29–30.

that Jesus, a false messiah who has infected Israel with perilous error (27:63–64), has, as necessity dictated, been destroyed.[18] In divine perspective, however, the end of Jesus' ministry is at the same time its culmination, for the cross is the place where Jesus "pours out" his blood for the forgiveness of sins (26:28) and consequently "saves" his people from their sins (1:21). In the cross, Jesus atones for sins (26:28) and, in fact, supersedes the temple and the Jewish cult (27:51) as the "place" of salvation.

Third, with this acclamation by the Roman soldiers, Matthew brings the third part of his story (16:21—28:20) to its initial climax. In declaring Jesus to be the Son of God, the Roman soldiers "think" about him as God "thinks" about him.[19] Accordingly, their evaluative point of view concerning Jesus' identity can be seen to be in alignment with that of God. Moreover, in contrast, for example, to Peter's confession on behalf of the disciples, no comment of any kind, narrative or otherwise, that can function as a command to silence follows the soldiers' acclamation (cf. 16:20). The reason for this is apparent: whereas Peter and the disciples near Caesarea Philippi correctly understood who Jesus is but were as yet ignorant of his passion, the Roman soldiers acclaim Jesus to be the Son of God at that juncture where he has completed his passion and, in fact, the whole of his earthly ministry.

Two consequences flow from this. The first is that the soldiers' acclamation becomes the place in Matthew's plot where Jesus is, for the first time, both correctly and publicly affirmed by humans to be the Son of God. And the second consequence is that, as a result of the soldiers' acclamation, the way is in principle now open for the task of "going and making disciples of all nations." Or, to put it differently, one could also say that the way is now open for the task of making the salvation Jesus has accomplished in his death owing to his conflict with Israel redound to the benefit of all humankind. Then, too, since the Roman soldiers are themselves Gentiles, they attest in this way as well that the time for embarking upon the universal mission is at hand.

The Resurrection of Jesus

Central to Matthew's resurrection narrative is the angel's declaration to the women that "he has been raised" (28:6). The passive voice here is the "divine passive," so that what the angel affirms is that "God has raised Jesus from the dead" (cf. 16:21). Earlier in Matthew's story, Jesus twice said to the disciples that "whoever loses his life will find it,"[20] and on the cross Jesus held fast to God in trust even as he relinquished his life (27:46, 50). In raising Jesus from the dead, God certifies the truth of Jesus' words and the

18. Cf. 12:14; 26:4; 27:1.
19. Cf. 3:17; 17:5; 16:23e.
20. Cf. 16:25; also 10:39.

efficacy of his trust, which is to say that God vindicates Jesus: God resolves Jesus' conflict with Israel by showing that Jesus is in the right. Within the world of Matthew's story, however, Israel as such will not see God's vindication of Jesus until the Parousia and the final judgment.[21] Still, Jesus has also been in conflict in Matthew's story with the disciples, a subject to be discussed at length in Chapter 8. God's vindication of Jesus in the resurrection is the point at which Jesus' conflict with the disciples comes to fundamental resolution. Because the resolution of this conflict is the topic with which the passage 28:16–20 deals, and because 28:16–20 constitutes the major climax not only of the third part of Matthew's story but also of his entire story, it is with it that this Chapter's study of Matthew's story will conclude.

Prior to his death and resurrection, Jesus' conflict with the disciples was over their unwillingness to appropriate Jesus' evaluative point of view according to which suffering sonship is a call to suffering discipleship, or to servanthood.[22] Because of such unwillingness, the disciples became apostate when confronted by the events of Jesus' passion: Judas betrayed Jesus (26:47–50), the disciples fled from him (26:56), and Peter denied him (26:69–75).

Notwithstanding the apostasy of the disciples, however, the angel of the Lord enjoins the women on Easter day to go and remind the disciples of Jesus' earlier promise that, following his resurrection, he would precede them to Galilee where, the angel adds, they will see him (28:5–7; 26:32). Moreover, as the women obey the angel and depart from the tomb, the resurrected Jesus himself meets them, and he likewise commands them to tell the disciples to make their way to Galilee, where they will see him (28:10). In making reference to the disciples, Jesus calls them "my brothers" (28:10).

The upshot of this sequence is that when the eleven disciples do make their way to Galilee and Jesus does appear to them on the mountain there, he meets them as the "brother" who has "gathered" them from their "having been scattered" (26:31; 28:16). In other words, the resurrected Jesus meets the disciples as the one who reconciles them to himself. True, some of the disciples worship him while others of them doubt (28:17). Nonetheless, doubt is "little faith," or weak faith, but is not "unfaith" (14:32), so that the assertion stands: the resurrected Jesus gathers the scattered disciples and reconciles them to himself.

As Jesus appears to the disciples atop the mountain in Galilee, he does so as the "Son of God" whom God, he himself, the disciples themselves, and

21. Cf. 13:36–43; 25:31–46; 26:64.
22. Cf. 16:21, 24; 20:28.

the Roman soldiers have all claimed him to be.[23] By the same token, he is both the crucified and the resurrected Son of God. Thus, he is the resurrected Son of God whose end-time glory God revealed proleptically to Peter, James, and John on the mountain of the transfiguration (17:2, 5). Yet, even as the resurrected Son of God, he remains the crucified Son of God ("the one who has been, and remains, the crucified"; 28:5). Indeed, he is the rejected "stone-son" whom God has placed "at the head of the corner," that is, raised from the dead and exalted to universal lordship (21:37, 42; 28:18). He is, in fact, Emmanuel, or "God with us," the Son conceived of the Spirit in whom God will abide with the disciples until the consummation of the age (1:20, 23; 28:20).

The disciples, in seeing Jesus Son of God as the resurrected one who remains the crucified one, see him, but also themselves, in new perspective. Because the Jesus the disciples see is the crucified, albeit also resurrected, Son of God, they now comprehend not only what they earlier perceived as well, that he is the Son of God (14:33; 16:16), but also the central purpose of his mission: death on the cross and the salvation from sins he thereby accomplished (26:28). Comprehending at last not only who Jesus is but also what he was about, the disciples necessarily gain insight into themselves as well: they finally understand and appropriate Jesus' evaluative point of view according to which suffering sonship is their call to suffering discipleship, or to servanthood (16:21, 24). Equipped with this insight, the disciples are not again commanded by Jesus, as previously, to silence concerning him (16:20; 17:9), but are instead commissioned to go and make all nations his disciples (28:19). In reconciling the disciples to himself and in giving them this commission, Jesus resolves the conflict he has had with them. With this conflict so resolved, the disciples move from Easter into the world Jesus predicted for them in his eschatological discourse (chaps. 24–25).

SUMMARY

In the third part of his story (16:21—28:20), Matthew employs the device of the "journey" (16:21—21:11) and the setting of Jerusalem and environs, including the temple (21:12—28:15 [16–20]), in order to forge a cohesive narrative from disparate materials. To inform the reader of the tenor of this narrative, Matthew employs three passion-predictions that tell of Jesus' suffering, death, and resurrection (16:21; 17:22–23; 20:18–19). Also, at the outset of the passion account itself he calls to mind these three predictions (26:2).

In line with Matthew's scheme, then, the conflicts Jesus has with Israel on the one hand and with the disciples on the other run their course here in

23. Cf. 3:17; 17:5; 21:37; 26:63–64; 14:33; 16:16; 27:54.

the third part to resolution. Jesus' conflict with the disciples is that he must lead them to appropriate his evaluative point of view that suffering sonship entails suffering discipleship (servanthood) (16:21, 24).

Jesus' conflict with Israel is to the death (16:21). Whereas the religious leaders conspire to have Jesus killed so as to destroy him (12:14; 26:2–3), God and Jesus desire Jesus' death because it will constitute the decisive, saving event in the history of salvation. In his parable of the wicked husbandmen, Jesus confronts the religious leaders with the claim that he is the Son of God, that is, God's supreme agent in the history of salvation (21:33–46). At his trial, the high priest abruptly puts Jesus' own claim to him in the form of a question, and when Jesus replies in the affirmative, the high priest and the Sanhedrin condemn him to death for having committed blasphemy against God (26:57–68). Delivering Jesus to Pilate, the religious leaders prevail upon Pilate to have Jesus crucified as an insurrectionist (27:11–37). In this way, the religious leaders, with the support of the crowds, bring about the death of Jesus and believe that in so doing they have acted in a God-pleasing manner in order to put to an end a movement initiated by one who was a false messiah (27:25, 63–64). What they have done in reality, however, is to show themselves to be blind to God's revelation that this Jesus is his royal Son whom he has sent them and, in making themselves responsible for Jesus' death, to call down God's wrath upon themselves and their nation (21:43; 22:7). Ironically, what also happens is that God turns Jesus' death to advantage for all humankind, for through his death, Jesus atones for sins and becomes the one through whom God henceforth grants salvation to all humans, Jews and Gentiles alike (1:21; 26:28). In the final analysis, therefore, God vindicates Jesus in his conflict with Israel, that is to say, he shows Jesus and not Israel to have been in the right. As proof of such vindication, God raises Jesus from the dead after three days (28:6), and at the end of time he will dispatch him in glory with angels to carry out the final judgment and to establish his Kingdom in splendor in sight of all the nations of the world (24:29–31; 25:31–46). In the meantime, the disciples of Jesus, having seen Jesus in Galilee as the crucified one whom God has raised, have at last comprehended that suffering sonship entails suffering discipleship (servanthood), and have received from Jesus the commission to go and make all nations his disciples (28:16–20). Empowered by this commission, they carry out their task within the world Jesus described for them in his eschatological discourse of chapters 24–25.

5
Jesus' Use of "the Son of Man"

Beginning with 8:20, Jesus not infrequently refers to himself throughout Matthew's story as "the Son of man" *(ho hyios tou anthrōpou)*. The purpose of this Chapter is to explore this designation in terms of its meaning and function.[1] As we shall see, the impact that Jesus' use of "the Son of man" has upon the plot of Matthew's story is that it enhances two features that have already become familiar, "repudiation" and "vindication."

Because "the Son of man" occurs exclusively on the lips of Jesus, one is tempted to seize on it and regard it as providing the key to Matthew's understanding of Jesus. We saw in Chapter 1, however, that Matthew has, by authorial choice, made God's evaluative point of view normative within the world of his story. If this is correct, it follows that what will be weightiest in Matthew's presentation of Jesus is the understanding of him that God conveys. As has been noted, God twice enters the world of Matthew's story as "actor" in order to announce that Jesus is his beloved Son (3:17; 17:5). Plainly, therefore, Matthean christology must be adjudged to be preeminently a Son-of-God christology, and one dare not lose sight of this in ascertaining the meaning and the function of "the Son of man."

"THE SON OF MAN" AS JESUS' SELF-DESIGNATION

"The Son of man" may be defined as the designation Jesus employs so as to refer to himself as "the (this) man" (earthly, suffering, vindicated). It is "in public" or with a view to the "public" or "world" (e.g., the crowds, the religious leaders, gentile opponents, Judas, or all those who submit to judgment at the latter day) that Jesus uses it, and through such use he calls

---

1. On Matthew's use of "the Son of man," cf. Kingsbury, "Figure of Jesus," 22–32. For a survey of recent Son-of-man research, cf. Lindars, *Jesus Son of Man*, chap. 1; Müller, *Ausdruck "Menschensohn" in den Evangelien*, 1–9, 245–60.

attention both to the divine authority on which he acts and the opposition he encounters.

What kind of a designation is "the Son of man"? Is it, more grandly, a christological title or, more modestly, a technical term? And what is the difference between the two?

A "christological title" is a designation that describes, wholly or partially, the identity and therefore also the significance of Jesus of Nazareth. By contrast, a "technical term" is some word or expression that bears, within the story-world of Matthew, a precise meaning. As these definitions indicate, the category of christological title is narrower and more restricted than that of technical term. Words or expressions such as "the Kingdom of Heaven," "the gospel of the Kingdom," and "righteousness" count in Matthew as technical terms, but obviously they cannot be said to be christological titles.

When examined with these definitions in mind, "the Son of man" proves to be a technical term in Matthew's story. It is not a christological title because Matthew does not use it to set forth the identity of Jesus, to explain "who he is." Strange as this statement may seem at first blush, the evidence to substantiate it is compelling.

How does Matthew make known the identity of Jesus? In the main, he does so through the use of four titles that are confessional in nature: "Messiah" (christos),[2] the "King of the Jews (Israel),"[3] the "Son of David,"[4] and especially the "Son of God."[5] One tactic Matthew employs with great effectiveness is to place these titles in formulas of identification ("predication formulas")[6] so as to advise the reader in words (declarations or questions) uttered by characters in the story that Jesus *is* the Messiah (cf. 16:16), or *is* the King of the Jews (Israel) (cf. 27:11, 42), or *is* the Son of David (cf. 12:23), or *is* the Son of God (cf. 14:33). Significantly, "the Son of man" never appears in a formula of identification. The result is that no character in Matthew's story, whether transcendent being or human being, ever makes any declaration, or asks any question, concerning Jesus such as the following: "You are the Son of man!"; "This is the Son of man!" "Are you the Son of man?"; or "Is this the Son of man?" The inference to be drawn from the conspicuous absence of such declarations or questions in Matthew's story is that "the Son of man" does not specify for the characters who Jesus is.

Another indication that "the Son of man" does not divulge the identity of

2. Cf., e.g., 1:1; 16:16; 26:63–64a.
3. Cf., e.g., 2:2; 27:11, 37, 42.
4. Cf., e.g., 1:1; 12:23; 22:42, 45.
5. Cf., e.g., 3:17; 14:33; 16:16; 17:5; 26:63–64a; 27:43, 54.
6. A "predication formula" is a statement (even if conditional) or question which attributes to Jesus some name, designation, or title of majesty in the interest of divulging "who he is" (cf. Kingsbury, "Figure of Jesus," 25–26).

Jesus is the fact that although Jesus frequently uses it in public in order to refer to himself, the thought occurs neither to the disciples, nor to any group of Jews, nor even to the high priest to construe it as an expression that, again, informs them of who Jesus is.

Observe the disciples in 4:17—16:20. As they accompany Jesus or he addresses them, he repeatedly speaks of himself as "the Son of man."[7] But despite this, the disciples never confess him to be the Son of man or even call upon him as such. To illustrate how striking this phenomenon is, one need only glance at the passages 8:18–27; 14:22–33; and 16:13–20. In 8:18–27, Jesus, in turning away a scribe who would arrogate to himself the authority to become his disciple, refers to himself in the presence of the disciples as "the Son of man" (8:20; cf. 8:18, 21a, 23). But this notwithstanding, when the disciples are depicted only seven verses later as asking themselves about the identity of Jesus because of the miracle he has performed in calming winds and sea, they do not adopt Jesus' reference to himself as the Son of man in order to acclaim him as such. Far from acclaiming him to be the Son of man, they wonder aloud: "What sort of man is this, that even winds and sea obey him?" (8:27).

Later, Jesus twice leads the disciples to give answer to this question they have raised, once when they are again out on the sea and once when they are in the regions of Caesarea Philippi. In both cases, however, the confession the disciples make is manifestly not "You are the Son of man," but "Truly you are the Son of God!" (14:33) and "You are the Messiah, the Son of the living God!" (16:15–16).

Or consider the Jews. In the full hearing of the crowds[8] and of the religious leaders,[9] Jesus more than once designates himself as "the Son of man." Still, when the question of his identity arises, the leaders and the crowds disregard completely these several Son-of-man references. Instead of understanding Jesus to be "the Son of man," the leaders think of him as "that deceiver" (27:63) who is in collusion with Beelzebul (9:34; 12:24), and the crowds hold him to be a "prophet," namely, "John the Baptist," "Elijah," "Jeremiah," or "one of the prophets" (16:14; 21:11, 46).

Or take the high priest. As Jesus stands trial before the Sanhedrin (26:57, 59–68), Matthew causes the entire pericope to turn on the question of Jesus' identity. Noteworthy is the fact that although Jesus has publicly referred to himself as the Son of man on a number of occasions heretofore in Matthew's story,[10] the high priest does not adjure him to say whether he is "the Son of man" but whether he is "the Messiah, the Son of God" (26:63).

Nor is this the whole of it. In immediate response to the high priest,

7. Cf. 8:20 with 8:18; 10:23 with 10:5; 12:8 with 12:1; 13:41 with 13:36; 16:13.
8. Cf. 8:20 with 8:18; 9:6 with 9:8; 11:19 with 11:7 and 11:16.
9. Cf. 8:20 with 8:19; 9:6 with 9:3; 12:8 with 12:2; 12:32 with 12:24; 12:40 with 12:38.
10. Cf. 8:20; 9:6; 11:19; 12:8, 32, 40.

Jesus affirms that he is in truth the Messiah, the Son of God ("[So] you have said"; 26:64a). Then, continuing his answer, Jesus makes a solemn prediction in which he tacitly refers to himself as "the Son of man" (26:64b). Apparently, this Son-of-man reference communicates nothing whatever to the high priest and the Sanhedrin about Jesus' identity. As proof of this, one has only to glance at the respective scenes attending the trial (26:67–68) and the crucifixion (27:41–43) in which Matthew depicts the Sanhedrin as mocking Jesus. In both scenes, members of the Sanhedrin make Jesus' identity the object of their ridicule. But regardless of the fact that they have all heard Jesus refer to himself as "the Son of man," in the first scene they taunt him as "Messiah" (26:68) and in the second as the "Son of God" (27:43). In these scenes, therefore, the members of the Sanhedrin pick up not at all on Jesus' reference to himself as "the Son of man" but instead cite in mockery the same titles the high priest had used as he had interrogated Jesus about his identity: " . . . tell us if you are the Messiah, the Son of God" (26:63). Plainly, Jesus' public reference to himself as "the Son of man" at his trial is not presented by Matthew as revealing his identity.

A third indication that "the Son of man" does not serve in Matthew's story to specify "who Jesus is" comes to the fore in the passage 16:13. Here Jesus asks the disciples who "men" say that "the Son of man" is. Now if "the Son of man" were indeed being used by Matthew to identify Jesus, a perfectly proper response to Jesus' question would be, "The Son of man is the Son of man!" This answer is, of course, absurd. Still, its very absurdity is yet another sign that, in Matthew's story, "the Son of man" does not explain who Jesus is.

A final indication that "the Son of man" functions other than to divulge the identity of Jesus has to do with the fact that it does not occur at all in the first part of Matthew's story (1:1—4:16). The aim of this part is to present Jesus to the reader so that he or she will know, throughout the rest of the story, precisely who Jesus is. This explains why the major designations by means of which Matthew identifies Jesus all stand out prominently in this part: "Jesus," "Jesus Christ," "Messiah," "Son of David," "King of the Jews," and "Son of God." By contrast, Matthew does not introduce the expression "the Son of man" into his story until as late as 8:20. Moreover, when he does introduce it, he does so unobtrusively, for the reader does not anticipate its sudden use, and the focus of the text is neither on the expression itself nor on the topic of Jesus' identity but on the theme of discipleship. Literally, the way Matthew first acquaints the reader with "the Son of man" is singularly ill-calculated to suggest that its purpose is to inform the reader of who Jesus is.

Though not a christological title that sets forth the identity of Jesus, "the Son of man" is nonetheless, as has been observed, a technical term. In fact, Matthew's very use of it attests already to its distinctiveness. Thus, in that

Jesus designates himself as "the Son of man" in connection with his earthly ministry, his suffering, death, and resurrection, and his anticipated Parousia, he calls attention to the peculiar contours of his ministry and so shows that "the Son of man" applies to him in a manner in which it can be applied to no other human being. Again, "the Son of man" also constitutes the phraseological point of view of exclusively Jesus: it occurs solely in his mouth; it is always definite in form ("the" Son of man); and when Jesus employs it, he does so to refer to himself alone. And third, Jesus fulfills OT prophecy as the one who designates himself "the Son of man," which is further indication that "the Son of man" possesses a special status in Matthew's story.

If "the Son of man" is a technical term, what does it mean? Literally, "the Son of man" means "the man," or "the human being." In four passages in particular this meaning comes to light. At 11:19, Jesus denounces this generation for dismissing the Son of man as the "man" who is a glutton and a drunkard, a friend of toll-collectors and sinners. At 9:6, Jesus declares that the Son of man has authority on earth to forgive sins and then validates this by healing a paralytic, whereupon the crowds respond by glorifying God for granting such authority to "men" (9:8). At 8:27, the disciples' question as to "what sort of man" (*potapos*) Jesus is picks up on Jesus' reference to himself as the Son of man in the preceding pericope (8:20). And in the interpretation of the parable of the tares, Jesus first identifies the Son of man with the "man" who in the parable has sown good seed (cf. 13:37 with 13:24) and then identifies this earthly Son of man with the future Son of man who will come at the consummation of the age to inaugurate the Great Assize (cf. 13:37 with 13:40–43).

But technically correct though it surely is to translate the Greek original of "the Son of man" as "the man," or "the human being," the latter nevertheless limps badly as an adequate English rendering of the former. To recognize this, one has only to move through Matthew's story and, each time "the Son of man" occurs, to substitute for it "the man." When one does this, one encounters difficulty virtually from the outset: although Jesus is, without exception, the one to whom "the Son of man" refers, the translation "the man" does not always make it as immediately obvious as it must be that Jesus is in fact the one being spoken of. To test this, consider the following two passages: "Foxes have holes and birds of the air nests, but 'the man' has nowhere to lay his head" (8:20); "And whoever says a word against 'the man' will be forgiven . . ." (12:32). To overcome this difficulty, it is preferable to render in English the Greek original of "the Son of man" with the expression "this man." "This man" is what may be termed a translational equivalent: it captures in English the force of the Greek original of "the Son of man."[11] Substitution of "this man" for "the Son of man"

---

11. On this point, cf., e.g., Vermes, *Jesus and the World of Judaism*, 99.

each time the latter occurs makes it unmistakably clear that "the man" being referred to is in each instance Jesus. To illustrate this, note the following three types of examples (earthly, suffering, future): "Foxes have holes and birds of the air nests, but *this man* has nowhere to lay his head" (8:20); *"This man* is to be delivered into the hands of men, and they will kill him, and he will be raised on the third day" (17:22–23); "But I tell you, hereafter you will see *this man* seated at the right hand of power and coming on the clouds of heaven" (26:64).

Earlier we discussed the curious phenomenon that Jesus can, in Matthew's story, openly speak of himself as "the Son of man" without at the same time ever having any character give even the slightest hint that he or she thinks that Jesus is thereby divulging his identity. Now should it be correct that "the man" is an accurate translation of the underlying Greek of "the Son of man" and that "this man" is its translational equivalent, then this phenomenon ceases to be a curiosity. If "the Son of man" has the force of "this man," then it can occur in Jesus' mouth frequently and in public and yet never occasion the disclosure of his identity.

Still, precisely because Jesus' use of "the Son of man" does not reveal his identity, the question necessarily arises: What specifically is the identity of Jesus the Son of man? On this score, Matthew is unambiguous, pointing the reader to the words Peter utters at Caesarea Philippi. Who, then, is Jesus the Son of man (i.e., Who is "this man" Jesus?) (16:13)? He is the Son of God (16:16). And lest one object that this answer is but the words of Peter, one will recall that the evaluative point of view Peter expresses in his confession is in accord with the evaluative point of view God has expressed at the baptism (3:17) and the transfiguration (17:5). Then, too, for one to recognize that the Son of man in Matthew's story is to be identified as the Son of God is also of benefit for gaining insight into yet another problem area. In the passages 16:27 and 25:34, the expressions "his Father" and "my Father" occur with reference to Jesus as the Son of man. Seen properly, these expressions likewise attest to the identity of Jesus the Son of man: Jesus the Son of man ("this man" Jesus), in referring to God as "my Father," tacitly bears witness that he is the Son of God.

From meaning we turn to purpose: How does "the Son of man" function in Matthew's story? It functions as a "public" designation and also to call attention to both the divine authority on which Jesus acts and the opposition he encounters.

In what sense is "the Son of man" a "public" designation? "The Son of man" is a "public" designation in the sense that it is primarily with an eye to "outsiders" or the "world," Jews and Gentiles and especially opponents, that Jesus calls himself the Son of man. To prove this, one has only to review Jesus' Son-of-man sayings. In the earthly Son-of-man sayings, it is in view of the Jewish public (16:13) or of the world (13:36–37) or in the audience of the crowds,[12] of some of the scribes,[13] and of the Pharisees[14] that Jesus refers to himself as the Son of man. In the suffering Son-of-man sayings, it is to some of the scribes and Pharisees (12:38, 40) or to the disciples but in view of Judas,[15] of "men"[16] and "sinners" (26:45), of the religious leaders (20:18), of Gentile opponents (20:19), and of the rulers of the Gentiles (20:25, 28) that Jesus speaks of himself as the Son of man. And in the future Son-of-man sayings, it is in view of all the nations (Israel, the Gentiles, the religious leaders, but also the disciples [since they, too, must at the Latter Day undergo judgment])[17] that Jesus terms himself the Son of man. In short, it is this orientation toward the "world" in Jesus' use of "the Son of man" that marks this designation as "public" in nature.

"Public" in character, "the Son of man" also functions in Matthew's story to call attention to the divine authority on which Jesus acts. If one leaves aside the passages 16:13 and perhaps 12:32, Jesus assumes to himself in the earthly Son-of-man sayings the power to forgive sins (9:6), to regulate the sabbath (12:8), to have table fellowship with toll-collectors and sinners (11:19), and to raise up in the world sons of the Kingdom (13:37-38). Paradoxically, he also asserts his authority by embracing a lifestyle that includes itinerancy born of rejection (8:19-20).[18] In the suffering Son-of-man sayings, Jesus evinces his authority by freely going the way of the cross in obedience to the will of God.[19] Indeed, as one who employs his authority not to be served but to serve, Jesus holds himself up as the example his disciples are to emulate in their life together (20:28). And in the future Son-of-man sayings, Jesus exercises his authority as the end-time judge who ushers in the consummated Kingdom and inaugurates the Great Assize.[20]

And last, "the Son of man" furthermore functions in Matthew's story to call attention to the opposition Jesus encounters. In the case of the earthly Son-of-man sayings, a strong aura of opposition surrounds them: Satan stands forth as the cosmic antagonist of Jesus (13:37-39); "men" prove themselves to be ignorant of Jesus' true identity and imagine him to be a prophet (16:13-14); "this generation" repudiates Jesus (11:19); a scribe wrongly attempts to arrogate to himself the right to become Jesus' disciple (8:19-20); and the religious leaders charge Jesus with blasphemy (9:3, 6),

12. Cf. 8:18, 20; 9:6, 8; 11:7, 19.
13. Cf. 9:3, 6; also 8:19-20.
14. Cf. 12:2, 8, 24, 32.
15. Cf. 26:2, 24-25, 45-46.
16. Cf. 17:22; also 17:12.
17. Cf. 10:23; 13:41-43; 16:27-28; 19:28; 24:27, 30-31, 37-39, 44; 25:31-32; 26:64.
18. On this point, cf. Kingsbury, "The 'Eager' Scribe and the 'Reluctant' Disciple."
19. Cf. 17:22-23; 20:18-19; 26:24, 45, 56; also 16:21.
20. Cf. 13:40-43; 16:27-28; 24:29-31; 25:31-46; 26:64.

accuse him of being in collusion with Satan (12:24, 32), and take him to task because his disciples have allegedly acted unlawfully on the sabbath (12:2, 8). In the suffering Son-of-man sayings, Jesus speaks directly of the opposition he faces by predicting his death (12:39–40), by telling his disciples what his enemies will do to him,[21] and by contrasting as opposites his will to serve with the will of the rulers of the world to lord it over others (20:25–28). And in the future Son-of-man sayings, Jesus sounds the note of opposition (but also of hope) by portraying himself as the judge who will hold the entire world accountable, consigning some to condemnation and inviting others to share in the bliss of God's presence.[22]

JESUS AS "THE SON OF MAN": REPUDIATION AND VINDICATION

Against the backdrop of this probe into the meaning and the function of "the Son of man," a final question arises: What impact does Matthew's use of "the Son of man" have upon his story? Perhaps the best way to answer this is to compare the overall role of this designation with that of the family of titles at the head of which stands the "Son of God."

Briefly, the title "Son of God" serves to identify Jesus for the reader. So it is, for example, that the first two parts of Matthew's story culminate, respectively, in the announcement by God that Jesus is his Son (3:17) and in the confession by Peter, which is in alignment with God's understanding, that Jesus is the Son of God (16:16–17). In the third part of Matthew's story, Jesus appropriates God's understanding of him as his Son in the parable of the wicked husbandmen he addresses to the Jewish leaders (21:37–39), and from this parable, in turn, the high priest derives the question concerning Jesus' divine sonship on which Jesus' trial turns and for which he is condemned to death for blasphemy (26:63–64a). Beyond this, upon Jesus' death the Roman soldiers, also uttering words that are in alignment with God's understanding of Jesus, likewise affirm Jesus to be God's Son (27:54). The significance of their affirmation is that with it Matthew has, in terms of narrating his story, guided it to a point where knowledge of the identity of Jesus also embraces, as far as the reader is concerned, a mature knowledge of the purpose of Jesus' earthly ministry. Finally, on a mountain in Galilee the disciples, to whom Jesus' identity had earlier been revealed (16:16; 14:33), see the resurrected Jesus as the crucified one (28:5–7) and hence comprehend at last not only who he is but also what he was about (26:28). Accordingly, they receive from the resurrected Jesus not a command to silence (16:20) but the commission to go and to make of all nations his disciples (28:16–20).

---

21. Cf. 17:12, 22–23; 20:18–19; 26:2, 24, 45–46.
22. Cf. 10:23; 13:40–43; 16:27–28; 19:28; 24:29–31, 37–39, 43–44; 25:31–46; 26:64.

Roughly parallel with this line of development (from 8:20 on), Jesus refers to himself in Matthew's story as "the Son of man." In so doing, he does not divulge his identity but instead speaks of himself as "the (this) man," or "the (this) human being." The purpose for which Jesus employs "the Son of man" is multiple: to assert his divine authority in the face of opposition; to tell his disciples what the "public," or "world" (Jews and Gentiles), is about to do to him; and to predict that he whom the world puts to death God will raise and that, exalted to universal rule, he will return in splendor as Judge and consequently be seen by all as having been vindicated by God. Through Jesus' use of the public designation of the Son of man, therefore, Matthew calls the reader's attention to the twin elements of "repudiation" and "vindication." In Matthew's purview, these mark the interaction that "this man" Jesus has with the public, or world, that does not receive him as the one he is, namely, the Son of God.

SUMMARY

In this chapter we have examined the meaning and the function of "the Son of man" in Matthew's story. As was observed, "the Son of man" is not of the nature of a christological title the purpose of which is to inform the reader of "who Jesus is." Instead, it is a self-designation that is also a technical term, and it describes Jesus as "the man," or "the human being" ("this man," or "this human being") (earthly, suffering, vindicated). It is "in public" or with a view to the "public," or "world" (Jews and Gentiles but especially opponents), that Jesus refers to himself as "the Son of man" ("this man"). Through his use of this self-reference, Jesus calls attention, for one thing, to the divine authority that he ("this man") exercises now and will also exercise in the future and, for another thing, to the opposition that he ("this man") must face. And should the question be raised as to who "this man" Jesus is, the answer is, as Peter correctly confesses, that he is the Son of God (16:13, 16).

6
The Great Speeches
of Jesus

Embedded in Matthew's story are five great speeches of Jesus. Although these speeches have been touched on in tracing the story-line of Jesus (Chaps. 2–4), they stand out so prominently that they merit special consideration. If a story, according to Chatman, is made up of events, characters, and settings, then "speeches" are particular types of events, or actions.[1] In Matthew, they afford Jesus the opportunity to address authoritatively other characters for a lengthy period of time.

THE DISPOSITION OF THE SPEECHES

Five times throughout Matthew's story the reader encounters the stereotyped formula: "And it happened when Jesus finished these words [these parables; instructing his twelve disciples] . . ." (7:28; 11:1; 13:53; 19:1; 26:1). Each time this formula occurs, it calls attention to the termination of a speech Jesus has delivered. With this formula as guide, one can readily distinguish the five great speeches, or discourses, of Jesus. They are: the Sermon on the Mount (chaps. 5–7); the missionary discourse (9:35—10:42); the discourse in parables (13:1–52); the ecclesiological discourse (17:24—18:35); and the eschatological discourse (chaps. 24–25).[2]

Since the ascendancy of the Two-Source hypothesis in the last century and the notion that Mark is the earliest Gospel, most scholars have viewed Matthew as being in some sense a revised version of Mark. Compare Matthew with Mark, and the feature that immediately catches the eye is the presence in Matthew of the five great speeches of Jesus. Focus attention on

1. Chatman, *Story and Discourse*, 45–46.
2. Because of the change in both "setting" (from the "temple" to the "Mount of Olives," 24:1–3) and "audience" (from the "crowds and the disciples," 23:1, to the "disciples," 24:1–3), chap. 23 ought not be grouped with chaps. 24–25 in determining the limits of the eschatological discourse.

these speeches, however, and it soon seems only logical to claim, along with Benjamin Bacon[3] at the beginning of this century and other scholars since then too numerous to mention, that Matthew consists fundamentally of two distinct elements, "story" and "speech."[4] Weigh the relative importance of these elements, and the conclusion seems compelling: "speech" is primary and "story" is secondary. In the view of many scholars, therefore, Matthew's Gospel is properly to be construed as a revised version of Mark whose crowning jewels are the five great speeches Jesus delivers.[5]

From a literary-critical standpoint, this understanding of Matthew's Gospel will not do. Matthew's Gospel is a unified narrative that tells the story of the conflict that Jesus Son of God has with Israel, the people of God. As we made clear (Chap. 4), the resolution of this conflict and therefore the climax of Matthew's story comes not in the great speeches of Jesus, but in the narration of his suffering, death, and resurrection (chaps. 26–28). By the same token, these speeches of Jesus, far from standing above, or apart from, the story being told, in reality have their proper place within it. A review of the story will make this clear.

Once Matthew has introduced Jesus (1:1—4:16), he describes Jesus' ministry to Israel and Israel's repudiation of him (4:17—16:20). In discharging his ministry to Israel (4:17—11:1), Jesus teaches, preaches, and heals (4:23; 9:35; 11:1). His first great speech, the Sermon on the Mount (chaps. 5–7), is the example par excellence of his teaching. Later, after Jesus himself has ministered to Israel, he broadens his outreach by sending the disciples out on a mission to Israel (10:1, 5–6). In his second great speech, the missionary discourse (10:5b–42), Jesus instructs his disciples in this mission.

Notwithstanding Jesus' ministry, Matthew portrays Israel as repudiating him (11:2—16:20). In his third great speech, the discourse in parables (13:1–52), Jesus himself reacts to Israel's repudiation of him by speaking to the crowds in parables, that is, in a mode of language they cannot comprehend (13:10–13). In so doing, Jesus characterizes Israel as a people that is blind, deaf, and without understanding (13:13).

In the lengthy end-segment of his story, Matthew depicts Jesus as journeying to Jerusalem, where he suffers, dies, and is raised (16:21—28:20). On his journey to Jerusalem, Jesus by and large teaches the disciples and heals the crowds or others (16:21—20:34). In his fourth great speech, the ecclesiological discourse (chap. 18), Jesus instructs the disciples on their life together. The characteristic mark of this life is "true greatness," that is, showing infinite concern for one another and forgiving one another.

3. Bacon, *Studies in Matthew*, xv, 47, 50, 81–82.
4. For a survey of this scholarly trend, cf. Kingsbury (*Matthew: Structure, Christology, Kingdom*, 2–4) and, more recently, Bauer ("Structure of Matthew's Gospel," 65–81).
5. For a parade example of this view of Matthew's Gospel, cf. the celebrated essay by Bornkamm, "End-Expectation and Church in Matthew."

Having reached Jerusalem and completed his activity in the temple, Jesus takes leave of the latter and goes to the Mount of Olives (24:1–3). In his fifth great speech, the eschatological discourse (chaps. 24–25), Jesus, atop the Mount of Olives and immediately prior to his passion, looks away from the present and foretells what the future holds for the disciples in the time following the resurrection and leading up to his Parousia (24:3). Plainly, all five of Jesus' great speeches fit seamlessly into the plot of the story Matthew tells.

THE AUDIENCE OF THE SPEECHES
Jesus presents none of his great speeches to the religious leaders, for there is never a time in Matthew's story when their ears are not deaf to his teaching. Instead, the audience he addresses are the crowds and especially the disciples. In the Sermon on the Mount, Jesus speaks to both the crowds and the disciples (5:1; 7:28–29), and it is primarily to the crowds that he also delivers the first half of his discourse in parables (13:1–35; but cf. 13:10–23). Otherwise, the recipients of Jesus' great speeches are exclusively the disciples: the latter half of the discourse in parables (13:36–52); and the missionary, ecclesiological, and eschatological discourses (chaps. 10; 18; 24–25).

Jesus as "Speaking Past" the Audience
One of the curious features of Jesus' great speeches is that they contain sayings that seemingly are without relevance for the characters in the story to whom they are addressed. Time and again, Jesus touches on matters that are alien to the immediate situation of the crowds or the disciples. This peculiar phenomenon—that Jesus speaks past his stipulated audience at places in his speeches—compels one to ask whether Jesus is not to be construed as addressing some person(s) other than simply the crowds or the disciples in the story. And if so, who might this person (these persons) be?

Representative examples of sayings of Jesus that appear to address a situation other than the one in the story in which the crowds or the disciples find themselves can readily be detected in all the speeches. Indeed, in one case, Jesus' eschatological discourse (chaps. 24–25), the whole of the speech envisages a different situation owing to the fact that it is prophetic in character and foretells the future (24:3). In the other speeches, examples of Jesus' sayings addressing another situation abound.

For instance, at 5:11 in the Sermon on the Mount Jesus pronounces eschatological blessing upon persons who, "on account of me," suffer persecution. The expression "on account of me" indicates that those here envisaged are "disciples" and that a time is in sight when Jesus is no longer physically present.[6] Accordingly, as a word directed to the Jewish crowds

6. On this last point, cf. esp. 10:18.

and the pre-Easter disciples, this saying describes circumstances that scarcely apply. Strictly speaking, Jesus delivers the Sermon on the Mount at a time when he has just called his first four disciples (4:18–22) and the crowds have only begun to follow him (4:24–25). For both groups, persecution and the absence of Jesus are quite beyond their horizon.

The same is also true of the words Jesus speaks in 7:15–23. Here Jesus predicts repudiation at the latter day for certain disciples who, although they prophesy, exorcise demons, and perform miracles in his name, are nevertheless condemned as workers of lawlessness. Clearly, neither the crowds nor the four disciples have thus far known any situation in which "Christians" who are false prophets are active.

Again, in 6:16–18 Jesus cites "fasting" as one of the three fundamentals of proper piety and enjoins his hearers to the true practice of it (i.e., without ostentation). But although the four disciples just called are plainly identified as hearers of Jesus, one learns only three chapters later (9:14–15) that, prior to his death, Jesus absolves his disciples of any necessity to fast. To leave the crowds aside for now, once more Jesus utters words in the Sermon on the Mount which have little import for the immediate situation of his pre-Easter disciples.

To turn to the missionary discourse (9:35—10:42), at least two examples of sayings of Jesus that seem to have no immediate relevance for the story-audience leap out. At 10:18, 22, Jesus warns the disciples that they will be dragged before governors and kings, "to bear testimony before them and the Gentiles," and be "hated by all." The anomaly of these words is that they presuppose a mission on the part of the disciples among Gentiles within a speech in which Jesus sends them solely to Israel and expressly forbids them to go to Gentiles (10:5b–6). As those being readied for an exclusive mission to Israel, the disciples are unprepared at this point in the story to entertain the notion of a mission among Gentiles.

At 10:41–42, Jesus speaks of the eventuality that the missionary-disciples he sends out may be received as a "prophet" or "righteous one" or "little one." Yet, because it was not until just prior to Jesus' missionary speech to them that the disciples had even been constituted as a group (10:2–4), one must ask how they can therefore be thought to recognize themselves in the above designations and to apply them to themselves.

In his discourse in parables (13:1–52), Jesus speaks past both audiences he addresses, crowds and disciples. In the first half of the discourse (13:1–35), Jesus primarily addresses the crowds. Still, the crowds, listen though they may to Jesus' parables, are, as Jesus explains to the disciples, unable to comprehend them (13:10–13). The ones who are to comprehend his parables are the disciples (13:11, 51).

But even considering that it is the disciples who are to comprehend Jesus' parables, one can observe that certain of Jesus' words have a time and situation in view that are completely foreign to them. Thus, as Jesus interprets the parable of the sower (13:18–23), he tells of persons who, having heard the word of the Kingdom and become Jesus' followers, surrender it when made to endure tribulation and persecution (13:20–21) or produce no fruit in their lives because they are either overcome by the cares of the world or give pride of place to the delight in riches (13:22). Similarly, in the interpretation of the seed growing secretly (13:36–43), Jesus suddenly depicts the whole "world" as the scene of combat between him and his followers and the devil and his followers (13:38). The point to be made is this: at this juncture in Matthew's story, the disciples are yet with Jesus in Israel; these circumstances of which Jesus speaks—a time of persecution and apostasy, seduction by the world, and struggle with the devil and his followers in the world—lie totally beyond their purview.

Finally, Jesus also utters words in the ecclesiological discourse (17:24–18:35) to which the disciples in the story can scarcely relate. In the passage 18:15–20, Jesus both outlines a procedure of "church discipline" and promises that he will be present whenever the community of disciples gathers "in his name." Once more, this passage presupposes the physical absence of Jesus and describes a situation completely beyond the disciples' present field of vision.

Jesus as "Speaking To" the Implied Reader

If in his great speeches Jesus periodically speaks past his story-audience of crowds or disciples, whom in addition to the latter is he addressing in these instances? From a literary-critical standpoint, he is addressing the implied reader(s).

To recognize this, one has only to remind oneself again of the peculiar position the implied reader occupies within the world of Matthew's story. This position is located, as has been said, in the time between the resurrection and the Parousia (27:8; 28:15). Now if Jesus' great speeches are "heard" from this particular vantage point, one sees at once that the implied reader is well able to relate to all those matters Jesus raises in his speeches which envisage a time or situation strikingly different from the one in which the crowds or disciples in the story find themselves.

For example, the implied reader can relate with ease to all such matters as these: the fact that Jesus is no longer physically present; that disciples are being persecuted; that certain Christians are proving themselves to be false prophets; that a mission is underway not only to Jews but also to Gentiles; that "prophet," "righteous one," and "little one" are designations that apply to various Christians in the community; that some Christians cannot endure persecution and tribulation and hence surrender their faith; that there are Christians who succumb to the cares of the world or to the delight in riches and hence "produce no fruit in their lives"; that the "world" is the battleground where the risen Jesus and his followers engage in combat with the devil and his followers; and that the Christian community is concerned to reconcile the erring brother or sister to itself and also assembles itself to decide its affairs in the name and presence of the risen Jesus. The very sayings in Jesus' speeches that are so ill-suited to address the immediate situation of the crowds or the pre-Easter disciples prove to be well-suited indeed to address the situation of the implied reader.

This phenomenon of having Jesus "speak past" his story-audience is by no means the only rhetorical device that Matthew as implied author utilizes in order to insure that the great speeches of Jes :s will relate directly to the implied reader. On the contrary, Matthew also utilizes to this end a variety of other devices.

To illustrate, the very structure Matthew has given these speeches enhances their capacity to serve as an immediate word of address to the implied reader. All the great speeches of Jesus are comparatively lengthy, which means that the implied reader, in hearing them, is exposed to long stretches of uninterrupted direct discourse.[7] The result is that these speeches enable Jesus to draw the implied reader to his side and to school him or her in his evaluative point of view on those ethical and eschatological issues that can be seen to be of the utmost importance within the world of Matthew's story.

Again, Matthew also makes effective use of such linguistic devices or modes of speech as the imperative mood, the pronoun "you" (whether singular or plural), "timeless expressions," and parables so as to turn Jesus' great speeches into a direct word of address to the implied reader. Indeed, the tone of Jesus' speeches is virtually that of a homily being addressed to the implied reader. For example, through the use of the imperative mood Jesus is made to exhort the implied reader: "Judge not, that you be not judged" (7:1); "Do not give dogs what is holy; and do not throw your pearls before swine" (7:6); "Ask, and it will be given you; seek and you will find; knock, and it will be opened to you" (7:7); "Enter by the narrow gate" (7:13); and "Beware of false prophets" (7:15). Or through the use of the pronoun "you" (singular and plural), Jesus is enabled to address the implied reader in a very personal and immediate way: "For I tell you" (5:20); "You have heard . . . but I say to you"[8] (cf. 5:21–22); "You, therefore, must be perfect" (5:48); or "You then pray like this" (6:9). Or also through the use of timeless expressions,[9] Jesus can be made to address the implied reader

7. On the rhetorical use of direct discourse and also the present tense, cf. Anderson, "Point of View in Matthew," 11–13; Chatman, Story and Discourse, 81–84; Hawkins, Horae Synopticae, 148–49.

8. On the rhetorical force of the formula "I say to you," cf. Aune, Prophecy in Early Christianity, 164–65.

9. Cf. Chatman, Story and Discourse, 80, 82.

as though the latter were his contemporary: "Not everyone who says" (7:21); "Every one then who hears" (7:24); "Whoever humbles himself" (18:4); "Whoever receives" (18:5); or ". . . whatever you bind . . . whatever you loose" (18:18). And through the vehicle of the parable, Jesus, the bearer of God's kingly Rule, conveys to the implied reader a vision of human existence as it is lived in the sphere of God's Rule: "The Kingdom of Heaven is like . . ." (13:31, 33); "The Kingdom of Heaven may be compared to . . ." (13:24); "Then the Kingdom of Heaven shall be compared to . . ." (25:1). The upshot of Matthew's use of these various rhetorical devices is that the implied reader, in hearing Jesus deliver his great speeches, is made to sense that he or she, along with the crowds or the disciples in the story, is being directly addressed by him.

THE PURPOSE AND THE THEMES
OF THE SPEECHES

What chief purpose do the great speeches of Jesus serve within the story of Matthew? To get at this, one needs to speak first of Matthew's overall depiction of the life of Jesus. In the story Matthew tells apart from the great speeches, Jesus is depicted as the Son of God who, in willing obedience to his Father, goes the way of the cross so as to save humankind by shedding his blood for the atonement of sins (1:21; 20:28; 26:28). Or to put it more simply, Jesus is depicted as the Son who, in devotion to the Father, serves humankind.

As the obedient Son who serves humankind, Jesus is himself the supreme exemplar of the greater righteousness. It is he in Matthew's story in whom the greater righteousness comes to perfect expression: Single-hearted in his devotion to God, he loves the neighbor as self (5:48; 22:37–40). In his great speeches, Jesus directly addresses, as was noted, not only the crowds or the pre-Easter disciples but also, and above all, the implied reader. The implied reader is, we know, a post-Easter disciple of Jesus who is at home in the time between the resurrection and the Parousia. Like all disciples, the implied reader, too, is summoned "to be like his teacher" (10:25; 16:24). To this end, he or she is summoned to hear and to internalize Jesus' speeches (cf., e.g., 7:24–27). To hear and to internalize Jesus' speeches is to be conformed to the shape of his life. This, then, is the chief purpose of Jesus' great speeches: to bring the life of the disciple, or the implied reader, into conformity with the shape of Jesus' life. At 16:24, Jesus, the Son of God, declares in Matthew: "If any man would come after me, let him deny himself and take up his cross, and let him follow me." By internalizing the speeches of Jesus, the disciple, or the implied reader, who through Jesus has become a "son of God" (5:45), realizes this saying in his or her life: In single-hearted devotion to God the Father, he or she serves the neighbor and indeed all humankind.

It remains for us to provide a brief overview of the great speeches of Jesus. Perhaps this can best be done by touching on the themes of the speeches and indicating the major parts into which each speech can be divided. For further treatment of the speeches, one may wish to consult the literature cited in the footnotes.

The theme of the Sermon on the Mount (5:3—7:27) is the "greater righteousness" (5:20) [10] This theme is developed in five major parts, to wit: (I) On Those Who Practice the Greater Righteousness (5:3-16); (II) On Practicing the Greater Righteousness toward the Neighbor (5:17-45); (III) On Practicing the Greater Righteousness before God (6:1-18); (IV) On Practicing the Greater Righteousness in Other Areas of Life (6:19—7:12); and (V) Injunctions on Practicing the Greater Righteousness (7:13-27).

The missionary discourse revolves around the theme of "the mission of the disciples to Israel" (10:6). It falls into three larger sections:[11] (I) On Being Sent to the Lost Sheep of the House of Israel (10:5b-15); (II) On Responding to Persecution (10:16-23); and (III) On Bearing Witness Fearlessly (10:34-42).

The discourse in parables (13:3-52) focuses on the theme of "instruction in the secrets of the Kingdom" (13:11).[12] It is divided into two main parts: (I) On the Secrets of the Kingdom as Being Revealed to the Disciples But Not to Israel (13:3-35); and (II) On the Secrets of the Kingdom as Urging Disciples to Obey Without Reserve the Will of God (13:36-52).

The theme that underlies the ecclesiological discourse (18:1-35) is "life within the community of the church" (18:18-20).[13] The two broad sections that make up this discourse are: (I) On True Greatness as Consisting in Humbling Oneself so as to Serve the Neighbor (18:1-14); and (II) On Gaining and Forgiving the Errant Disciple (18:15-35).

Finally, the theme addressed in the eschatological discourse is that of the "last times" (24:3).[14] Here, three larger sections comprise the discourse: (I) On Understanding Aright the Signs of the End (24:4-35); (II) On Being on the Alert for Jesus' Coming at the Consummation of the Age (24:36—25:30); and (III) On the Second Coming of Jesus and the Final Judgment (25:31-46).

10. For further reading, cf. Kingsbury, "Place, Structure, and Meaning of the Sermon on the Mount," 131–43; Guelich, *Sermon on the Mount*.

11. These divisions are those advocated by Weaver, "Missionary Discourse in Matthew," 123–27.

12. For further reading, cf. Kingsbury, *Parables of Jesus in Matthew 13*.

13. For further reading, cf. Pesch, *Matthäus der Seelsorger*, 15–16, 32–33; Thompson, *Matthew's Advice to a Divided Community*; Patte, *Gospel According to Matthew*, 244–60.

14. For further reading, cf. Lambrecht, "Parousia Discourse," 309–42; Thompson, "Historical Perspective in the Gospel of Matthew," 243–62; Brown, "Matthean Apocalypse," 2–27; Burnett, *Testament of Jesus-Sophia*.

SUMMARY

Contrary to what many scholars have claimed over the years, the great speeches of Jesus do not constitute the climactic feature of Matthew's Gospel nor do they stand apart from the rest of the story being told. On the contrary, each speech can be seen to be appropriately situated within the story's plot. One of the unique features of these speeches is that Jesus can be found at places to speak past the story-audience, the crowds or the disciples, and to address directly the implied reader in his or her own situation in the time between the resurrection and the Parousia. Accordingly, the implied reader, and not the crowds or the disciples in the story, is the one who is to be thought of as comprehending the whole of each speech. Intended to be heard and internalized, the great speeches of Jesus have as their chief purpose to bring the life of the disciple, or the implied reader, into conformity with the shape of Jesus' own life, which is one of single-hearted devotion toward God and loving service toward the neighbor. The several themes Jesus treats in his speeches have to do with such matters as the greater righteousness, the mission of the disciples to Israel, the secrets of the Kingdom of Heaven, the nature of the disciples' life together, and the last things. Together, these speeches comprise the bulk of Jesus' teaching, which Matthew would have all disciples everywhere observe to the end of time (28:20).

7

The Antagonists
of Jesus

In discussing "conflict" as the central element of plot in Matthew's story (Chap. 1) and in tracing the story-line of Jesus (Chaps. 2–4), we have already, of course, dealt with the religious leaders. Nevertheless, Matthew develops a story-line apropos of the leaders that begs to be explored in its own right.[1]

If Jesus is the protagonist of Matthew's story, then the religious leaders, as his principal opponents in the human realm, are the antagonists. As persons who, by virtue of time-honored privilege (23:2), occupy positions of authority in Israel, they lay proud claim to be called "leaders."[2] Except for Jesus himself, they are the ones in Matthew's story who influence most the development of the plot. Although they go by many names—Pharisees, Sadducees, chief priests, elders, scribes, and Herodians—they form a united front against Jesus and hence can be treated, as we saw in Chapter 1, as a single character. In terms of the traits they exhibit, they are "flat" and not "round." The reason is that Matthew presents the plethora of traits they possess as in reality offshoots of one "root trait," namely, "evilness." Accordingly, the picture the reader gets of the religious leaders in Matthew's story is not historically objective but wholly negative and polemical. Just as Jesus is the Son of God who invariably "thinks the things of God," so the leaders are quintessentially those who never "think the things of God" and only "think the things of humans" (16:23e). As the antagonists of Jesus, the religious leaders are cast by Matthew in a singularly villainous role (13:38–39; 15:13).

---

1. At the basis of a significant portion of this chapter is the following article: Kingsbury, "Developing Conflict between Jesus and the Jewish Leaders." For a full-scale literary-critical treatment of the religious leaders in Matthew's story, cf. Powell, "Religious Leaders."
2. Observe that the religious authorities are acknowledged to be "leaders" even in such pejorative passages as 15:14; 23:16; 23:24.

The story of the religious leaders develops in concert with the story of Jesus. In the first part (1:1—4:16), Matthew introduces, along separate lines, both Jesus and the leaders to the reader. In the second part (4:17—16:20), while highlighting Jesus' ministry to Israel of teaching, preaching, and healing (4:17—11:1), Matthew likewise describes the initial controversies that flare up between Jesus and the leaders (chap. 9). Also in this part, Matthew portrays, within the broader context of Israel's repudiation of Jesus (11:2—16:20), the escalation of the conflict between Jesus and the leaders to the point where it becomes irreconcilably hostile (12:14). And in the third part (16:21—28:20), as Matthew dwells on events associated especially with Jesus' stay in Jerusalem and with his suffering, death, and resurrection, he correspondingly treats of the last great confrontation Jesus has with the leaders in the temple (21:12—23:39) and of the resolution of Jesus' conflict with them (chaps. 26–28).

THE PRESENTATION OF THE
RELIGIOUS LEADERS

In the first part of his story (1:1—4:16), Matthew introduces the religious leaders to the reader. He does this in three segments, the first of which is found in chapter 2. Here Herod the Great figures prominently. When asked by the Magi where the King of the Jews has been born, Herod and all Jerusalem become frightened at hearing news of such a birth (2:1–3). Moreover, to discover the whereabouts of the Messiah-King, Herod assembles "all the chief priests and scribes of the people" and makes inquiry of them (2:4). In giving reply to Herod, they announce that the place of the Messiah's birth is Bethlehem, and to prove it they cite scripture (2:5–6).

Fleeting though this initial appearance of the religious leaders in Matthew's story is, two things stand out. For one thing, it is as allies of Herod that the leaders make their debut. Like Herod and as part of all Jerusalem, they react with fright and not joy to the news of the Messiah's birth. Also, in searching scripture, they do Herod's bidding. For another thing, the manner in which the leaders "read" scripture shows that although they are well-versed in it, the truth of it escapes them. Scripture tells them that the one born in Bethlehem is Israel's end-time King. The irony, however, is that when they later confront this King, they will charge him with making common cause with Satan (9:34; 12:24) and repudiate him as being a fraud, or false messiah (27:63).

It was just said that it is as allies of Herod that the religious leaders make their debut in Matthew's story. Throughout chapter 2, Herod proves himself to be incorrigibly "evil": he is "implacably opposed" to Jesus Messiah, and he not only takes Jesus to be a fraud (political throne pretender) but also plots to destroy him. As one who thus exemplifies evil, Herod presents himself in Matthew's story as the "precursor" of the religious leaders.

The selfsame character traits Herod exhibits in chapter 2, the leaders will exhibit later in the story. To enumerate the most obvious of these, Herod shows himself to be "spiritually blind" (2:3), "fearful" (2:3), "conspiratorial" (2:7), "guileful" and "mendacious" (2:8), "murderous" (2:13, 16), "wrathful" (2:16; cf. 21:15), and "apprehensive of the future" (2:16).[3]

The first major appearance of the religious leaders in Matthew's story occurs in conjunction with the ministry of John the Baptist (3:7–10). The importance of their appearance here has to do with the fact that John is the forerunner of Jesus. As such, the attitude that John assumes toward the leaders is predictive of the attitude that Jesus will assume toward them. Seeing the Pharisees and Sadducees coming out to him, John attacks them. He denounces them as a "brood of vipers," that is, as persons who are "evil" at the very center of their being (3:7; 12:34). He warns them not to suppose that appeal to Abraham as father can serve as a substitute for repentance or enable them to persevere in the approaching judgment (3:8–9). What they must do is reflect in their lives the fruit that only repentance can produce (3:10). That John's preaching elicits no such repentance in the religious leaders is something that they themselves will later acknowledge (21:25) and Jesus will confirm (21:32).

The final pericope in 1:1—4:16 that informs the reader of the religious leaders is the temptation (4:1–11). Still, owing to the fact that the temptation makes no reference to the leaders, it seems at first blush not to have anything to do with them. Only from a later vantage point in Matthew's story does it become clear that the temptation does in fact shape the reader's understanding of them.[4] In the case of John the Baptist, his encounter with the religious leaders anticipates Jesus' later encounters with them because John is the forerunner of Jesus. In the case of the temptation, Jesus' encounter with Satan likewise anticipates Jesus' later encounters with the leaders because Satan is the Evil One with whom they have affinity (12:34; 13:38–39). As the Tempter, the transcendent fountainhead of all evil (4:3; 6:13), Satan three times puts Jesus to the test (4:1–10). As those who are also evil (3:7), the religious leaders will similarly repeatedly put Jesus to the test.[5] In debate with Satan, Jesus has the last word, so that Satan leaves the scene (4:10–11). In debate with the leaders, Jesus will again have the last word, so that, reduced to silence, they, too, will leave the scene (22:46—23:1). If Jesus ultimately bests Satan in conflict, he will also ultimately best the leaders in conflict.

In the first part of Matthew's story, then, the reader becomes acquainted with the religious leaders. In their initial appearance (2:4–6), they are

---

3. For a similar view of the character traits of Herod, cf. Fiore, "Characterization in Matthew," 5.

4. Cf., e.g., 12:34; 13:38–39; 16:1–4; the body of the Chapter.

5. Cf. 16:1 and 4; 19:3; 22:18, 35.

depicted as standing in the service of Herod, who is their "precursor." In their first major appearance (3:7–10), John, the forerunner of Jesus, denounces them as "evil" and declares them to be ripe for end-time judgment. And in the temptation (4:1–11), the groundwork is laid for a later point in the story at which they will be seen to have affinity with Satan, the Tempter and fountainhead of all evil.

THE MOVEMENT TOWARD IRRECONCILABLE HOSTILITY

The second part of Matthew's story (4:17—16:20) falls into two sections. In the first section (4:17—11:1), Jesus discharges his ministry to Israel of teaching, preaching, and healing, thereby proffering it salvation (4:17). Because Jesus' proffering Israel salvation is the motif that dominates this section, the conflict between Jesus and the religious leaders that suddenly flares up (chap. 9) essentially serves the purpose of preparing the reader for the more intense conflict soon to follow, in the second section of part two. Still, to describe the conflict of 4:17—11:1 as "preparatory" is not to say that it is not grave. It involves, among other things, the same charge of blasphemy that becomes, at the trial of Jesus, the grounds on which Jesus is condemned to death (9:3; 26:65–66).

Prior to the actual outbreak of conflict between Jesus and the religious leaders in 4:17—11:1, Matthew leads the reader to anticipate such conflict. Almost from the outset, Jesus or Matthew as narrator utter statements envisaging the religious leaders which are negative in general or suggestive of conflict in particular. In the Sermon on the Mount, for example, Jesus predicts persecution for the disciples after the manner of the Old Testament prophets (5:10–12), disparages the righteousness of the scribes and Pharisees as falling short of what is necessary for gaining entrance into the Kingdom of Heaven (5:20), and castigates the "hypocrites" in the synagogues for performing their acts of piety not in worship of God but so as to win public acclaim for themselves (6:1–18). Following the sermon, Matthew bluntly tells the reader that, in contrast to Jesus, the scribes are "without authority" in their teaching (7:28–29). Later, implored by a centurion to heal his slave, Jesus asserts in view of the centurion's faith that whereas the "sons of the Kingdom" will be cast into the outer darkness, Gentiles will share in the bliss of the future Kingdom with Abraham, Isaac, and Jacob (8:10–12). And last, about to embark on a journey across the sea, Jesus turns away a scribe who would claim for himself the prerogative to become his disciple (8:18–20).[6]

With the onset of chapter 9, the anticipated conflict between Jesus and

6. For a detailed discussion of this disputed passage, cf. Kingsbury, "The 'Eager' Scribe and the 'Reluctant' Disciple."

the religious leaders finally materializes. But again, this conflict, fierce as it is, is still preliminary to the more intense conflict to come. Three things give clear indication of this.

The first is that this conflict does not become so virulent that it incites the religious leaders to mobilize themselves against Jesus. One looks in vain in chapter 9 for any narrative comment to the effect that the leaders go off and conspire how to destroy Jesus (cf. 12:14). In chapter 9, Jesus' conflict with the leaders is not yet to the death.

The second thing indicating that the conflict of chapter 9 is still preliminary is the fact that none of the issues that provoke the religious leaders (or, in one instance, the disciples of John) to attack Jesus—forgiving sins and then demonstrating by performing a miracle that God has given him such authority (9:1–8), having table fellowship with toll-collectors and sinners (9:11), temporarily releasing the disciples from the obligation to fast as dictated by prevailing piety (9:14), and exorcising a demon (9:32–34)— touches on Mosaic law as such. Now it is true, of course, that not every matter, to be "utterly serious" within the world of Matthew's story, must have to do with Mosaic law. After all, for forgiving sins and affirming that he is the Son of God, Jesus incurs the potentially capital charge of blasphemy (9:3; 26:63–66). But this notwithstanding, it is a mark of the enormous importance Matthew attaches to Mosaic law that he does not state that the religious leaders take counsel on how to do away with Jesus until the conflict between Jesus and them has shifted to focus on a precept of Mosaic law (12:2, 10, 14). Hence, the circumstance that the conflict of chapter 9 occurs both prior to, and apart from, controversy over Mosaic law also attests to the preliminary nature of this conflict.

The third thing indicating that the conflict of chapter 9 is preliminary in nature is that it is not so acutely confrontational as later conflict: Jesus is not himself directly challenged for something he himself does.[7] A glance at the pertinent pericopes illustrates this well. The scribes, watching Jesus forgive a paralytic his sins, declare only "within themselves" that Jesus is guilty of committing blasphemy (9:3–4). The Pharisees, in seeing Jesus sit at table with toll-collectors and sinners, take offense at his behavior but go to the disciples with their complaint (9:10–11). The disciples of John, siding on one occasion with the Pharisees, object to the fact that Jesus' disciples are not observing the custom of fasting but, though they do approach Jesus and put their question to him, it concerns not him but the disciples (9:14). And the Pharisees, after witnessing the exorcism of a demon by Jesus, cast

---

7. In Mark, by comparison, the conflict between Jesus and the religious leaders becomes acutely confrontational much more rapidly, as Dewey (*Markan Public Debate*, 116) shows in her study.

aspersions on his feat, but they do so either to themselves alone or merely in the hearing of the crowds (9:32–34).[8]

If the conflict between Jesus and the religious leaders in 4:17—11:1 is preliminary in nature and portends more intense conflict to come, this more intense conflict follows rather quickly. It erupts in 11:2—16:20, which is the latter half of the second part of the story. In this section, Matthew's purpose is no longer to tell of Jesus' ministry of teaching, preaching, and healing but of Israel's response to him, which is that of repudiation.[9] Because Jesus' conflict with the religious leaders becomes part and parcel of this leitmotif of repudiation, it rapidly escalates to the point where it becomes "mortal" and will henceforth remain this way. To call attention to this dramatic change in the tenor of the conflict in 11:2—16:20, the three features that are so conspicuously absent from chapter 9 now become exceedingly prominent: (a) Debate becomes increasingly confrontational, which is to say that for the first time Jesus is himself directly attacked for an act he himself is about to perform (12:9–13). (b) Debate centers on Mosaic law itself (12:1–8, 9–13). And (c) debate becomes so rancorous that it incites the religious leaders to conspire to take Jesus' life (12:14).

To trace this trend of events, Jesus, after giving answer to the Baptist's question from prison (11:2–6) and censuring the crowds for their un-willingness to repent (11:16–24), again enters into conflict with the re-ligious leaders (12:1–8, 9–14). Unlike earlier conflict, the Mosaic law itself, or, more particularly, violation of the command to rest on the sabbath, is the issue that sparks controversy. In the two debates of interest, there is progression as one moves from the first debate to the second in terms of how acutely confrontational each is. In the first debate, the Pharisees confront Jesus, but the charge they raise is against the disciples: in pluck-ing, or "reaping," grain to eat, the disciples have "worked," and this the Pharisees adjudge to be unlawful (12:1–2). In the second debate, the Phar-isees again confront Jesus, but this time, and indeed for the first time in Matthew's story, the accusation they make in the question they raise con-cerns an act Jesus himself intends to perform: if Jesus heals a man on the sabbath who is not in danger of dying, he will have broken the command of Moses that enjoins rest (12:10). In the case of both charges, Jesus rebuts the Pharisees by asserting that meeting human need in these instances is not only not unlawful but is necessitated by God's will that mercy be shown or

---

8. The verse 9:34 relates to 9:33 the same way as 12:24 relates to 12:23. In the case of 12:23–24, the words in 12:25a ("But [Jesus], knowing their thoughts, said . . .") indicate that it is solely "to themselves" or "within themselves" that the Pharisees say, "It is only by Beelzebul, the prince of demons, that this man casts out demons." If 12:25a reveals how 9:34 is to be understood in relation to 9:33, then in 9:34, too, the Pharisees speak the words "He casts out demons by the prince of demons" solely "to themselves."

9. Cf. 11:6, 16–24, 25; 13:57.

that good be done (12:3–8, 11–12). In immediate response to Jesus' pitting himself against the law of Moses as they interpret it, the Pharisees take leave of Jesus and consult together on how to destroy him (12:14). With this sudden shift in the action, Matthew's story has arrived at that juncture where the conflict between Jesus and the religious leaders has intensified to the point of becoming irreconcilably hostile. Then, too, the narrative comment to the effect that Jesus "withdraws" in the face of danger corroborates this (12:15).

Once the conflict between Jesus and the religious leaders turns irreconcilably hostile in Matthew's story, any hope for amelioration becomes otiose. Throughout the rest of this half of part two, Jesus and the religious leaders continue to clash in fierce debate. For example, the leaders accuse Jesus for a second time of acting on the authority of the prince of demons, and he assails them for being evil, like a "brood of vipers" (12:24–37). They demand of him a sign to prove that he acts on the authority of God and not of Satan,[10] and he again assails them, for being both evil and faithless to God (12:38–45). They attack his disciples for transgressing the tradition of the elders by eating with unwashed hands, and he attacks them for employing their tradition to subvert God's command that one should care for one's parents (15:1–11). And they once more insist, likewise for a second time, that he give them a sign, and he reiterates his charge that they are both evil and faithless to God (16:1–4). In other respects, until the time finally arrives for him to set out on his journey to Jerusalem (16:21), he also continues his custom of avoiding harm's way by prudently withdrawing to places where he is inaccessible to the leaders (14:13; 15:21; 16:4).

To recapitulate, the focus in the first of the two sections comprising the second part of Matthew's story (4:17—16:20) rests on Jesus' ministry to Israel of teaching, preaching, and healing (4:17—11:1). Toward the end of this section, conflict between Jesus and the religious leaders flares up (chap. 9). Still, this conflict is "preparatory" in nature in the sense that it readies the implied reader for the more intense conflict soon to follow. By the same token, the initial charge that some scribes make "within themselves" against Jesus, that he is guilty of blasphemy, is the selfsame charge that is later made against him at his trial (9:3). In the second section (11:2—16:20), the leitmotif of the story centers on Israel's repudiation of Jesus. Correlatively, Jesus' conflict with the religious leaders becomes an essential part of this motif, and this conflict differs from that of 4:17—11:1 in noticeable ways: debate is more keenly confrontational, for now Jesus is himself directly challenged for an act he himself is about to perform (12:9–13); debate involves Mosaic law itself (12:1–8, 9–13); and debate engenders

10. For a discussion of Gospel pericopes on the request for a sign, cf. Linton, "Sign from Heaven." 112–29.

such rancor in the religious leaders that they go off and take counsel how to destroy Jesus (12:14). Then, too, once the conflict between Jesus and the religious leaders attains this high level of intensity, there is no more opportunity in Matthew's story for it to abate.

CONFRONTATION IN THE TEMPLE AND DEATH AS THE RESOLUTION OF THE CONFLICT

The leitmotif that governs the third part of Matthew's story (16:21—28:20) is Jesus' journey to Jerusalem and his suffering, death, and resurrection.[11] As is apparent, integral to this leitmotif is Jesus' recurrent conflict with the religious leaders. This conflict is to the death. The question is how Matthew sustains the high level of the intensity of this conflict.

As Jesus makes his way to Jerusalem, he teaches the disciples and heals the sick (16:21—21:11). Only once does he clash with the religious leaders (19:3-9), over the question of divorce (19:3-9). He denies that God had ever intended divorce,[12] and he uses this controversy as a vehicle for instructing the disciples (19:10-12). Still, the ill will that pervades this controversy is palpable (cf. 19:4, 8).

Prior to the passion itself, the temple in Jerusalem becomes the site for the last great confrontation between Jesus and the religious leaders (21:12—22:46). This is significant, because the temple is both the place of God's presence and the seat of the religious leaders' authority. Extreme tension suffuses the several controversies that take place here, and to heighten the reader's awareness of this, Matthew makes effective use of at least four literary devices.

For example, the tone of all these controversies is acutely confrontational, so that it is consistently Jesus who is himself directly challenged over issues that pertain to what he himself teaches or does.[13] Again, these controversies occur unremittingly over a period of two days (21:17), as one after another the various groups that comprise the united front of religious leaders face Jesus so as to call him to account, or to best him in argument, or, at the last, even to be challenged by him: the chief priests and the scribes (21:15), the chief priests and the elders of the people (21:23; cf. 21:45), the disciples of the Pharisees with the Herodians (22:16), the Sadducees (22:23), a lawyer of the Pharisees (22:35), and the Pharisees (22:41). Third, the several questions that spark debate are all of critical importance within the world of Matthew's story: they concern such matters as Jesus' right to be acclaimed as the messianic Son of David (21:15-16), the "authority" on

11. Cf. 16:21; 17:22–23; 20:18–19; 26:2.
12. On the meaning of the so-called "exceptive clause" (19:9) in this much-discussed passage on divorce, cf. above, p. 66 n. 12.
13. Cf. 21:16, 23; 22:15–17, 23, 34–36.

which he acts (21:23), and the correct way to read and interpret the law[14] or scripture (22:42–45). And last, the atmosphere in which all these controversies take place is one of deep-seated animosity. To emphasize this, Matthew sprinkles narrative comments throughout 21:12—22:46 so as to inform the reader of the religious leaders' psychological point of view as they clash with Jesus in the temple. In these comments, Matthew observes, variously, that the chief priests and scribes address Jesus "in anger" (21:15–16); or that the reaction of the chief priests and the Pharisees to his parables is to want to "seize" him on the spot (21:45–46); or that the secret intent of the disciples of the Pharisees and the Herodians is to "ensnare" Jesus in his speech (22:15–17); or that the reason the lawyer of the Pharisees puts his question to Jesus is to "tempt" him (22:35).

How does this whole series of controversies in the temple end? As Matthew remarks, Jesus reduces all the religious leaders to silence, and they, in turn, lose all heart for further debate (22:46). In consequence, the leaders resort to the one option they believe is still open to them as a means by which they can resolve their conflict with Jesus: they take leave of him in the temple (cf. 4:11) and gather to consult on how to bring about his arrest and death (22:46; 26:3–5).

With this latter act, the events of the passion account itself have already begun (chaps. 26–28). As far as the religious leaders themselves are concerned, Matthew captures the tenor of the passion with yet another narrative comment of psychological import: ". . . and they took counsel together in order to arrest Jesus 'by deceit' and kill him" (26:4). In portraying the leaders throughout the passion, Matthew orchestrates numerous variations both on this theme of "deception" and on the related theme of "self-deception."

To illustrate, the first move the religious leaders make against Jesus is to obtain custody of him, and they accomplish this only through deceit: they enlist Judas, one of the Twelve, to betray him (26:14–16, 48–50a–c); and they send the crowds, whom Jesus had daily taught in the temple, to arrest him and hand him over (26:47, 50d, 55, 57). Next, as Jesus stands trial before them, the strategy the leaders at first employ to secure a sentence of death against him is, similarly, one of deceit: false witnesses step forward to bear false testimony, but nothing comes of this and Jesus acquits their fraudulent proceedings with silence (26:59–62a). Moments later, when Jesus does at last break his silence and affirm under oath that he is the Messiah Son of God, the reaction of the leaders constitutes, ironically, a massive act of self-deception: in condemning Jesus to death for having blasphemed God, they delude themselves into thinking that they know the mind of God

14. Cf. 22:17, 24, 36.

(26:63b–68; 3:17). At Jesus' hearing before Pilate the following morning, the leaders once again resort to deceit, this time to win Pilate to their side: they accuse Jesus of "many things," but because their accusations are false, Jesus does not so much as reply (27:1–2, 12–14). Meanwhile, the leaders have also involved themselves, unwittingly, in yet a second act of self-deception: in being concerned to be "lawful" in the way they dispose of the money Judas has returned to them, they belie the fact that what they are dealing with is "blood money" (27:3–10). Again, the leaders furthermore practice deceit in the scene in which Pilate grants Barabbas release but delivers Jesus to the Roman soldiers to be crucified: although Barabbas is known to be a "notorious prisoner" and their motive for acting against Jesus is envy, or "malice," they persuade the crowds, who in turn prevail upon Pilate, to choose freedom for Barabbas but crucifixion for Jesus (27:15–26). And finally, in their ostensible moment of triumph as Jesus hangs upon the cross, the leaders ensnare themselves in yet another act of self-deception: in mocking Jesus as "the King of Israel" and the "Son of God," they unwittingly attest to the very truths they earlier repudiated as Jesus stood trial before them ("Son of God"; 26:63–66) and was interrogated by Pilate ("King of the Jews"; 27:11).

What, at last, is the resolution of the conflict between Jesus and the religious leaders? In seeing to it that Jesus is brought to the cross, the leaders are firmly convinced that they are doing the will of God (26:65–66) and purging Israel of the fraud he has perpetrated (27:63–64). The irony, however, is that God shows, by raising Jesus from the dead and exalting him to universal rule (28:6, 18), that Jesus is in reality to be adjudged as having been in the right in his conflict with them. Not only that, but God also establishes Jesus' death as the means whereby Jesus atones for the sins of all people (1:21; 26:28). As Matthew's story draws to a close, therefore, Jesus' cross becomes the symbol, not of his destruction at the hands of his enemies, but of the salvation God accomplishes in him on behalf of all humankind, whether Jew or Gentile (1:21; 20:28; 26:28).

What is to be said at the end of the story regarding the religious leaders? Two things, the first of which is tragically ironic. Owing to the leaders' abject repudiation of Jesus, they unwittingly effect, not the salvation of Israel as they had anticipated, but just the opposite, Israel's demise as God's special people: they bring a curse upon themselves and the people (27:25); they provoke the destruction of Jerusalem (22:7); and they unknowingly make themselves responsible for the transfer of God's Rule to another nation, the church, which becomes God's end-time people (21:43; 16:18; 13:38).

The second thing to be said regarding the religious leaders is that not even does Jesus' death and burial put an end to the opposition they mount against him. At the height of his ministry, Jesus gave the leaders the "sign of Jonah," which was a prediction of his death and resurrection (12:39–40). Recalling this sign after Jesus had died and been buried, the leaders gather before Pilate and request that Jesus' tomb be made secure by guard (27:62–64). When Pilate refuses to act himself but leaves the matter to them, they themselves place a guard (26:65–66). Their aim is to prevent the disciples from stealing the body of Jesus and proclaiming a resurrection (27:64). Despite the guard, Jesus of course does rise from the dead (28:6). When certain of the soldiers bring the leaders this news, they not only do not change their minds about Jesus (cf. 21:32) but they bribe the soldiers to spread the lie that the disciples did indeed come and, finding the guard asleep, make off with Jesus' body (28:11–15). Accordingly, not content to bring Jesus to the cross, the religious leaders continue their active opposition against him even in the aftermath of the cross and Easter.

THE QUESTION OF AUTHORITY

The religious leaders are the antagonists of Jesus in Matthew, and their story is one of conflict. Thus far, the concern has been to trace their story: after being introduced to the reader in the first part of Matthew, they become embroiled with Jesus in ever more intense conflict in the second part, and, in the third part, they clash one last time with him in the temple and then resolve their conflict with him by bringing about his death. The one thing yet to be discussed is the issue that lies at the heart of their conflict with Jesus.

The issue is the "authority" of Jesus.[15] Matthew first raises this issue in the narrative comment he makes following the Sermon on the Mount in which he remarks that Jesus, unlike the scribes, teaches with authority (7:29).[16] Shortly thereafter, Matthew again refers to this issue, though indirectly, when he depicts Jesus as turning away a scribe from following him who would claim for himself the authority to become his disciple (8:19–20). Throughout the rest of his story, Matthew makes it exceedingly plain that, whether directly or indirectly, the issue of authority underlies all the controversies Jesus has with the religious leaders and that it is therefore pivotal to his entire conflict with them.

Essentially, the religious leaders attempt to impugn the authority of Jesus in two ways. On the one hand, they dispute his right to act as he does: to forgive sins (9:2–8); to have table fellowship with toll-collectors and sinners (9:10–13); to release his disciples temporarily from the obligation to fast (9:14–17); to set aside, radicalize, or otherwise interpret the law or scripture according to his knowledge of the will of God;[17] to overrule the tradition of

---

15. This point is properly stressed by Powell ("Religious Leaders," 202–10).
16. On the significance of the passage 7:28–29 within Matthew's story, cf. ibid., 55–58.
17. Cf. 12:1–8, 9–13; 19:3–9; 22:15–22, 23–33, 34–40, 41–46.

the elders (15:1–20); or to "cleanse" the temple or to heal there or indeed to receive there the messianic acclamation of the children (21:12–16, 23–27).

On the other hand, the religious leaders also attack Jesus personally: they charge him with having allied himself with the prince of demons (9:32–34; 12:24); they cast aspersions on his integrity by demanding that he prove by means of a "sign" that he acts on the authority of God and not of Satan;[18] they treat as a lie the claims he makes about himself, say, in his parables (21:33–46); or, following his death, they brand him as a "deceiver," or false messiah (27:63).

The point in Matthew's story where the religious leaders' assault on Jesus' authority reaches its climax is at his trial before the Sanhedrin. Here the high priest adjures Jesus to say whether he is the Messiah, the Son of God (26:63). By breaking his silence and responding to the high priest in the affirmative, Jesus openly claims in effect that he enjoys a unique filial relationship to God and that he is God's supreme agent in the history of salvation (1:18–25; 3:17; 21:33–44). Still, in thus claiming for himself the identity of Messiah Son of God, Jesus is at the same time claiming for himself divine authority (3:16–17; 11:27). Correspondingly, the high priest, by declaring Jesus' claim to be blasphemous (i.e., an infringement upon the majesty of God), is refusing Jesus this particular identity and the divine authority it entails (26:65–66). Then, too, as the religious leaders later mock Jesus at the foot of the cross as the "King of Israel" (= Messiah) and the "Son of God," they are merely reiterating their earlier denial of his claim to divine sonship and divine authority (27:41–43).

The resolution of the religious leaders' conflict with Jesus over the issue of his authority occurs in the resurrection. In the resurrection, God vindicates Jesus' claim to divine authority and indeed exalts him to universal rule. Vindicated and exalted, the risen Jesus declares triumphantly at the close of Matthew's story: "All authority in heaven and on earth has been given to me . . ." (28:18). Although the religious leaders are not privy to this declaration, the reader knows that they will have no alternative but to acknowledge the truth of it when Jesus returns in splendor as Judge at the consummation of the age (26:64).

SUMMARY

Next to Jesus, the protagonist, the character-group influencing most the plot of Matthew's story is the religious leaders. In the latter half of the second part of the story (11:2—16:20), the conflict Jesus has with them becomes central to the flow of events, and this is also the case in the third part of the story (16:21—28:20). This explains why the story of the religious leaders is closely correlated with the story of Jesus.

18. Cf. 12:38–45; 16:1–4.

In the first part of Matthew (1:1—4:16), the reader is introduced to the religious leaders. Herod the Great shows himself to be their "precursor" in the story (chap. 2), John the Baptist identifies "evilness" as the "root trait" characterizing them (3:7–10), and Satan, the Tempter and the Evil One, proves, later, to be the one with whom they have affinity (4:3; 13:38–39).

In the second part of Matthew (4:17—16:20), two phases distinguish the conflict Jesus has with the religious leaders. In the one phase (4:17—11:1), the anticipation of conflict finally gives way to the occurrence of conflict (chap. 9). Although the first charge leveled against Jesus, that of blasphemy made by some scribes "within themselves," is also the charge for which Jesus is at the last condemned to death (9:3; 26:65–66), this initial conflict essentially serves the purpose of preparing the reader for the more intense conflict soon to follow. In the second phase (11:2—16:20), this more intense conflict takes place. Three marks characterize it: debate is acutely confrontational, for Jesus is now himself directly attacked for an act he himself intends to perform (12:9–13); debate involves the Mosaic law (12:1–8, 9–13); and debate gives rise to such ill will that the leaders conspire to kill Jesus (12:14). Once the conflict Jesus has with the religious leaders takes this turn toward irreconcilable hostility, it never again ameliorates.

In the third part of Matthew (16:21—28:20), the conflict between Jesus and the religious leaders retains the three marks, or variations thereof, just cited. Beyond this, to sustain or even to heighten the intensity of the conflict, Matthew situates Jesus in the temple of Jerusalem and describes the several groups that together comprise the whole gamut of Jewish officialdom as approaching Jesus, one after the other, to engage him in controversy (21:12—22:46). Prior to the passion, these continual clashes with the religious leaders constitute Jesus' last great confrontation with them. Because at the end Jesus reduces all of the leaders to silence (22:46), the one thing still open to them is to resolve their conflict with him by putting him to death (26:3–5). In bringing Jesus to the cross, the leaders are convinced that they are purging Israel of a false messiah and the fraud he has perpetrated (27:63–64). The resurrection, however, reveals this outlook to be itself fraudulent, for through it God vindicates Jesus in his conflict with them (28:6, 18–20). The result is that the death of Jesus, which the religious leaders had envisaged would be the sign of Jesus' destruction, becomes instead the means whereby God achieves salvation for the world, Jew and Gentile alike (1:21; 20:28; 26:28).

8
The Disciples of Jesus

Because Jesus is the protagonist in Matthew's Gospel, the main story-line concerns him. Opposite Jesus stand his antagonists, the religious leaders, who also have a story-line. As those whom Jesus calls to be with him, the disciples, too, have a story-line.

Since Matthew begins his story by presenting Jesus to the reader, the disciples make no appearance in the first part (1:1—4:16). By contrast, in the second and third parts of the story they have a prominent role to play.[1] Still, only marginally does their role determine the plot of Matthew's story.

Matthew's story of the disciples, like that of the religious leaders, follows the contours of his story of Jesus. In the second part (4:17—16:20), Matthew tells of the ministry of Jesus to Israel (4:17—11:1). Parallel to this, he tells of the call of the disciples and of their mission to Israel (4:17—11:1). Also in the second part, Matthew tells of Israel's response to Jesus, which is one of repudiation (11:2—16:20). Parallel but contrasting to this, he tells of the disciples as being the recipients of divine revelation (11:2—16:20). In the third part (16:21—28:20), Matthew tells of Jesus' journey to Jerusalem and of his suffering, death, and resurrection. Parallel to this, he shows how the disciples are led to appropriate Jesus' evaluative point of view according to which suffering sonship is a summons to suffering discipleship, or to servanthood.

Jesus has conflict not only with Israel but also with the disciples. The two conflicts, however, are fundamentally different in nature. Jesus has conflict with Israel because it repudiates the evaluative point of view he espouses and judges that because of this point of view, he must be put to death. Jesus has conflict with the disciples because although they aspire to appropriate his evaluative point of view, they falter at times or fail badly. Through his

1. For two other studies of the disciples in Matthew, the first redaction-critical and the second literary-critical, cf. Luz, "Disciples in the Gospel," 98–128; Edwards, "Uncertain Faith," 47–61.

conflict with the disciples, Jesus aims to instruct them or to mediate to them new insight or perception.

The level of conflict between Jesus and the disciples varies in Matthew's story. In the second part (4:17—16:20), for example, one hears relatively little of conflict. Nevertheless, it does occur, as when the disciples prove themselves to be persons of little faith, or do not understand at once what Jesus endeavors to teach them, or leave untapped the authority Jesus would make available to them because they forget that it is at their disposal. In the third part (16:21—28:20), however, the conflict Jesus has with the disciples becomes intense. It has to do with the disciples' imperceptiveness, and at times resistance, to the notion that servanthood is the essence of discipleship. Not until the end of Matthew's story is this conflict resolved. When Jesus appears to the disciples atop the mountain in Galilee, he finally leads them to adopt his evaluative point of view on discipleship.

THE CALL OF THE DISCIPLES AND
THEIR MISSION TO ISRAEL

As Jesus begins his public activity in Israel (4:17), he stands before the reader as the Son of God whom God has chosen and empowered for messianic ministry (3:16–17). Almost immediately Jesus calls his first disciples, two pairs of brothers (Peter and Andrew; James and John), thus taking to himself eye- and ear-witnesses (4:18–22). The pattern that governs the calling of each pair of brothers is the same: Jesus sees, Jesus summons, and at once those summoned leave behind everything—nets, boat, and father—in order to follow him (4:18–20, 21–22). The force of this pattern is clear: Jesus authoritatively calls those whom he himself chooses to be his disciples, and those who obey his call abandon their former way of life (with all its commitments of family, goods, and occupation) and join themselves to him by giving him their total allegiance.

In calling disciples, Jesus thus forms a new community, which he elsewhere designates as "my church" (16:18; 18:17) or alludes to as a "(new) nation" (21:43). What are the nature and purpose of this new community? Its purpose is plainly stated by Jesus: to be "fishers of men," that is, to engage in mission in line with the broad schema of first Israel (10:5b–6) and then the nations (28:19). The nature of this new community derives from the call Jesus extends: through Jesus, who is the unique Son of God in whom God's Kingdom is a present reality, those who make up this community enter, and live in, the sphere of God's end-time Rule. In this sphere, God is their Father (6:9), and they, in turn, are sons of God,[2] disciples of Jesus,[3] and brothers both of Jesus (28:10) and of one another (23:8). In a

2. Cf. 5:9, 45; 13:38.
3. Cf. 10:1; 26:17.

word, the new community Jesus forms is a brotherhood of the sons of God and of his disciples.

Intrinsic to this description of Jesus and his new community are two features Matthew is at pains to emphasize throughout his story: on the one hand, the uniqueness of Jesus as the Son of God; and on the other hand, his close association with the disciples as sons of God and brothers. Thus, Jesus stands out from the disciples as the obvious figure of authority. The relationship he has with them is characterized as that of "teacher and learner," of "master and slave" (10:24–25). Consistently, they address him as "Lord" and acknowledge thereby his exalted station and divine authority.[4] Moreover, it is he who summons, dispatches, commands, and teaches, and it is they who follow, go, obey, and heed.

By the same token, Matthew also highlights the close association the disciples have with Jesus. This comes to clear expression in the concept of "being with Jesus."[5] The Greek preposition translated as "with" (*meta* + genitive case) is frequently employed to denote accompaniment (cf., e.g., 12:3: "David . . . and those who were 'with him' "). Noteworthy is the way Matthew carefully restricts the circle of those who share in the presence, or the company, of Jesus. Except for Mary his mother (2:11) and toll-collectors and sinners (9:11), the list of those who are "with Jesus" or of whom it is said that Jesus is "with them" includes only Peter (26:69, 71), one of Jesus' followers (26:51), Peter and the two sons of Zebedee,[6] and the twelve or eleven disciples.[7] Noticeably absent from this list are such as the Jewish crowds or their leaders. Indeed, the fact that Judas eats with Jesus is played down in favor of merely mentioning that he dips his hand with Jesus in the dish, in this manner marking himself as the one who will betray Jesus (26:23; cf. Mark 14:18). In point of fact, Jesus is only "with Israel" as with a "faithless and perverse generation" from whom he will withdraw his presence (17:17), and the critical principle obtains: "He who is not *with me* is against me, and he who does not gather *with me* scatters" (12:30).

In Matthew's story, then, Jesus grants the privilege of his company almost without exception only to his own. Before the resurrection, these are his disciples. After the resurrection, they are his church (16:18). The disciples before the resurrection follow along "with Jesus" as he leads them to the cross (16:21; 20:17–19). The church after the resurrection makes its way toward the consummation of the age and the Parousia on the promise of the exalted Jesus that he will surely be "with them [you]" (28:20).

What such close association with Jesus means is explained by Matthew in the key passages 1:23 ("Emmanuel . . . God [is] *with us*"), 18:20 ("there am I

4. Cf. 8:21, 25; 14:28, 30; 16:22; 17:4; 18:21; 26:22.
5. Cf. Frankemölle, *Jahwebund und Kirche Christi*, chap. 1.
6. Cf. 26:37–38, 40.
7. Cf. 26:18, 20, 36; 28:20.

in the midst of them"), and 28:20 ("I am *with you* always"). It means that through his presence Jesus Messiah, the earthly and exalted Son of God, mediates to his disciples or church the gracious, saving presence of God and his Rule.

The final feature in 4:18–22 that begs to be considered is the order in which the disciples are called: Peter is cited as being first (4:18). Later, at 10:2, Matthew makes specific mention of this: "The names of the twelve apostles are these: first Simon, who is called Peter . . ." By depicting Peter as the first of the disciples to be called and by making reference to this in listing the names of the Twelve, Matthew informs the reader of the manner in which he conceives of Peter's "primacy": it is temporal, or better, "salvation-historical," in nature.

What impact does Peter's "salvation-historical primacy" have on his relationship to the other disciples throughout Matthew's story? Ruled out is the notion that it elevates Peter to a position of authority over the other disciples, for at 23:8 Jesus himself says to the disciples: "But you are not to be called rabbi, for one is your teacher [the Messiah], and all you are brothers." Peter's primacy is consequently that of being "first among equals." This explains why he functions as the "spokesman" of the disciples and is also, in his behavior, "typical" of them, both positively and negatively. It is in line with Peter's salvation-historical primacy that he makes confession of Jesus near Caesarea Philippi (16:16). It is also in line with this primacy that he is promised in return that he will be the rock on which the church will be built and that he will be given the keys of the Kingdom, which are the authority to bind and to loose (to decide matters of church doctrine and of church discipline) (16:17–19). This authority, incidentally, is one that Peter likewise shares with the other disciples (16:17–19; 18:18). So again, Matthew in his story pointedly ascribes primacy to Peter, but this primacy is one of being first among equals (4:18; 10:2; 23:8–12).[8]

Accordingly, the disciples, through the call of Jesus, enter into the sphere of God's end-time Rule. In the Sermon on the Mount, Jesus describes both the kinds of persons his disciples are and the quality of life they lead in the sphere of God's Rule. The kinds of persons Jesus' disciples are comes to light in the beatitudes he pronounces (5:3–10). For example, "the poor in spirit" are those who may or may not be economically deprived but who in any case stand before God with no illusions of self-righteousness or self-sufficiency. "Those who mourn" are those who grieve over sin and evil in the world. "The meek" are those who are lowly and powerless, whose only hope is God. "Those who hunger and thirst for righteousness" are those who yearn for the final salvation that only God can effect. "The merciful" are those who eschew judgment and forgive. "The pure in heart"

8. Cf. Kingsbury, "Peter in Matthew's Gospel," 67–83.

are those who are undivided in their allegiance to God. "The peacemakers" are those who work for the wholeness and well-being that God wills for a broken world. And "those who are persecuted for righteousness' sake" are those who incur tribulation because, as disciples of Jesus, they serve God.

The quality of life that is indicative of disciples who live in the sphere of God's end-time Rule is designated by Jesus as the "greater righteousness" (5:20). "Righteousness" (*dikaiosynē*) is a term that Jesus predicates to both God and humans. The righteousness of God is his justice, which will issue at the consummation of the age in salvation or condemnation for humans (5:6). The "greater righteousness" to which Jesus refers envisages to be sure human conduct ("your righteousness"; 6:1), but a human conduct that contrasts sharply with that of the scribes and Pharisees (5:20). The conduct Jesus imputes to the scribes and Pharisees is "hypocrisy," which he further defines as "lawlessness" (23:28). As the antithesis of lawlessness, the greater righteousness is doing the will of God, including the law (5:17), as Jesus teaches this.[9] One does God's will when one is perfect, or whole-hearted, in one's devotion to God (5:48), and one is such when one loves God with heart, soul, and mind and the neighbor as self (22:37–40). At the center of the greater righteousness, then, is undivided fealty toward God and selfless love of the neighbor (5:21—6:18).

The community Jesus forms in calling disciples to follow him and to reflect in their lives the ethic of the greater righteousness has an ethos all its own. Matthew 8:18–22 captures well some of the flavor of this ethos.[10] This passage comprises an introduction (8:18) and two contrasting scenes. In the first scene (8:19–20), a scribe approaches Jesus and offers to become his disciple: "Teacher," he says, "I will follow you wherever you go." Jesus, however, turns the scribe away with the remark, "Foxes have holes, and birds of the air have nests; but the Son of man has nowhere to lay his head."

Is there proof to substantiate the contention that Jesus turns the scribe away? The proof lies in the fact that the words of the scribe fracture the pattern one finds in pericopes that portray the call of true disciples. In these pericopes, the pattern is such as to place the initiative squarely with Jesus: Jesus sees, Jesus summons, and those who are summoned follow him (4:18–20, 21–22; 9:9). In the scene of 8:19–20, however, the scribe arrogates to himself the authority to make of himself a disciple of Jesus. He believes that he has within him the capacity to embark upon, and to sustain, the life of discipleship. In his reply to the scribe, Jesus asserts in effect that so rigorous is the life of discipleship that no one, apart from his enabling call, is capable of embarking upon this life and sustaining it.

9. Cf. 6:10; 7:21; 12:50; 18:14.
10. On the interpretation of 8:18–22, cf. Kingsbury, "The 'Eager' Scribe and the 'Reluctant' Disciple."

Is there further evidence to support the contention that Jesus turns the scribe away? It is noteworthy that the scribe addresses Jesus as "teacher" and that Jesus refers to himself in his reply as "the Son of man." "Teacher" is not the term of address employed by those in Matthew's story who approach Jesus in "faith." These persons call on Jesus as "Lord." "Teacher" is the term of human respect that is used, for example, by the opponents of Jesus. Similarly, "the Son of man" is the term by which Jesus refers to himself in public or with a view to the public, especially his opponents. In sum, the use of the two terms "teacher" and "the Son of man" in the scene of 8:19–20 has the effect of highlighting the distance that exists between Jesus and the scribe: they are not of one mind and one will. Jesus turns the scribe away.

The second scene (8:21–22) concerns a man described as already being a disciple of Jesus. The man's use of the term "Lord" and not "teacher" and Jesus' use of the pronoun "me" and not "the Son of man" are also proof of this. Earlier, Jesus had ordered the disciples to board a boat and set sail for the other side of the sea (8:18). With a view to Jesus' command, this unnamed disciple comes to him with a request: "Lord," he asks, "let me first go and bury my father." Jesus' answer to the disciple is: "Follow me, and leave the dead to bury their own dead."

The problem inherent in the request of the unnamed disciple is that he desires to suspend for a time his commitment to follow Jesus. Moreover, his request is exceedingly well-founded: he has a prior obligation to which he must attend, namely, the sacred trust to go and look after the burial of his father (cf. Gen. 50:5–6). Jesus' response to the disciple's request is swift and sharp. The commitment of discipleship, he declares in essence, brooks no suspension. No obligation exists that can be permitted to take precedence over it. The resolution of this conflict is clear: the unnamed disciple boards the boat.

If the life of discipleship cannot be undertaken apart from the enabling call of Jesus but, once entered upon, brooks no suspension, it is also a life always open to attacks of "little faith." The latter is the truth illustrated by the pericope on the stilling of the storm (8:23–27). Having ordered the disciples to the other side of the sea (8:18), Jesus now boards the boat and the disciples follow him in (8:23). Out on the sea, Jesus sleeps, while the disciples encounter a fierce storm (cf. 24:7–8). Fearing for their lives, the disciples awaken him and plead in prayerlike petition that he save them. Jesus grants their plea, calming winds and sea, but not before he has chided them for being cowardly and hence exhibiting little, or weak, faith. They have, in fact, allowed cowardice to frustrate his command to sail across the sea.

Two contrasting themes dominate this episode. The first theme has to do with the phenomenon of "little faith," which provokes conflict between

Jesus and the disciples. Here as elsewhere in Matthew's story, little faith manifests itself as a "crisis of trust." In this instance, it thwarts the disciples' ability to carry out the task, or mission, Jesus has given them. Jesus fully expects that the disciples should obey his command and sail across the sea. They succumb, however, to the malady of little faith, which assumes the guise of cowardice, and do not complete their task. Far from showing the disciples sympathy, Jesus expresses surprise that they should have been so beset by weakness (8:26). And the second, contrasting theme is that, despite the fact that the disciples have fallen victim to a crisis of trust, Jesus does not leave them to their own devices but hears their plea and assists them in their plight. The life of discipleship is susceptible to bouts of little faith. Such little faith is not to be condoned. Nevertheless, Jesus does not abandon his disciples at such times but stands ever ready with his saving power to sustain them so that they can in fact discharge the mission he has entrusted to them.

The pericope on the call of Matthew (9:9) illustrates yet another aspect of discipleship, to wit: the broad spectrum of those whom Jesus summons to follow him. The pattern governing the narration of the pericope reveals that the call of Matthew is the call of a true disciple: Jesus sees, Jesus summons, and the one summoned follows after Jesus (9:9; 10:3). In the case of the calling of Peter and Andrew and of James and John, Jesus summoned fishermen to become his disciples, persons who were accounted as being upright citizens. Matthew, however, is a toll-collector.[11] As such, he is looked upon by the Jewish society of Matthew's story as no better than a robber and one whose testimony would not be honored in a Jewish court of law. Nevertheless, Jesus makes him one of the Twelve (10:3). Not only the upright are called by Jesus, but also the despised.

Thus far, the focus has been on Jesus' calling of disciples. But this changes in 9:35—10:42, and the disciples' mission to Israel becomes the topic.[12] To indicate that the circle of the twelve disciples is now complete and that the disciples are to be "fishers of men" in Israel, Matthew recites the names of the Twelve and terms them "apostles" ("ones who are sent"; 10:2–4). The mission Jesus gives them is plainly an extension of his own: he endows them with the authority on which they are to act (10:1); they are to go only to the lost sheep of the house of Israel (10:6; 15:24); the message they are to proclaim is the nearness of the Kingdom (10:7; 4:17); and they are to heal every disease and every infirmity (10:1; 9:35).

Despite the command that the disciples go only to Israel, the instructions Jesus gives them are such that their mission to Israel becomes emblematic

11. Cf. Donahue, "Tax Collectors and Sinners," 39–61.
12. For a detailed treatment of the section 9:35–10:42, cf. Weaver, "Missionary Discourse in Matthew."

of their later, universal mission to the nations. The place in time of Matthew, the implied author, and of the implied reader lies between the resurrection and the Parousia.[13] When Jesus' discourse is "heard" also from this vantage point, it depicts realities that smack of the familiar. To illustrate, consider the following, selected references: the disciples will be like sheep in the midst of wolves (10:16); they will be persecuted by both Jews and Gentiles and be hated by all (10:17–23); they will be subject to the same harsh treatment Jesus had to endure (10:24–31); they are to give fearless confession of Jesus (10:32–33); they are to place allegiance to Jesus and the life of servanthood above any other good (10:34–39); and they are to discharge the mission entrusted to them in anticipation of the "reward" they will receive at the latter day (10:40–42). In these missionary instructions of Jesus to the Twelve, "the particular" is not without the quality of "the typical."

To conclude, in the first half of the second part of his story (4:17—11:1) Matthew tells of the ministry of Jesus to Israel and, in conjunction with this, of the call of the disciples and of their mission to Israel. In calling disciples, Jesus creates a new community described as a brotherhood of the sons of God and of the disciples of Jesus. The purpose of this new community is to engage in missionary activity (4:18–22). The ethic that distinguishes Jesus' disciples is that of the "greater righteousness" (5:20). Not only to begin but also to sustain the life of discipleship, the enabling power of Jesus is indispensable (8:19–20). Moreover, the commitment to which Jesus summons his disciples is enduring and takes precedence over all competing obligations (8:21–22). Called to mission as the disciples are, they are always susceptible to bouts of little faith. At the same time, they can always rest assured that Jesus stands ever ready to sustain them in their needs (8:23–27). As a group, the disciples form no exclusive community of the holy. Just the opposite, Jesus invites into their circle not only the upright but also the despised and the outcast (9:9). And commissioned to preach and to heal in Israel, the disciples receive instructions that portend intense conflict for them and that present this first mission as foreshadowing in numerous particulars the later mission they will undertake to the Gentiles (9:35—10:42).

THE DISCIPLES AS THE RECIPIENTS
OF DIVINE REVELATION

In the latter half of the second part of his story (11:2—16:20), Matthew tells of Israel's repudiation of Jesus. In contrast to Israel, the disciples stand out as the recipients of divine revelation. The incidence of conflict between

13. Cf. 24:15; 27:8; 28:15.

Jesus and the disciples, which was low in 4:17—11:1, is only marginally more frequent in this section and by no means high.

Although the fame of Jesus has spread and the crowds throng to him, this does not mean that Israel has accepted him. On the contrary, it repudiates him. In private prayer, Jesus attributes his repudiation to the will of God himself: it has pleased God to hide his revelation from Israel (11:25–26). But though God has hidden his revelation from Israel, he has nonetheless also made it known, to "infants," that is to say, to Jesus' disciples (11:25). Within the surrounding context of chapters 11–12, this hiding of divine revelation and making it known corresponds to the fact that whereas all Israel turns away from Jesus (11:16–19; 12:14, 24), the disciples continue to adhere to him (12:49–50).

God, then, while hiding his divine revelation from Israel, imparts it to the disciples. But what is the nature and substance of this revelation? As elaborated in the context, it concerns in greatest measure two matters. The one matter is the mysteries of the Kingdom of Heaven (13:11). And the other is insight into Jesus' identity as the Son of God (14:33; 16:16).

The mysteries of the Kingdom of Heaven made known to the disciples but hidden from Israel are contained in Jesus' discourse in parables (chap. 13).[14] These mysteries may perhaps be listed as follows. First, the Kingdom of Heaven, or the end-time Rule of God, confronts people in the person of Jesus as a present, though hidden, reality tending toward its consummation in the final judgment Jesus will conduct at the end of the age (13:31–32, 33). Second, through hearing the proclamation of the gospel of the Kingdom, people are called to decision: On the one hand, those ultimately decide against this proclamation who cannot be moved by it to give God their wholehearted allegiance; or who are not prepared to endure the persecution that acceptance of it entails; or who value the pursuit of wealth more than the good news the proclamation announces (13:3b–7, 19–22). On the other hand, those (like the disciples) decide for this proclamation who receive it with understanding and are led by it to love God with heart, soul, and mind and the neighbor as themselves (13:8, 23). Third, until the consummation of the age, the entire world is the site where people live under the influence of one of two opposing spheres of power: either people live in the sphere of God's end-time Rule under the aegis of the earthly and exalted Jesus, or they live in the sphere of the kingdom of evil under the aegis of Satan (13:24–30, 36–43). Fourth, disciples of Jesus living in the sphere of God's end-time Rule are summoned to be single-mindedly dedicated to the doing of God's will as taught by Jesus (13:44–46). And last, as

14. On the interpretation of Jesus' parable discourse, cf., e.g., Kingsbury (Parables of Jesus) and Gerhardsson ("Parable of the Sower," 165–93).

disciples lead their lives against that time when this age will end, they must guard themselves against any false sense of security, for at the latter day they, too, will undergo judgment (13:47–50).

At the end of his discourse in parables, Jesus asks the disciples whether they have understood the mysteries of the Kingdom he has taught them. Their reply is unequivocally yes! (13:51). Yet, on other occasions the disciples show that they can falter in their understanding, and this engenders conflict between Jesus and them. For example, twice in deserted places Jesus expects the disciples to act on their awareness that he has endowed them with authority (10:1) and hence to feed, respectively, the five thousand and the four thousand men (14:16; 15:32–33). In both instances, however, the disciples give no hint of being aware that they have been endowed with such authority. On the contrary, they stand overwhelmed by Jesus' expectations, so that he himself must feed the men and demonstrate that he has not placed demands upon them incapable of fulfillment (14:13–21; 15:32–38).

Again, shortly after the second of these episodes Jesus and the disciples are on the east side of the Sea of Galilee (16:5). Already the disciples have forgotten that authority is available to them to satisfy human need. As a result, they become agitated because they are without bread (16:7). Jesus' concern at this point is to warn the disciples of the "leaven of the Pharisees and Sadducees." What Jesus means by "leaven" is the "(corrupting) teaching" of the religious leaders, and he becomes annoyed that the disciples do not comprehend this. Indeed, not until Jesus has explained himself do the disciples finally grasp the warning he is giving them (16:9–12). In principle, the disciples in Matthew's story do in fact possess the gift of understanding (13:11, 16–17, 51). But this does not foreclose the possibility that they can falter in making use of this gift and that such faltering can spark conflict between Jesus and them.

The other area in which the disciples are the recipients of divine revelation has to do with knowledge of Jesus' identity as the Son of God. In the pericope on the walking on water (14:22–33), Jesus compels the disciples to board the boat and to go before him to the other side of the sea. Underway on the water, the disciples witness Jesus, in sequence, walk on the water, command Peter to get out of the boat and come to him, rescue Peter from drowning when because of fear and doubt he begins to sink and cries out for rescue, and calm the wind. Because Peter's fear and doubt constitute a crisis of trust (attack of little faith) that prevents him from carrying out the order Jesus has given him, Jesus reprimands him. But be that as it may, in witnessing all these events, the disciples are led to worship Jesus and to confess him to be the Son of God (14:33). They in effect give answer to the question they themselves had raised earlier in another episode out on the sea, "What sort of man is this, that even winds and sea obey him?" (8:27).

The disciples' confession of 14:33 is a prelude to Peter's climactic confession of Jesus near Caesarea Philippi. Here Peter, on behalf of all the disciples, affirms Jesus to be the Son of God (16:15–16). Noteworthy, however, is Jesus' response to Peter's confession. He declares with no little fervor that only by revelation from the Father is knowledge of his divine sonship possible (16:17). In perceiving Jesus to be the Son of God, the disciples perceive that God is uniquely present and at work in Jesus (11:27). Without revelation from the Father, no human can grasp this truth. To be sure, Jesus, after lauding Peter, also commands the disciples to silence about his divine sonship (16:20). But this is necessitated by the fact that, at this juncture, they do not as yet know that his being the Son of God also involves death on the cross. Peter and the disciples, in affirming Jesus to be the Son of God, espouse an evaluative point of view concerning Jesus' identity that is at once aligned with the evaluative point of view of God (3:17) and opposed to the evaluative point of view of the Jewish public. The latter, which has rejected Jesus (11:16–24), holds him to be but a prophet of one sort or another (16:13–14).

In summary, at the same time Matthew portrays Israel as reacting to Jesus' ministry by repudiating him, he also marks out the disciples as the recipients of divine revelation (11:2—16:20). The revelation imparted to the disciples concerns in the main the mysteries of the Kingdom of Heaven (chap. 13) and the knowledge that Jesus is the Son of God (14:33; 16:16). Although conflict between Jesus and the disciples flares up in this latter half of the second part of Matthew's story, it does not occur with great frequency and it serves the larger purpose of enabling Jesus to instruct the disciples or to mediate new insight to them.

SERVANTHOOD AS THE ESSENCE OF DISCIPLESHIP

The leitmotif of the third part of Matthew's story (16:21—28:20) is Jesus' journey to Jerusalem and his passion and resurrection. In harmony with this, the motif that dominates Matthew's story of the disciples is that servanthood constitutes the essence of discipleship.

Matthew begins this part of his story with a narrative comment, and he follows this rather closely with a word of Jesus. In his narrative comment Matthew reports:

> From that time Jesus began to *show* his disciples that he must go to Jerusalem and suffer many things from the elders and chief priests and scribes, and be killed, and on the third day be raised. (16:21)

And the word Jesus speaks is this: "If any man would come after me, let him deny himself and take up his cross, and let him follow me" (16:24). The emphasis in the narrative comment on "showing" *(deiknyein)* is significant, for its use here is such that it necessarily encompasses both words and deeds, both speaking and doing. Combine these two passages while keep- ing this latter observation in mind, and the following Matthean axiom regarding discipleship emerges: Jesus reveals to his disciples, in all he says and in all he does beginning with 16:21, that God has ordained that he should go to Jerusalem to suffer, and that his way of suffering is a summons to them also to go the way of suffering (i.e., the way of servanthood) (cf. 20:28). In other words, Matthew alerts the reader through the key passages 16:21 and 16:24 that suffering, defined as servanthood, is the essence of discipleship and that Jesus will show the disciples in what he says and does that this is in fact the case.

Peter's immediate reaction to Jesus' prediction of his passion is to take Jesus aside and censure him: "God forbid, Lord!" exclaims Peter, "This shall never happen to you!" (16:22). In reply, Jesus reproves Peter, warning him that in taking exception to the notion that Jesus must suffer and die he is functioning as the mouthpiece not of God, but of Satan (16:23). Then, addressing all the disciples, Jesus tells them that the corollary to suffering sonship is suffering discipleship (16:24). These words Jesus has with the disciples here at the outset of the third part of the story adumbrate the conflict he will henceforth have with them: Jesus' struggle will be to wean the disciples from an evaluative point of view which can make them more akin to Satan than to God and to bring them to realize that suffering, or servanthood, is indeed the essence of discipleship.

In the pericopes on the transfiguration (17:1–9) and on the coming of Elijah (17:10–13), indication is given by no lesser authorities than God and scripture of how crucial it is in Matthean perspective for the disciples to be led to adopt Jesus' evaluative point of view concerning both his own fate and the essence of discipleship. Atop the high mountain, Peter, James, and John gaze on Jesus in transfigured splendor and hear the voice from the bright cloud declare, "This is my beloved Son, in whom I take delight; hear him!" (17:5). This declaration contains both an affirmation of Jesus' divine sonship and an injunction to hear him. The affirmation, uttered by God himself, confirms the fact that the earlier confessions made by Peter (16:16) and the disciples (14:33) to the effect that Jesus is the Son of God are true. The injunction to hear Jesus is an exhortation, likewise from God, that the disciples are to attend carefully to Jesus' words regarding the necessity both of his own going the way of suffering (16:21) and of their emulating him (16:24). As soon as the transfiguration is past, Jesus and the three disciples descend from the mountain. On the way down, Jesus speaks of John the Baptist as fulfilling also by his suffering the end-time expectations associated with Elijah; in this way, too, John was his forerunner (17:10–13). In sum, therefore, what Jesus tries to impress upon the disciples in these two pericopes is that, according to God's evaluative point of view, both "forerunner" and "disciples" are to reflect in their persons and lives the person and life of himself, Jesus.

Sharp conflict occurs when Jesus and the three disciples return to the crowd and the other disciples below (17:14–20). In Jesus' absence, a man had appealed to the disciples to exorcise a demon from his son, but they had been unable to do so. Taking control from the disciples, Jesus exorcises the demon and, in private, tells the disciples that the reason they failed is that they were hampered by "little faith" (17:20). Much earlier, Jesus had endowed the disciples with authority to exorcise demons as part of their mission to Israel (10:1, 8). Consequently, he expects them to draw on this authority. But if they approach the tasks of their mission forgetful of their empowerment and encumbered by a crisis of trust, they render themselves ineffectual. Says Jesus: "For truly I say to you, if you have faith as a grain of mustard seed . . . nothing will be impossible to you" (17:20).

Gathered with his disciples in Galilee before leaving for Jerusalem, Jesus predicts his passion a second time (17:22–23). His prediction "grieves" the disciples: what he has said they understand, but why he does not turn aside from the events he has foretold escapes them (cf. 16:21–22).

In the house at Capernaum a final time, Jesus first engages Peter in dialogue (17:24–27) and then delivers his ecclesiological discourse to all the disciples (18:1–35).[15] In the latter, Jesus instructs the disciples in their life together as a community. Toward those on the outside, the disciples, as sons of God and Jesus' followers, are in principle free and responsible only to God. At the same time, they do not lead lives in society that are less than exemplary or employ their freedom to give needless offense to others and hence foreclose the possibility that others may become Jesus' followers. Toward one another, the disciples lead lives befitting a community presided over by Jesus. In recognition of their total dependence on God, they deal with one another in the spirit of loving concern, of circumspection, of mutuality, and of forgiveness.

Guided by his divinely appointed goal to reach Jerusalem (16:21), Jesus at last departs from Galilee and enters the regions of Judea beyond the Jordan (19:1). Concomitantly, the extent to which he moves closer to Jerusalem is also the extent to which his conflict with the disciples becomes increasingly intense. To be sure, the disciples continue to follow him and to function as eye- and ear-witnesses to his activity, to be instructed by him, and to carry out obediently assignments he gives them (cf. 21:1–7; 26:17–19). Nonetheless, it likewise becomes ever more apparent that the evaluative point of view Jesus advocates differs in obvious respects from the one the disciples advocate. The basis of Jesus' evaluative point of view is devotion to God and love of the neighbor, which lead him to suffering and death. The basis

---

15. On the ecclesiological discourse, cf. Thompson, *Divided Community.*

of the disciples' evaluative point of view is self-concern, which is the opposite of servanthood: it counts as important having status in the eyes of others, possessing wealth, exercising authority over others, overcoming might with might, and "saving one's life" no matter what the cost. The end to which the disciples' evaluative point of view leads them is apostasy.

Examples abound of the conflict the disciples' evaluative point of view incites. Thus, the disciples arouse Jesus' ire when they rebuke those who bring children to him (19:13–15). They would turn the children away, for they are "no-accounts" and without status in the society of Matthew's story (19:13–15).

Again, the disciples, like the world around them, look on the possession of wealth as a sign of God's favor. Consequently, they are nonplussed when Jesus tells them not only that the rich do not have any advantage over others in attaining eternal life, but also that it will be difficult, indeed impossible, for them to do so. But if those who enjoy God's favor are unable to be saved, the disciples wonder, who, then, can be? For all humans alike salvation is an impossible attainment, is Jesus' reply, because salvation is of God (19:23–26). But if this be granted, what, then, do the disciples ultimately have to look forward to, Peter wants to know. Answers Jesus: the hope in which the disciples live lies, finally, in anticipation of the reward, or gift, of eternal life (19:27–30).

On another occasion, immediately following Jesus' third prediction of his passion (20:17–19), the mother of James and John approaches Jesus with the request that he award her sons the positions of first and second honor when he comes into his Rule (20:20–23). As the other ten disciples hear of this request, they become indignant, not because their motives are purer, but because they covet these same positions of honor for themselves (20:24).

Finally, on the day following Jesus' entry into Jerusalem, as he is returning to the city from having spent the night in Bethany, he curses and causes to wither a fig tree that had failed to produce fruit (21:18–19). Wrongly, the disciples are astonished at this feat. Jesus seizes on this and reminds them once more that if only they will trust and not give place to doubt, or little faith, they will be able to do far greater things than this (21:20–22; cf. 17:20).

As one moves on to the events of the passion (26:1–2), one can observe that the disciples stray still further from Jesus' evaluative point of view. The upshot is that they are unable to cope with these events. What Jesus says of Peter in Gethsemane, with an eye to James and John as well, is true of all of the disciples during the passion: "The spirit is willing, but the flesh is weak" (26:41). The disciples are divided in their intentions and loyalties. To be undivided, to be wholehearted, is to be "perfect" (5:48). Jesus, therefore, is perfect; the disciples are not.

Accordingly, as the disciples face with Jesus the events of his passion, they show themselves to be enmeshed in circumstances manifestly beyond either their comprehension or their control. For instance, in the house of Simon the leper in Bethany, the disciples misinterpret as a waste of money the woman's anointing Jesus with expensive anointment. They do not perceive that she is, in reality, preparing him for burial (26:6–13).

More tragically, Judas, in selling his services to the chief priests to betray Jesus, unwittingly acts in a manner that is the exact opposite of "servanthood": Jesus is the servant par excellence, for he delivers himself to death in order that others might gain life; by contrast, Judas delivers Jesus to death in order that he might gain advantage for himself (24:14–16).

On another note, at the Last Supper Jesus shares with the disciples, he predicts that one of them will betray him. Hearing this, each of the disciples, with a great display of grief, asks Jesus, "Is it I, Lord?" In its Greek wording, this question assumes that, were Jesus to reply to each disciple, his answer would be, "No [it is not you]." Seen for what they are, the disciples' grief and question are in reality massive expressions of false confidence: none of the disciples actually believes that he could ever do such a thing as betray Jesus (26:20–22).

Like the others, Judas also asks Jesus whether he will be the one to betray him (26:25). Judas, however, addresses Jesus not as "Lord," but as "rabbi" ("Is it I, rabbi?"). In just the use of this term "rabbi," Judas has already attested to the fact that he is not of one heart and mind with Jesus. When, therefore, Judas likewise frames his question so as to anticipate that Jesus' answer to him will be no, he makes of himself, in the very asking of his question, a liar (cf. 26:14–16).

Along this same line, Jesus predicts, on the way to the Mount of Olives, that all the disciples will fall away from him in that night and that Peter will deny him. In a grand gesture of self-delusion, Peter, joined by all the disciples, solemnly affirms that he will die with Jesus rather than deny him (20:30–35).

In similar fashion, Peter, James, and John, enjoined by Jesus to watch with him while he is at prayer in Gethsemane, are unable to do so and instead fall asleep. Although they boasted that they would die rather than desert Jesus, they do not possess so much as the inner strength to stay awake. Indeed, such boasting on the one hand and such falling asleep on the other bear eloquent testimony to the fact that the disciples are in truth divided in their loyalties toward Jesus.

In a different vein, in the hour of Jesus' arrest one of the disciples, in an act of utter futility, endeavors to meet might with might by drawing his sword and cutting off the ear of the slave of the high priest (26:51). Completely forgotten by this disciple are all the words Jesus has spoken to the Twelve concerning his passion.

Last, the disciples complete, once Jesus is in the custody of his opponents, the entire series of their failures exactly as Jesus said they would: all desert him and flee (26:56); and Peter later denies him (26:58, 69–75). To adapt a word of Jesus: Their spirit indeed was willing, but their flesh was weak (26:41).

With the exception of Judas (27:3–10), Jesus' conflict with the disciples does not, however, end in failure for them. Through a series of words given to, or meant for, the eleven disciples,[16] Jesus directs "his scattered brothers"[17] to a mountain in Galilee. There he appears to them as the resurrected Son of God who remains the crucified Son of God (28:5–6, 16–17). In seeing him, some of the disciples worship him, whereas others doubt (28:17). Still, even those who doubt, though they are weak in faith (14:31), are nonetheless not without faith. Thus, as the risen Jesus gathers about him the eleven who had been scattered, he cleanses them of their sin of apostasy and reconciles them to himself. By the same token, as they see him not only as the risen one but also as the crucified one, they recognize by the "marks on his person" that the central purpose of his ministry was in fact death on the cross (16:21). In comprehending at last the essence of his ministry, they comprehend as well the essence of their ministry: servanthood (16:24; 20:28). In this full knowledge of Jesus and of themselves, they receive from the resurrected and crucified Son of God the commission to go and make all nations his disciples (28:18–20). Having, then, received this commission, they make their way from the mountain in Galilee to the world that Jesus has described for them in his end-time discourse of chapters 24–25. If the resolution of the conflict between Jesus and Israel results tragically in alienation, the resolution of the conflict between Jesus and the disciples results happily in reconciliation.

SUMMARY

Matthew's story of the disciples follows the contours of his story of Jesus. As Matthew tells of Jesus' ministry to Israel (4:17–11:1) and of Israel's repudiation of him (11:2–16:20), he also tells of the call of the disciples and of their ministry to Israel (4:17–11:1) and of the divine revelation that is imparted to them (11:2–16:20). And as Matthew tells of Jesus' journey to Jerusalem and of his passion and resurrection (16:21–28:20), he also tells of the way whereby Jesus finally leads the disciples to comprehend that servanthood is the essence of discipleship (16:21–28:20).

As Jesus Son of God calls disciples to live in the sphere of God's end-time Rule, he forms a new community (16:18; 21:43). This new community is a brotherhood of the sons of God and of the disciples of Jesus and has as its purpose missionary activity (4:18–22). The ethic that distinguishes the lives

16. Cf. 26:32; 28:7, 10.
17. Cf. 26:31; 28:10.

of the disciples is that of the "greater righteousness" (5:20). Sustained in person and mission by the power of Jesus (8:18–22), the disciples are nonetheless vulnerable to attacks of little, or weak, faith (8:23–27). Moreover, in their ranks are not only the so-called upright but also the despised and the outcast (9:9). As described by Jesus, the ministry of the disciples to Israel foreshadows in many respects their later ministry to the nations (10:5b–42). Then, too, against the backdrop of Israel's repudiation of Jesus, the disciples stand out as the recipients of divine revelation (11:25–26). They are given to know the mysteries of the Kingdom of Heaven (13:11) as well as the identity of Jesus as the Son of God (14:33; 16:16–17). But this notwithstanding, Jesus must also enter into intense conflict with them because they resist the related notions that he must suffer and that his suffering is a summons to them to servanthood (16:21, 24; 20:28). Their resistance even leads them to the point where they commit apostasy (26:47–50, 56, 69–75). Nevertheless, Jesus overcomes their failure and reconciles them to himself (28:7, 10, 16–17). What is more, in appearing to them as the risen Son of God who remains the crucified Son of God (28:5–6, 16–17), he leads them to comprehend both that death on the cross was the central purpose of his ministry and that servanthood is the essence of discipleship. In the end, therefore, the resolution of Jesus' chief conflict with the disciples is that they appropriate his evaluative point of view concerning both himself and them and receive from him the Great Commission (28:18–20).

9
The Community
of Matthew

Thus far, we have explored the world of Matthew's story. Here we shall focus attention on the community of Christians for which Matthew's story was originally written. These Christians are best referred to as the "intended readers" of Matthew. What kind of people were they? And what were the conditions—social, economic, and religious—in which they lived?[1]

One way to approach these issues is to use the implied reader of Matthew's story as an index, even if only approximate, of the intended readers.[2] If this approach is valid, one can infer from Matthew's story the kind of things the implied reader is expected to know or the events or circumstances of which he or she is expected to be aware. Thereby one can derive information that will enable one to sketch a picture of the intended readers. Also, to supplement this information, occasional glances at Mark or Luke or at other historical data will prove to be of benefit.

The initial clue as to the place in history of the Matthean community comes from Matthew himself, as implied author. In such passages as 24:15 ("let the reader understand"), 27:8 ("until this day"), and 28:15 ("until this day"), Matthew bursts the bounds of the story he is telling of the life and ministry of Jesus in order to address the implied reader directly. Temporally, these passages locate the implied reader at a point after the resurrection but short of the Parousia. Matthew himself describes this point as

1. On the situation in life reflected in Matthew's Gospel, cf. Kingsbury, "Verb *Akolouthein* ('to follow') as an Index of Matthew's View of His Community," 56–73; Kilpatrick, *Origins of the Gospel*, chap. 7; Hare, *Jewish Persecution of Christians*; Schweizer, *Matthäus und Seine Gemeinde*; Farmer, "Post-Sectarian Character," 235–47; Waetjen, *Origin and Destiny*, chap. 2; S. Brown, "Matthean Community," esp. 213–21; Brown and Meier, *Antioch and Rome*, chap. 3; Smith, *Easter Gospels*, 55–67.
2. For an insightful discussion of how a literary critic may go about determining who the intended readers of John's Gospel were, cf. Culpepper, *Anatomy of the Fourth Gospel*, chap. 7.

the time of the messianic woes, which will ultimately issue in the final judgment (24:8). The time of the messianic woes, therefore, is also the time in which the intended readers of Matthew's Gospel were living.

CONSTITUENCY

More prosaically, the time of the messianic woes would seem to refer to the latter part of the first century and the intended readers of Matthew's Gospel to Greek-speaking Christians of Jewish or gentile origin who were perhaps at home in Antioch of Syria. To ascertain the date of the Gospel, a glance at the parable of the great supper may prove helpful. At 22:7, one finds what many scholars consider to be a clear allusion to the destruction of Jerusalem (A.D. 66–70). From the first evangelist's own vantage point in history, this event apparently already lies in the past (cf. 21:41). Add to this the datum that Ignatius, writing shortly after the turn of the century (ca. A.D. 110 or 115), seemingly has knowledge of the Gospel of Matthew,[3] and one arrives rather quickly at A.D. 85 or 90 as the date of writing.

The text of Matthew's Gospel itself is testimony that the language the intended readers spoke was Greek, and this, in turn, suggests that the Gospel's place of origin was most probably a city. A good conjecture is Antioch of Syria. Thus, the quality of the Gospel's language is such that it is by no means "translation Greek," the secondary rendering, for example, of a Hebrew or an Aramaic original. In an analysis of the language of the Gospel, one scholar states that although the first evangelist betrays a feeling for "Semitic atmosphere" and has at times taken over Semitisms from his sources or even himself given a phrase a Semitic twist (cf. 7:28; 11:1; 13:53; 19:1; 26:1: "*And it happened* when Jesus finished . . ."), he can be seen on the whole to have been "an educated person commanding sound Greek with a considerable vocabulary."[4] Then, too, if the observation is even roughly accurate that in the first century Aramaic was the language of the populace in the rural regions of Syria and Palestine but Greek the dominant language of the cities,[5] then the Greek of Matthew's Gospel would place the intended readers in an urban environment. This does not prove that Antioch of Syria was the place where Matthew's Gospel was written, but neither does it challenge this view.

If the language of the intended readers was Greek, does this rule out the notion that they may also have spoken Hebrew or especially Aramaic? While one cannot simply deny the possibility that the intended readers were bilingual, it is difficult to make a case for it. Neither the isolated

3. Cf. Ign. *Eph.* 19:2–3; *Smyrn.* 1:1; 6:1; *Pol.* 1:3; 2:2; also Brown and Meier, *Antioch and Rome,* 24–25. For a table listing the passages in Matthew and in the letters of Ignatius most commonly cited as being parallel, cf. Trevett, "Ignatian Correspondence," 62–63.

4. Moule, *Birth of the New Testament,* 219; also Turner, *Style,* 4:37–38.

5. Cf. Theissen, "Itinerant Radicalism," 133.

instances in which the first evangelist employs a Semitic word without translating it[6] nor the Semitic idiom of his speech as such are sufficient to prove bilingualism. Indeed, they prove no more than that the evangelist presupposed the intended readers would not find such words or idiom incomprehensible. By the same token, three times the evangelist does provide a translation of Semitic words (1:23; 27:33, 46), and if it can be assumed that he had Mark available as a source, he has also chosen several times not to take over Semitic words that stand out prominently in that Gospel.[7] As for the evangelist's use of the OT, only the so-called formula-quotations would suggest that the Septuagint was not his Bible. Then, too, the evangelist could just as easily as not have appropriated these quotations from an obscure Greek version of the OT or from an early Christian collection in Greek of OT testimonies.[8]

The intended readers of Matthew's Gospel appear to have been people of Jewish and of gentile background. This is suggested by the contents of the Gospel, which presuppose knowledge of Jewish thought, history, and traditions on the one hand and openness toward Gentiles on the other. Features of the Gospel suggesting that the first evangelist wrote for a sizable Jewish-Christian constituency are numerous. To begin with, many of the key terms in the Gospel are thoroughly Jewish in tone. The sanctified life of the disciple is known as "righteousness" (*dikaiosynē;* cf. 5:20; 6:1), and part and parcel of it are "almsgiving" (6:2), "prayer" (6:5), and "fasting" (6:16). The preferred designation for the Rule of God is "the Kingdom of Heaven" instead of "the Kingdom of God," which is the expression Mark and Luke employ. God is often referred to as "your heavenly Father" or as "your Father who is in heaven" (cf. the Sermon on the Mount) and the disciples as "sons of God" (5:9), "sons of your Father who is in heaven" (5:45), or "sons of the Kingdom" (13:38). The archadversary of Jesus is designated as "the devil" (4:1–11), "Satan" (4:10; 16:23), "the Enemy" (13:39), and "the Evil One" (13:19), and in his service stands "Beelzebul, the prince of demons" (12:24; 10:25). The end of time and the final day are termed, respectively, "the consummation of the age" (13:39, 40, 49) and "the day of judgment" (11:22, 24; 12:36). These are but a sampling of the evangelist's penchant for Jewish-like phraseology.

The first evangelist's picture of Jesus is likewise Jewish in hue. He is the "Son of Abraham," the one in whom the entire history of Israel reaches its culmination (1:1–17). He is furthermore the "Messiah" (chap. 1) or "Coming One" (11:2–3) who has been sent specifically to the "lost sheep of the house of Israel" (15:24). He is also the "Son of David," the royal figure who stands

6. Cf., e.g., "*hraka*" (5:22), "*mamōna*" (6:24), "*Beelzeboul*" (10:25; but cf. 12:24), and "*korbanan*" (27:6).

7. Mark 3:17; 5:41; 7:11, 34; 10:46, 51; 14:36.

8. On this question, cf. Stendahl, *School of St. Matthew*, iii–v.

in the line of David (chap. 1; 21:5, 9), and the "King of the Jews [Israel]," who suffers on behalf of his people (chap. 27). Indeed, Jesus is, in sum, the "Son of God," or "Emmanuel," the one in whom God has drawn near to dwell with his people to the end of the age[9] and who will, in fulfillment of OT Son-of-man prophecy, return to judge all humankind (25:31–46).

The ministry of Jesus, too, has a particularly Jewish aura about it in Matthew's Gospel. The first evangelist is at pains to show that this ministry takes place almost exclusively within the confines of Israel (15:24; 10:5–6). Galilee is the place of Jesus' activity, and he traverses the whole of it (4:23; 9:35; 11:1). It is from Galilee that news of him spreads throughout all Syria (4:24), and it is to Galilee that the crowds from the Decapolis, Jerusalem, Judea, and across the Jordan come to be with him (4:25). When Jesus leaves Galilee, it is only briefly.[10] In fact, on one occasion when he withdraws into the regions of Tyre and Sidon, it appears that he merely crosses the border, for it is said of the Canaanite woman that she "came out" toward him (15:21–28). Only once does Jesus undertake a journey during his public ministry that is actually regarded as taking him away from the environs of Galilee, and this is his fateful trip to Jerusalem (19:2).

In point of fact, the first evangelist's treatment of the region of Galilee reveals that he actually construes it as the wider setting for Jesus' activity, for he locates numerous events in and around the city of Capernaum. This seems to be the case, for instance, with all but two of the ten miracles he records in chapters 8—9 (8:23—9:1). As for Capernaum itself, neither Mark nor Luke ever reports that Jesus "dwells" anywhere, but the first evangelist, taking up on his previous notation that Joseph "went and *dwelt* in a city called Nazareth" (2:23), documents with a formula-quotation the circumstance that Jesus "left Nazareth and went and 'dwelt' in Capernaum" (4:13–16). Indeed, Capernaum is designated as "his own city" (9:1), and it may be that the "house" there is to be thought of as belonging to him.[11]

Until Easter, the disciples in Matthew's Gospel also share in Jesus' concentration on Israel. To stress this, the first evangelist devotes the whole of the section 9:35—10:42 to their projected mission to Israel, which goes beyond anything one finds in either Mark or Luke.

The attitude Jesus takes toward the Mosaic law and the tradition of the elders is yet another factor suggesting that the first evangelist wrote for a strong Jewish-Christian constituency. Although the law retains its validity until the consummation of the age only as interpreted by Jesus, it is nonetheless not set aside (5:17–20). And although Jesus wages a vigorous polemic against the tradition of the elders (15:1–9), he does not simply

9. Cf. 1:23; 2:15; 28:20.
10. Cf., e.g., 3:13—4:13; 8:23—9:1; [14:22]; 15:21; 16:4c–5, 13.
11. Cf. 9:10, 28; 12:46 and 13:1; 13:36; 17:25.

abolish it (23:2–3, 23). The Marcan Jesus, by contrast, appears to overthrow the legal system of the Jews (cf. Mark 7:1–23).

Finally, the manner in which the first evangelist treats certain other details also argues for the Jewishness of a large segment of the intended readers of his Gospel. Unlike Mark, the first evangelist does not explain such Jewish regulations as the washing of hands before meals (cf. 15:2 with Mark 7:2–4), and neither does he explain the custom of wearing amulets and tassels (23:5). As has been noted, if at times he translates Semitic words (1:23; 27:33, 46), at other times he leaves them untranslated (cf. *"hraka,"* 5:22; *"mamōna,"* 6:24; *"Beelzeboul,"* 10:25; *"korbanan,"* 27:6). In addition, he also assumes his readers will be familiar with a peculiarly Jewish turn of phrase (cf., e.g., "straining out the gnat," 23:24; "whitewashed tombs," 23:27).

But if the unmistakable Jewishness of much of Matthew's Gospel favors the thesis that the first evangelist wrote with a sizable Jewish-Christian constituency in mind, the attitude he takes toward the mission to the nations shows that he also wrote with a view to intended readers of gentile origin. One looks in vain in Matthew's Gospel for traces of the fierce controversy surrounding the gentile mission which are so prominent in Paul (Galatians 2) and Acts (15). On the contrary, one can detect in the Gospel from beginning to end a pronounced "gentile bias." Already in the genealogy of Jesus, four non-Israelite women are listed as the ancestors of Jesus ("Tamar," "Rahab," "Ruth," and "the wife of Uriah" [Bathsheba]; 1:3, 5–6). In chapter 2, the "Magi from the East" are described as "worshiping" Jesus and presenting him gifts that befit a king (2:1–2, 11). Jesus' settling in "Galilee of the Gentiles" to begin his ministry to Israel prefigures the post-Easter return of the disciples to Galilee, from where they will undertake their mission to the nations.[12] As the second of a series of ten miracles, Jesus heals the servant of a centurion, and attendant to this he declares:

> Truly, I say to you, not even in Israel have I found such faith. I tell you, many will come from east and west and sit at table with Abraham, Isaac, and Jacob in the Kingdom of Heaven. (8:10–11)

At 12:21, the evangelist quotes from the OT in order to proclaim Jesus as the one in whom the "Gentiles will hope," and at 13:38 he writes that it is in the "world" that "sons of the Kingdom" will be raised up. In the parables of the wicked husbandmen (21:33–46) and of the great supper (22:1–14), the evangelist employs figurative speech to depict the influx of the Gentiles into the church (21:41; 22:9–10), and in 24:14 and 26:13 he has Jesus announce that it is throughout the entire world that the gospel of the Kingdom will be proclaimed.

To conclude, from what can be inferred from the text of Matthew's Gospel the intended readers were Christians both of Jewish and of gentile

---

12. Cf. 4:12, 15; 28:7, 16–20.

origin. Their language was Greek, their place in history the latter part of the first century (A.D. 85 or 90), and they were probably at home in a city, perhaps Antioch of Syria.

SOCIAL STANDING

Apparently, the intended readers of Matthew's Gospel were well-to-do, and it also seems that home for them was in an urban area. In comparison with Mark, who uses the word "city" *(polis)* eight times and the word "village" *(kōmē)* seven times, the first evangelist uses the word "village" only four times but the word "city" no fewer than twenty-six times. The latter statistic is all the more striking when one observes that the "city" is the setting for a significant part of Jesus' life and ministry and for the ministry of the disciples as well. Thus, Jesus grows up in the city of Nazareth (2:23; 21:11). In discharging his ministry, he makes the city of Capernaum home base (4:13; 9:1). When he leaves Capernaum, he visits all the cities of Galilee (9:23; 9:35; 11:1). Finally, he completes his ministry in the city of Jerusalem (21:1—28:15). As for the disciples, Jesus similarly describes them in his missionary discourse as carrying out their ministry within the setting of the city.[13] Perhaps, then, the intended readers of Matthew's Gospel were members of a "city church."

Indications are strong that the intended readers were also well-to-do. The Lucan Jesus, for example, pronounces a blessing on "the poor" (6:20) but the Matthean Jesus on "the poor in spirit" (5:3). The Marcan Jesus commands the disciples in conjunction with their missionary journey to take with them no "copper coin" (i.e., small change; Mark 6:8), but the Matthean Jesus commands them to take neither "gold, nor silver, nor copper coin" (10:9). The Lucan Jesus tells a parable about "minas" (Luke 19:11–27) but the Matthean Jesus about "talents" (25:14–30), one of the latter being worth approximately fifty times one of the former. The Lucan Jesus says in the words of the household in the parable of the great supper: "Go out quickly to the streets and lanes of the city, and bring in the poor and maimed and blind and lame" (14:21). By contrast, the Matthean Jesus makes no such explicit reference to the disenfranchised but merely says in his version of these words: "Go therefore to the thoroughfares, and invite to the marriage feast as many as you find" (22:9). And in Mark (15:43) and Luke (23:50–51), Joseph of Arimathea is a member of the council who is looking for the Kingdom of God, but in Matthew he is a "rich man . . . who also was a disciple of Jesus" (27:57).

It seems, in fact, that the intended readers of Matthew's Gospel were well accustomed to dealing in a wide range of money. Whereas Luke mentions

13. Cf. 10:11, 14, 15, 23; 23:34.

"silver" and a few kinds of money[14] and Mark mentions an assortment of
what on the whole were the lesser denominations, the first evangelist
makes no reference whatever to the *lepton*, the smallest unit of money cited
in the Gospels (a small copper coin = ca. ⅛ cent), but does refer to all the
following: the *kodrantēs* ("quadrans" = ca. ¼ cent), the *assarion* ("assarion"
= ca. 1 cent), the *dēnarion* ("denarius" = ca. 18 cents), the *didrachmon*
("double drachma" = ca. 36 cents), the *statēr* ("stater" = ca. 80 cents), the
talanton ("talent" = ca. $1,080); and *chalkos* ("copper coin"), *argyrion* ("sil-
ver"), *argyros* ("silver"), and *chrysos* ("gold"). Indeed, if one takes the three
terms "silver," "gold," and "talent," one discovers that they occur in Matthew's Gospel no fewer than twenty-eight times, which may be compared
with the single use of the word "silver" by Mark and the fourfold use of it
by Luke. Against a background of wealth such as these terms indicate, it
makes sense that the first evangelist should appropriate in 13:22 Mark's
warning against riches (Mark 4:19) and sharpen the saying of Jesus at 19:23
so that difficulty in entering the Kingdom is predicated not merely to
"those who have means" (Mark 10:23), but to the "rich man."

Accordingly, in light of the preceding there is further reason to postulate
that the intended readers of Matthew's Gospel lived in or near a city, such
as Antioch of Syria, and it also seems safe to infer that they were pros-
perous and in no sense materially disadvantaged.

SOCIAL CLIMATE

It appears certain that the social and religious climate in which the
intended readers of Matthew's Gospel found themselves was one of intense
conflict. On the one hand, it looks as though they were living in close
proximity to hostile pagans. Whether or not their mission to the nations
was the sole reason, they were seemingly being hauled into court by gentile
authorities, judicially harassed ("handed over to tribulation"), hated "by
all," and even put to death.[15] Plainly, these Christians were enduring
persecution at the hands of their gentile neighbors.[16]

On the other hand, it likewise seems that they were living in close
proximity to a vigorous Jewish community. The evidence for this is multiple. For instance, it is possibly with a view to the church's relationship to
Israel that the first evangelist reports Jesus as saying in the parable of the
tares, "Let both grow side by side until the harvest" (13:30).[17] In a similar
vein, if the story of the payment of the temple tax (17:24–27) can be
interpreted to mean that the Jewish Christians in Matthew's community

14. Cf., e.g., 7:41; 12:6, 59; 19:13.
15. Cf. 10:18, 22; 13:21; 24:9.
16. Cf. Hare, *Jewish Persecution of Christians*, 106–8, 124.
17. Cf. Kingsbury, *Parables of Jesus*, 63–76.

were being encouraged, despite their "freedom," not to offend Jews by refusing to participate in the collection of contributions throughout Jewry in support of the Patriarchy at Jamnia,[18] then this unit, too, may speak for close contact between Jews and the intended readers of Matthew's Gospel.

Perhaps the first evangelist's presentation of Jesus, of the disciples, and of the religious leaders also indicates that the intended readers were living in close proximity to Jews. Thus, it may secondarily be with an eye to the Jews about him that the evangelist has portrayed Jesus Son of God as the ideal Israelite[19] and has elevated him above Moses as the supreme teacher of the will of God (cf. the Sermon on the Mount). In addition, the evangelist's description of Christian piety as the righteousness "greater" than that of the scribes and Pharisees may also have the Jews "next door" in mind (5:20). Similarly, this could furthermore be the case for the many invectives that are hurled at the religious leaders throughout the Gospel (cf. chap. 23). On another level, although the primary task of the intended readers was to make disciples of the nations (28:18–20), this does not mean, as was mentioned earlier, that missionary activity among the Jews had ceased. The missionary discourse of chapter 10, which has to do with evangelization especially among Jews though also among Gentiles,[20] continued to be of relevance for these Christians. What is more, the passage 23:34 is an unmistakable reference to missionary activity among the Jews seemingly taking place in the evangelist's own day. In short, the Christian mission to the Jews had not met with success and the essential task henceforth was to go to the Gentiles, but continued work among the Jews points to no lack of interaction between the intended readers of Matthew's Gospel and the Jewish community.

Still, if the intended readers were living in close proximity to a strong Jewish community, they are not to be thought of as a "splinter group" that was nevertheless a member of the Jewish league of synagogues.[21] The place of the intended readers was no longer within Judaism but outside it. Several factors support this conclusion.

To begin with, the first evangelist, more rigorously than either Mark or Luke, makes of Jesus and his disciples a group set apart from the Jewish crowds and their leaders. This comes to the fore already both in the way he has persons address Jesus and in the way he develops his ecclesiological concept of "being with Jesus." As for the latter, we noted in Chapter 8 that the evangelist very carefully reserves for the disciples alone the privilege of sharing in the company, or presence, of Jesus. As a result, it is not said of Judas or of the crowds or of the religious leaders that they are "with Jesus"

18. Cf. Thompson, *Divided Community*, 66–68.
19. Cf., e.g., 4:1–11.
20. Cf. 10:17–18, 22–23.
21. Cf., e.g., Hummel, *Auseinandersetzung*, 28–33, 159–61.

or that he is "with them." Correlatively, the evangelist distinguishes sharply, as was also noted, between the manner in which Jesus is approached by the disciples on the one hand and persons without faith on the other: whereas the disciples address Jesus as "Lord," opponents and persons without faith address him only as "rabbi" or "teacher." The "apartness" of Jesus and his disciples in the Gospel's story reflects, it would seem, the religious distance of the intended readers of Matthew's Gospel from the Jewish community.

Further indications that the intended readers had already broken with Judaism are the first evangelist's use of the expression "their [your] synagogue(s)," his massive polemic against Judaism as an institution, and the apparent organizational autonomy of the community to which he belonged. To take the last point first, Matthew's community was not at all, as will be seen, under Jewish religious control but had its own form of organization which dealt with such weighty matters as those of doctrine and church order. In addition, by regularly appending the modifying genitive "your" or "their" to the noun "synagogue(s),"[22] the evangelist attests idiomatically to the disassociation of his community from Judaism. Also, except to acknowledge that the "scribes and the Pharisees are seated on the chair of Moses" (23:2),[23] he has virtually nothing good to say of Judaism as a religious institution. Typically, there is no "friendly scribe" in Matthew's Gospel, as there is in Mark's, of whom it is written: "And when Jesus saw that he answered wisely, he said to him, 'You are not far from the Kingdom of God'" (Mark 12:34). On the contrary, the one scribe in Matthew's Gospel who requests of Jesus that he become his disciple is turned away with the words: "Foxes have holes, and birds of the air have nests; but the Son of man has nowhere to lay his head" (8:20).[24] Indeed, far from evincing affinity for contemporary Judaism, the first evangelist has mounted a massive polemic against it in his Gospel. In his eyes, contemporary Judaism was, as a saying of Jesus puts it, a "plant which my heavenly Father has not planted [and] will be rooted up" (15:13). And if "persecution" characterized the relationship of the intended readers of the Gospel to the Gentiles, this was all the more the case as far as contemporary Judaism was concerned. From what can be inferred, Matthean Christians, and especially the missionaries, were subject to abuse that was both verbal (5:11) and

22. Cf. 4:23; 9:35; 10:17; 12:9; 13:54; 23:34.

23. In light of such passages as 23:8–10 and 16:6–12, those scholars are doubtless correct who contend that the seemingly positive words Jesus utters in 23:2–3 concerning the religious leaders serve not so much to pay tribute to them as to highlight the cleavage between what they say and what they do (cf. 23:3c). On this view, then, the function of these positive words is to serve as a contrast to the negative judgment that follows and in this way to lend greater prominence to the latter. Cf. most recently Cook, "'Pro-Jewish' Passages," 135–46.

24. Cf. Kingsbury, "The 'Eager' Scribe and the 'Reluctant' Disciple."

physical, including floggings in the synagogues and measures aimed at expulsion or resulting, apparently, even in death (10:17, 23; 23:34).[25]

Consequently, the intended readers of Matthew's Gospel, a community with members of Jewish and gentile background which stood outside the orbit of official Judaism but lived in close proximity to both Jews and Gentiles, encountered from without persecution by both Jew and Gentile. What is to be said of the internal structure of this community?

ORGANIZATION

Called through baptism to follow Jesus, the risen and exalted Son of God who presides over and resides in his "church,"[26] the intended readers of Matthew's Gospel knew themselves to be "sons of God"[27] and "brothers" of Jesus and of one another.[28] As sons of God, they were also "little ones," for they understood themselves to be totally dependent on their heavenly Father (18:3, 6, 10). As the brothers of Jesus and of one another, they were at the same time the "servants" and the "slaves" of one another (20:25–28). And as followers of Jesus, they were likewise "disciples" (mathētai), for they had taken upon themselves his yoke and they were "learning" from him.[29] Internally, therefore, the intended readers of Matthew's Gospel saw themselves as comprising the church, that is to say, a community, or brotherhood, of the sons of God and the disciples of Jesus.

Within this community, two or three groups can be distinguished. One group was that of the "prophets" (10:41; 23:34). In principle, the entire community regarded itself as standing in the tradition of the OT prophets and the twelve disciples of Jesus (5:12; 13:17). It appears, however, that there were also certain Christians in the community who were specifically thought of as being "prophets." They seem to have been itinerant missionaries who proclaimed the gospel of the Kingdom to Jews[30] but especially to Gentiles.[31]

Whether these Christian prophets functioned exclusively beyond the confines of the Matthean community is difficult to say. In 7:15–23, reference is made to prophets who were, it seems, active within the community. These prophets are denounced as being "false," as being "ravenous wolves . . . who come to you in sheep's clothing" (7:15). Also, they were "enthusiasts," for it is said that in the name of Christ they have prophesied, cast out

25. Cf. Hare, *Jewish Persecution of Christians*, 126; Stanton, "Matthew and Judaism," 275–77; Kingsbury, *Parables of Jesus*, 57–59.

26. Cf. 28:19–20; also 1:23; 16:18; 18:17, 20.

27. Cf. 5:9, 45; 13:38.

28. Cf. 12:49–50; 18:35; 23:8; 25:40; 28:10.

29. Cf. 11:29; 10:1, 24–25; 23:10.

30. Cf. 10:41 with 10:6, 17, 23; 23:34 with 23:29a.

31. Cf. 10:41 with 10:18; 24:14; 26:13; 28:19.

demons, and performed many miracles (7:22). Their works, however, are castigated as contravening their profession of the name of Christ (7:16–20). The result is that they are condemned in words of Jesus as "workers of lawlessness" whom the exalted Jesus will banish from his presence at the latter day (7:23). The point is: Is one to infer from such reference to false prophets as active within the community that, conversely, legitimate Christian prophets, too, are to be thought of as having engaged in ministry not only as missionaries beyond the community but also as preachers of the gospel of the Kingdom within the community?[32] One can only conjecture.

One or possibly two groups within the Matthean community have been identified: the "prophets" and the "false prophets." Another identifiable group is those who functioned as "teachers." They were designated variously. Thus, the "righteous man" (*dikaios*; 10:41) was a teacher of righteousness,[33] and the "rabbi" (*hrabbi*; 23:8), the "scribe" (*grammateus*; 23:34), and the "wise man" (*sophos*; 23:34), were those expert in matters pertaining to the scripture and the law.[34] The verses 10:41 and 23:34, in which three of these four terms occur, show that Christian teachers, too, served as missionaries to the Jews, perhaps conversing or debating with them about the meaning of the scriptures, the law, and the traditions in light of the coming of Jesus Messiah.

But these Christians who served as teachers were likewise active within the community, as can be presupposed from 23:8–12 (cf. 13:52). What their exact competencies were is hard to know. Still, at one point this question becomes acute, because it touches on the matter of the regulation of the life of the community.

Indications are that by A.D. 85 or 90 the Matthean community had already developed a structure for governing its communal life. The outlines of this structure can be discerned in the evangelist's portrait of the disciples. In 16:19, for example, Peter is depicted as receiving from Jesus the promise of the power of the "keys of the Kingdom of Heaven." He receives this promise, however, in his capacity as the "first" of the disciples to be called[35] and therefore as the one who is their "spokesman" and who is "typical" of them and of later Christians.[36] Peter's "primacy," therefore, is not that of being elevated to a station above the other disciples but is "salvation-historical" in nature: he is, again, the "first" disciple whom Jesus called to follow him. Because Peter is the first among the disciples all of whom have been called and are in this sense equal, the power of the keys Jesus

<hr>

32. On a less cautious note, Boring (*Sayings of the Risen Jesus*, 45) asserts that "prophets" constituted the "recognized leadership" of the Matthean church.
33. Cf. Cothenet, "Les prophètes chrétiens," 294.
34. Cf. Wilckens, "Sophia," 7:505.
35. Cf. 4:18–20; 10:2; 16:16.
36. Cf. Kingsbury, "Peter in Matthew's Gospel," 67–83.

promises him is perhaps best equated with the power of "binding and loosing," which the other disciples exercise as well as he (cf. 16:19 with 18:18). The power of "binding and loosing," in turn, pertains to the regulation of church doctrine and church discipline.[37] Accordingly, whatever the particular contribution of those who served as teachers, it was the entire Matthean community that decided the matters of doctrine and discipline. As the passage 18:18–20 indicates, this community made such decisions gathered together in the name and hence in the presence and on the authority of the exalted Son of God. Moreover, as it did so, it was conscious of the fact that the touchstone of whatever it decided is that it was to be in keeping with the injunction given by Jesus to "observe all that I have commanded you" (28:20).

The Matthean community, then, was without a peculiar "teaching office" such as contemporary Judaism was in the process of developing. Indeed, with an eye toward those engaged in teaching, it counteracted the problem of position and status they could well have posed by invoking sayings of Jesus. These sayings expressly forbade those who taught to arrogate to themselves a station setting them above the rest of the community. They were not, for instance, to assume the title of "rabbi" or "teacher" (didaskalos, kathēgētēs), for there is only one from whom the church receives its teaching, Jesus Messiah, the Son of God (23:8, 10). Neither were they to assume the title of "Father," for there is only one who can lay just claim to this title, God himself (23:9). In point of fact, they were to be the opposite of the "scribes and Pharisees" in contemporary Judaism who had office and authority but who "shut the Kingdom of Heaven against men," neither entering it themselves nor allowing those who would enter to go in (23:13). On the contrary, in the church "all . . . are brothers" (23:8), and the eschatological maxim applied that "whoever exalts himself will be humbled, and whoever humbles himself will be exalted" (23:12).

To recapitulate, the intended readers of Matthew's Gospel thought of themselves as the church, which is to say that they understood themselves to be a community, or brotherhood, of the sons of God and of the disciples of Jesus. Within this community, two or three groups stand out: those who were "prophets" or "false prophets," and those who served as "teachers." But though these groups can be distinguished, they did not constitute a select leadership that decided matters of church doctrine and church discipline. On the contrary, the entire community, gathering in the presence of the exalted Son of God, decided matters of this nature, in line with the injunction of Jesus to "observe all that I have commanded you."[38]

---

37. Cf. Bornkamm, " 'Bind' and 'Loose,' " 1:37–50; Brown, Donfried, and Reumann, Peter in the New Testament, 95–101.

38. Cf. 16:19; 18:18–20; 28:20.

THE FIRST EVANGELIST

A word is in order about the evangelist himself, the real author of the First Gospel. In greatest measure, scholarly opinion does not identify the first evangelist with Matthew the apostle. One reason is that if the First Gospel is in some sense dependent on the Gospel of Mark as a source, as most scholars believe, it is difficult to explain how it could happen that the apostle Matthew, an eyewitness to the ministry of Jesus, should have taken the greater part of his Gospel from Mark, who no one claims was a disciple or eyewitness of Jesus. Another reason is that the theological outlook of the writer of the First Gospel seems to be that of the second, not the first, generation of Christians to follow Jesus. One might also ask, if it is correct that the First Gospel was written about A.D. 85 or 90, whether the apostle Matthew could reasonably be expected to have lived long enough to write it.

It could be, however, that the apostle Matthew, although not the author of the First Gospel, was associated at one time with the church in which the Gospel arose and was esteemed as a founder or "patron disciple" of this church. This would explain why the story of the call of Matthew (9:9) substitutes in the First Gospel for the story of the call of Levi (Mark 2:14; Luke 5:27), and why the list of the disciples of Jesus has been adjusted accordingly.[39]

Still, some scholars, while they agree that Matthew the apostle did not write the First Gospel, nevertheless hold that his association with it was more direct than this. Appealing to a notice of the second-century church father Papias which reads that "Matthew wrote [collected] the oracles [accounts] in the Hebrew language and every one interpreted them as he was able,"[40] they contend that Matthew the apostle was the author of a primitive Aramaic document subsequently taken up into the First Gospel. In its various forms, this thesis has been thoroughly debated over the years, but the results have been inconclusive.

Can, then, the real author of the First Gospel be identified? The answer is no. It is sometimes suggested that the First Gospel was produced not by an individual, but by a school.[41] Most scholars, however, prefer to think in terms of individual authorship. A few argue that the Gospel was written by a gentile Christian, basing their case on the author's alleged "distance" from Judaism, on his use of the Septuagint and treatment of certain Semitic words and other terms, and on the supposed relationship within the Gospel between tradition (= Jewish Christian) and redaction (= gentile

39. Cf. 10:3 ("Matthew the toll-collector") with Mark 6:18 and Luke 9:15.
40. Cf. Eusebius, *Ecclesiastical History*, 3.39.16.
41. Cf. Stendahl, *School of St. Matthew*, 30–35.

Christian).[42] But the majority of scholars regard the author as a Christian of Jewish background, and they point to many of his theological emphases, to his oftentimes rabbinic mode of thinking and arguing, and to the architectonic structure of his work as proof of this. Perhaps, therefore, the first evangelist can best be described as a Greek-speaking Jewish Christian of the second generation after Jesus who possessed a universal missionary outlook and had most probably enjoyed rabbinical training.

SUMMARY

By the last two decades of the first century, the church of Matthew was a firmly established community. Greek was its language, and the constituency was of both Jewish and gentile origins. It was furthermore urban and well-to-do, located perhaps in or near Syrian Antioch, and its neighbors were Jews and Gentiles. The atmosphere in which it lived was one of conflict, both from within and from without. From without, it encountered gentile but especially Jewish persecution. From within, it was troubled by miracle-working false prophets, among others. Still, this community, having had its ties with contemporary Judaism severed, conceived of itself as a brotherhood of the sons of God and of the disciples of Jesus. It knew the exalted Son of God to reside in its midst, and it traced its teaching and ethics to him. Groups within the community can be distinguished, but hierarchical tendencies were resisted. There were, for example, the itinerant prophets who proclaimed the gospel of the Kingdom among Jews and Gentiles, though the primary mission of the community was to the latter. And there were those engaged in teaching, who, although they, too, undertook missionary activity, instructed the community in the will of God as taught by Jesus. But whatever the contribution of the latter, when it came to making final decisions concerning matters of doctrine and church discipline, the entire community, under the aegis of the exalted Son of God, decided.

---

42. Cf. Strecker, *Weg der Gerechtigkeit*, 15–35; also Meier, *Vision of Matthew*, 17–25.

10
Concluding
Remarks

The gospel story Matthew narrates is of the life and ministry of Jesus of Nazareth (1:18—28:20). The context in which Matthew places this story is that of the history of salvation.[1] Constitutive of this history are two epochs: the time of the OT, which is the time of prophecy; and the time of fulfillment, which is the time of Jesus (cf. the formula-quotations). The time of Jesus extends from conception and birth (1:23) to Parousia (25:31), and encompasses the ministries to Israel of John (3:2), of Jesus (4:17), and of the pre-Easter disciples (10:7) and the ministry to the nations of the post-Easter disciples (24:14). The focus, however, is on the ministry of Jesus, for John is the forerunner of Jesus (11:10) and the pre-Easter and post-Easter disciples receive from Jesus their commission (10:5; 28:18–20).

Matthew's story of Jesus' life and ministry possesses a clearly defined beginning, middle, and end and hence falls into three parts: (I) The Presentation of Jesus (1:1—4:16); (II) The Ministry of Jesus to Israel and Israel's Repudiation of Jesus (4:17—16:20); and (III) The Journey of Jesus to Jerusalem and His Suffering, Death, and Resurrection (16:21—28:20). In the first part, Matthew presents Jesus as the Davidic Messiah-King, the royal Son of God (1:1—4:16). To show that Jesus is preeminently the Son of God, Matthew depicts God as announcing within the world of the story that Jesus is his Son (3:17). As the Son of God, Jesus stands forth as the supreme agent of God who authoritatively espouses God's evaluative point of view.

In the second part of his story (4:17—16:20), Matthew tells of Jesus' ministry to Israel (4:17—11:1) and of Israel's repudiation of Jesus (11:2—16:20). Sent to Israel, Jesus teaches, preaches, and heals (4:23; 9:35; 11:1). He also calls disciples, and commissions them to a ministry in Israel modeled on his own (4:17—11:1). Israel's response to Jesus, however, is one of repudiation (11:2—16:20). Still, even as Israel repudiates him, it wonders

1. Cf. 1:2–17; 21:33–46; 22:1–14; chaps. 24–25.

and speculates about who he is. Wrongly, the religious leaders think of him as one who acts in collusion with Satan (9:34; 12:24), and the Jewish public imagines him to be a prophet (16:13–14; 21:46). In stark contrast to Israel, the disciples, as the recipients of divine revelation, are led by Jesus to think about him as God "thinks" about him, namely, as the Messiah Son of God (16:15–17; 14:33). Nevertheless, because the disciples do not know at this point in the story that the central purpose of Jesus' mission is death, Jesus commands them to silence concerning his identity (16:20).

In the third part of this story (16:21—28:20), Matthew describes Jesus' journey to Jerusalem and his suffering, death, and resurrection (16:21; 17:22–23; 20:17–19). Jesus' first act is to tell his disciples that God has ordained that he should go to Jerusalem and there be made by the religious leaders to suffer and die (16:21). On hearing this, Peter rejects out of hand the idea that such a fate should ever befall Jesus (16:22), and Jesus reprimands Peter for thinking the things not of God, but of humans (16:23). Then, too, Peter's inability to comprehend that death is the essence of Jesus' ministry is only part of the malady afflicting the disciples: they are also incapable of perceiving that servanthood is the essence of discipleship (16:24).

Still, key to the resolution of Jesus' conflict with both Israel and the disciples is precisely his death on the cross. Guided by the religious leaders, Israel desires the death of Jesus (27:20–25). As the leaders see it, Jesus threatens the overthrow of law and tradition and the destruction of the nation (12:1–14; 15:12; 21:43). In claiming to be the Son of God and the decisive figure in the history of salvation,[2] Jesus makes himself guilty of blasphemy against God and is deserving of death (26:65–66). Accordingly, in effecting the death of Jesus, the leaders understand themselves to be purging Israel of the error with which a false messiah would pervert the nation (27:63–64). The irony, however, is that in abjectly repudiating Jesus, the leaders achieve the opposite of what they had intended: far from purging Israel from error, they plunge it into fatal error, for they make both themselves and the people responsible for the death of the one who is in fact the Son of God and through whom God proffers salvation to Israel; unwittingly, therefore, the leaders make themselves responsible for Israel's loss of its privileged place among the nations as God's chosen people (15:13–14; 21:37–43; 22:7; 27:20–25).

But however this may be, God and Jesus also desire the death of Jesus (16:21; 26:39, 42). Through death, Jesus accomplishes the gracious purposes of God, which is to say that he atones for sins and offers forgiveness to all humankind (1:21; 26:28; 27:51). Moreover, to demonstrate that Jesus, in enduring the humiliation of the cross, did not die as a false messiah but as

2. Cf. 21:33–42; 26:63–64.

the Son who did his Father's will (21:37–39), God vindicates Jesus by raising him from the dead (28:5–6). Consequently, when Jesus appears to the disciples on the mountain in Galilee (28:16–17), it is as the crucified Son of God whom God has vindicated through resurrection (28:5c–6). Although some disciples show, in doubting, that they are yet weak of faith (28:17; 14:32), they all see on the person of Jesus that crucifixion, or suffering sonship, was the essence of his ministry (21:42). Correlatively, they also grasp at last that servanthood is the essence of discipleship (16:24; 20:25–28). As ones, therefore, who comprehend, in line with God's evaluative point of view (17:5), not only who Jesus is but also what he was about and what it means to be his followers, the disciples receive from Jesus the Great Commission and embark on a mission to all the nations (28:18–20; chaps. 24–25).

In narrating in this fashion the story of the life and ministry of Jesus, Matthew advances a bold theological claim. This claim is, as the passages 1:23 and 28:20 reveal (cf. 18:20), that in the person of Jesus Messiah, his Son, God has drawn near to abide to the end of time with his people, the church, thus inaugurating the end-time age of salvation. This claim, which lies at the heart of "the gospel of the Kingdom," is, in Matthew's view, of decisive significance for Israel and the Gentiles alike (4:23; 9:35; 24:14). The disciples, whom the risen Jesus commissions to a worldwide ministry at the end of Matthew's story, understand this, and so does the reader. It is apparent that the first evangelist, who wrote this story, would also have wanted any real reader both to understand this and to act on it.

Selected
Bibliography

Abrams, M. H. *A Glossary of Literary Terms.* 4th ed. New York: Holt, Rinehart & Winston, 1981.

Anderson, Janice Capel. "The Implied Reader in Matthew." Paper presented at the SBL Group on Literary Aspects of the Gospels and Acts, 1983.

_____. "Point of View in Matthew: Evidence." Paper presented at the SBL Symposium on Literary Analysis of the Gospels and Acts, 1981.

Aune, David E. *Prophecy in Early Christianity and the Ancient Mediterranean World.* Grand Rapids: Wm. B. Eerdmans, 1983.

Bacon, Benjamin W. *Studies in Matthew.* London: Constable & Co., 1930.

Banks, Robert. "Matthew's Understanding of the Law: Authenticity and Interpretation in Matthew 5:17–20." *JBL* 93 (1974): 226–42.

Barth, Gerhard. "Matthew's Understanding of the Law." In *Tradition and Interpretation in Matthew,* by G. Bornkamm, G. Barth, and H. J. Held, 58–164. Eng. trans. P. Scott. NTL. Philadelphia: Westminster Press, 1963.

Bauer, David R. "The Structure of Matthew's Gospel." Ph.D. diss., Union Theological Seminary in Virginia, 1985.

Betz, Hans Dieter. "The Hermeneutical Principles of the Sermon on the Mount (Matt. 5:17–20)." In *Essays on the Sermon on the Mount,* 37–53. Eng. trans. L. L. Wellborn. Philadelphia: Fortress Press, 1985.

_____. "The Sermon on the Mount: Its Literary Genre and Function." *JR* 59 (1979): 285–97.

Booth, Wayne C. *The Rhetoric of Fiction.* 2d ed. Chicago: Univ. of Chicago Press, 1983.

Boring, M. Eugene. *Sayings of the Risen Lord: Christian Prophecy in the Synoptic Tradition.* SNTSMS 46. New York and Cambridge: Cambridge Univ. Press, 1982.

Bornkamm, Gunther. "The Authority to 'Bind' and 'Loose' in the Church in Matthew's Gospel." In *Jesus and Man's Hope,* ed. D. G. Buttrick, 1:37–50. Pittsburgh: Pittsburgh Theological Seminary, 1970.

_____. "End-Expectation and Church in Matthew." In *Tradition and Interpretation in Matthew,* by G. Bornkamm, G. Barth, and H. J. Held, 15–51. Eng. trans. P. Scott. NTL. Philadelphia: Westminster Press, 1963.

Boucher, Madeleine. *The Mysterious Parable: A Literary Study.* CBQMS 6. Washington, D.C.: Catholic Biblical Association of America, 1977.

Bourke, Myles. "The Literary Genus of Matthew 1—2." *CBQ* 22 (1960): 160–75.

Broer, Ingo. *Freiheit vom Gesetz und Radikalisierung des Gesetzes: Ein Beitrag zur Theologie des Evangelisten Matthäus.* SBS 98. Stuttgart, W. Ger.: Katholisches Bibelwerk, 1980.

Brown, Raymond E. *The Birth of the Messiah: A Commentary on the Infancy Narratives in Matthew and Luke.* New York: Doubleday & Co., 1977.

Brown, Raymond E., and John P. Meier. *Antioch and Rome: New Testament Cradles of Catholic Christianity.* New York: Paulist Press, 1983.

Brown, Raymond E., Karl P. Donfried, and John Reumann, eds. *Peter in the New Testament.* Minneapolis: Augsburg Pub. House, 1973.

Brown, Schuyler. "The Matthean Apocalypse." *JSNT* 4 (1979): 2–27.

_____. "The Matthean Community and the Gentile Mission." *NovT* 22 (1980): 193–221.

_____. "The Mission to Israel in Matthew's Central Section (Mt 9:35—11:1)." *ZNW* 69 (1978): 73–90.

_____. "The Two-fold Representation of the Mission in Matthew's Gospel." *ST* 31 (1977): 21–32.

Burnett, Fred W. *The Testament of Jesus-Sophia: A Redaction-Critical Study of the Eschatological Discourse in Matthew.* Washington, D.C.: Univ. Press of America, 1981.

Catchpole, D. R. "The Answer of Jesus to Caiphas (MATT. XXVI. 64)." *NTS* 17 (1970/71): 213–26.

Chatman, Seymour. *Story and Discourse: Narrative Structure in Fiction and Film.* Ithaca, N.Y.: Cornell Univ. Press, 1978.

Chilton, Bruce. "Introduction." In *The Kingdom of God,* 1–26. IRT 5. Philadelphia and London: Fortress Press and SPCK, 1984.

Combrink, H. J. B. "The Structure of the Gospel of Matthew as Narrative." *TynBul* 34 (1983): 61–90.

Cook, Michael J. "Interpreting 'Pro-Jewish' Passages in Matthew." *HUCA* 54 (1983): 135–46.

Cope, O. Lamar. *Matthew: A Scribe Trained for the Kingdom of Heaven.* CBQMS 5. Washington, D.C.: Catholic Biblical Association of America, 1976.

Cothenet, É. "Les prophètes chrétiens dans l'Évangile selon saint Matthieu." In *L'Évangile selon Matthieu: Rédaction et Théologie,* ed. M. Didier, 281–308. BETL 19. Gembloux: Duculot, 1972.

Culpepper, R. Alan. *Anatomy of the Fourth Gospel: A Study in Literary Design.* FFNT. Philadelphia: Fortress Press, 1983.

Dewey, Joanna. *Markan Public Debate.* SBLDS 48. Chico, Calif.: Scholars Press, 1980.

Donahue, John. "Tax Collectors and Sinners." *CBQ* 33 (1971): 39–61.

Donaldson, Terence L. *Jesus on the Mountain: A Study in Matthean Theology.* JSNTSS 8. Sheffield: JSOT Press, 1985.

Duling, Dennis C. "The Therapeutic Son of David: An Element in Matthew's Christological Apologetic." *NTS* 24 (1978): 392–410.

Edwards, Richard A. *Matthew's Story of Jesus.* Philadelphia: Fortress Press, 1985.

_____. "Uncertain Faith: Matthew's Portrait of the Disciples." In *Discipleship in the New Testament*, ed. F. F. Segovia, 47–61. Philadelphia: Fortress Press, 1985.

Farmer, William R. *Jesus and the Gospel: Tradition, Scripture, and Canon.* Philadelphia: Fortress Press, 1982.

_____. "The Post-Sectarian Character of Matthew and Its Post-War Setting in Antioch of Syria." *PRS* 3 (1976): 235–47.

Fiore, Benjamin. "Characterization in Matthew." Paper presented at the CBA Task Force on the Literary Study of Matthew, 1984.

Forster, E. M. *Aspects of the Novel.* New York: Harcourt, Brace & World, 1954.

Frankemölle, Hubert. *Jahwebund und Kirche Christi: Studien zur Form- und Traditionsgeschichte des "Evangeliums" nach Matthäus.* NTAbh 10. Münster, W. Ger.: Aschendorff, 1974.

Frye, Roland Mushat. "A Literary Perspective for the Criticism of the Gospels." In *Jesus and Man's Hope*, ed. D. G. Miller and D. Y. Hadidian, 2:193–221. Pittsburgh: Pittsburgh Theological Seminary, 1971.

Garland, David E. *The Intention of Matthew 23.* NovTSup 52. Leiden, Neth.: E. J. Brill, 1979.

Gerhardsson, Birger. "Du Judéo-christianisme a Jésus par le Shema." *RSR* 60 (1972): 23–36.

_____. "Gottes Sohn als Diener Gottes." *ST* 27 (1973): 73–106.

_____. "Jésus livré et abandonné d'après la Passion selon saint Matthieu." *RB* 76 (1969): 206–27.

_____. "The Hermeneutic Program in Matthew 22:37–40." In *Jews, Greeks, and Christians: Essays in Honor of William David Davies*, ed. R. Hamerton-Kelly and R. Scroggs, 129–50. Leiden, Neth.: E. J. Brill, 1976.

_____. *The Mighty Acts of Jesus According to Matthew.* Eng. trans. R. Dewsnap. ScrMin. Lund, Swed.: C. W. K. Gleerup, 1979.

_____. "The Parable of the Sower and Its Interpretation." *NTS* 14 (1967/68): 165–93.

_____. *The Testing of God's Son.* ConBNT 2:1. Lund, Swed.: C. W. K. Gleerup, 1966.

Gnilka, Joachim. *Das Evangelium nach Markus.* EKK 2/1. Cologne and Neukirchen-Vluyn: Benziger Verlag and Neukirchener Verlag, 1978.

Goulder, M. D. *Midrash and Lection in Matthew.* London: SPCK, 1974.

Guelich, Robert A. *The Sermon on the Mount: A Foundation for Understanding.* Waco, TX: Word, 1982.

Gundry, Robert Horton. *The Use of the Old Testament in St. Matthew's Gospel.* NovTSup 18. Leiden, Neth.: E. J. Brill, 1967.

Hare, Douglas R. A. *The Theme of Jewish Persecution of Christians in the Gospel According to St. Matthew.* SNTSMS 6. Cambridge: Cambridge Univ. Press, 1967.

Hawkins, John C. *Horae Synopticae: Contributions to the Study of the Synoptic Problem.* 2d ed. Oxford: Clarendon Press, 1909.

Held, Heinz Joachim. "Matthew as Interpreter of the Miracle Stories." In *Tradition and Interpretation in Matthew*, by G. Bornkamm, G. Barth, and H. J. Held, 165–299. Eng. trans. P. Scott. NTL. Philadelphia: Westminster Press, 1963.

Hummel, Reinhart. *Die Auseinandersetzung zwischen Kirche und Judentum im Matthäusevangelium.* BEvT 33. Munich: Chr. Kaiser, 1963.

Iser, Wolfgang. *The Act of Reading: A Theory of Aesthetic Response.* Baltimore: Johns Hopkins Univ. Press, 1978.

Jeremias, Joachim. *Jerusalem in the Time of Jesus: An Investigation into Economic and Social Conditions during the New Testament Period.* Eng. Trans. M. E. Dahl. Philadelphia: Fortress Press, 1975.

Johnson, Marshall D. *The Purpose of the Biblical Genealogies.* SNTSMS 8. Cambridge: Cambridge Univ. Press, 1969.

Katz, Steven T. "Issues in the Separation of Judaism and Christianity after 70 C.E.: A Reconsideration." *JBL* 103 (1984): 43–76.

Keck, Leander E. "Ethics in the Gospel According to Matthew." *IR* 40 (1984): 39–56.

Kilpatrick, G. D. *The Origins of the Gospel According to Matthew.* Oxford: Clarendon Press, 1946.

Kingsbury, Jack Dean. "The Developing Conflict between Jesus and the Jewish Leaders in Matthew's Gospel: A Literary-Critical Study." *CBQ* 49 (1987): 57–73.

———. "The Figure of Jesus in Matthew's Story: A Literary-Critical Probe." *JSNT* 21 (1984): 3–36.

———. "The Figure of Jesus in Matthew's Story: A Rejoinder to David Hill." *JSNT* 25 (1985): 61–81.

———. "The Figure of Peter in Matthew's Gospel as a Theological Problem." *JBL* 98 (1979): 67–83.

———. *Matthew.* Proclamation Commentary. 2d ed. Philadelphia: Fortress Press, 1986.

———. *Matthew: Structure, Christology, Kingdom.* Philadelphia and London: Fortress Press and SPCK, 1975.

———. "On Following Jesus: The 'Eager' Scribe and the 'Reluctant' Disciple (Matt. 8. 18–22)." *NTS* 34 (1988): 45–59.

———. "The Parable of the Wicked Husbandmen and the Secret of Jesus' Divine Sonship in Matthew: Some Literary-Critical Observations." *JBL* 105 (1986): 643–55.

———. *The Parables of Jesus in Matthew 13.* London and St. Louis: SPCK and Clayton Pub. House, 1977.

———. "The Place, Structure, and Meaning of the Sermon on the Mount within Matthew." *Int* 41 (1987): 131–43.

———. "Reflections on 'the Reader' of Matthew's Gospel." Forthcoming in *NTS.*

———. "The Title 'Son of David' in Matthew's Gospel." *JBL* 95 (1976): 591–602.

———. "The Verb *Akolouthein* ('to follow') as an Index of Matthew's View of His Community." *JBL* 97 (1978): 56–73.

Krentz, Edgar. "The Extent of Matthew's Prologue." *JBL* 83 (1964): 409–14.

Kretzer, Armin. *Die Herrschaft der Himmel und die Sohne des Reiches.* SBM 10. Stuttgart, W. Ger.: KBW Verlag, 1971.

Lambrecht, J. "The Parousia Discourse, Composition and Content in Mt., XXIV–XXV." In *L'Évangile selon Matthieu: Rédaction et Théologie,* ed. M. Didier, 309–42. BETL 19. Gembloux: Duculot, 1972.

Lanser, Susan Sniader. *The Narrative Act: Point of View in Prose Fiction.* Princeton: Princeton Univ. Press, 1981.

Lategan, Bernard C. "Structure and Reference in MT 23." *Neot* 16 (1982): 74–87.

Lindars, Barnabas. *Jesus Son of Man*. London: SPCK, 1983.

Linton, Olaf. "The Demand for a Sign from Heaven (Mk 8, 11–12 and Parallels)." *ST* 19 (1965): 112–29.

Loader, W. R. G. "Son of David, Blindness, Possession, and Duality in Matthew." *CBQ* 44 (1982): 570–85.

Lohr, Charles H. "Oral Techniques in the Gospel of Matthew." *CBQ* 23 (1961): 403–35.

Lotman, J. M. "Point of View in a Text." *NLH* 6 (1975): 339–52.

Luz, Ulrich. *Das Evangelium nach Matthäus*. EEK 1/1. Cologne and Neukirchen-Vluyn: Benziger Verlag and Neukirchener Verlag, 1985.

————. "Die Erfüllung des Gesetzes bei Matthäus (Mt 5, 17–20)." *ZTK* 75 (1978): 398–435.

————. "The Disciples in the Gospel According to Matthew (1971)." In *The Interpretation of Matthew*, ed. G. Stanton, 98–128. IRT 3. Philadelphia and London: Fortress Press and SPCK, 1983.

Matera, Frank J. *Passion Narratives and Gospel Theologies: Interpreting the Synoptics through Their Passion Stories*. TI. New York: Paulist Press, 1986.

————. "The Plot of Matthew's Gospel." *CBQ* 49 (1987): 233–53.

Martin, Brice L. "Matthew on Christ and the Law." *TS* 44 (1983): 53–70.

Meier, John P. *Law and History in Matthew's Gospel*. AnBib 71. Rome: Biblical Institute Press, 1976.

————. *The Vision of Matthew: Christ, Church and Morality in the First Gospel*. TI. New York: Paulist Press, 1979.

Mohrlang, Roger. *Matthew and Paul: A Comparison of Ethical Perspectives*. SNTSMS 48. Cambridge: Cambridge Univ. Press, 1984.

Moule, C. F. D. *The Birth of the New Testament*. New York: Harper & Row, 1962.

Müller, Mogens. *Der Ausdruck "Menschensohn" in den Evangelien: Voraussetzungen und Bedeutung*. AThD 17. Leiden, Neth.: E. J. Brill, 1984.

Nolan, Brian M. *The Royal Son of God: The Christology of Matthew 1—2 in the Setting of the Gospel*. OBO 23. Göttingen, W. Ger.: Vandenhoeck & Ruprecht, 1979.

Oepke, Albrecht. "*Gyne*." *TDNT* 1 (1964): 776–89.

————. "*Pais*." *TDNT* 5 (1967): 636–54.

Patte, Daniel. *The Gospel According to Matthew: A Structural Commentary on Matthew's Faith*. Philadelphia: Fortress Press, 1987.

Pesch, Rudolf. *Das Markusevangelium*. HTKNT 2. 2 parts. Freiburg: Herder, 1976–77.

Pesch, Wilhelm. *Matthäus der Seelsorger*. SBS 2. Stuttgart: KWB Verlag, 1966.

Petersen, Norman R. *Literary Criticism for New Testament Critics*. GBS. Philadelphia: Fortress Press, 1978.

————. " 'Point of View' in Mark's Narrative." *Semeia* 12 (1978): 97–121.

————. "The Reader in the Gospel." *Neot* 18 (1984): 38–51.

Powell, Mark A. "The Religious Leaders in Matthew's Gospel: A Literary-Critical Study." Ph.D. diss., Union Theological Seminary in Virginia, 1988.

Prince, Gerald. "Notes Toward a Categorization of Fictional 'Narratees.' " *Genre* 4 (1971): 100–106.

Reicke, Bo. *The New Testament Era*. Eng. trans. D. E. Green. Philadelphia: Fortress Press, 1968.

Reumann, John. "*Righteousness*" *in the New Testament.* Philadelphia: Fortress Press, 1982.

Rhoads, David. "Narrative Criticism and the Gospel of Mark." *JAAR* 50 (1982): 411–34.

Rhoads, David, and Donald Michie. *Mark as Story : An Introduction to the Narrative of a Gospel.* Philadelphia: Fortress Press, 1982.

Rotfuchs, Wilhelm. *Die Erfüllungszitate des Matthäus-Evangeliums.* BWANT 8. Stuttgart, W. Ger.: Kohlhammer, 1969.

Sand, Alexander. *Das Gesetz und die Propheten: Untersuchungen zur Theologie des Evangeliums nach Matthaus.* BU 11. Regensburg: Verlag Friedrich Pustet, 1974.

Sandmel, S. "Herodians," *IDB* 2 (1962): 594–95.

Schrage, Wolfgang. "*Typhlos.*" *TDNT* 8 (1972): 270–94.

Schweizer, Eduard. *The Good News According to Matthew.* Eng. trans. D. E. Green, Atlanta: John Knox Press, 1975.

———. *Matthäus und seine Gemeinde.* SBS 71. Stuttgart, W. Ger.: KBW Verlag, 1974.

Senior, Donald. *The Passion of Jesus in the Gospel of Matthew.* Wilmington: Michael Glazier, 1985.

Smith, Robert H. *Easter Gospels: The Resurrection of Jesus According to the Four Evangelists.* Minneapolis: Augsburg Pub. House, 1983.

Snodgrass, Klyne. *The Parable of the Wicked Tenants: An Inquiry into Parable Interpretation.* WUNT 27. Tübingen: J. C. B. Mohr, 1983.

Stanton, Graham N. "The Gospel of Matthew and Judaism." *BJRL* 66 (1984): 264–84.

Stendahl, Krister. *The School of St. Matthew.* Philadelphia: Fortress Press, 1968.

Sternberg, Meir. *The Poetics of Biblical Narrative: Ideological Literature and the Drama of Reading.* Bloomington: Indiana Univ. Press, 1985.

Strecker, Georg. *Der Weg der Gerechtigkeit: Untersuchungen zur Theologie des Matthäus.* FRLANT 82. Göttingen, W. Ger.: Vandenhoeck & Ruprecht, 1984.

———. Die Bergpredigt: Ein exegetischer Kommentar. Göttingen, W. Ger.: Vandenhoeck & Ruprecht, 1984.

Suggs, M. Jack. *Wisdom, Christology, and Law in Matthew's Gospel.* Cambridge: Harvard Univ. Press, 1970.

Suleiman, Susan R., and Inge Crosman, eds. *The Reader in the Text: Essays on Audience and Interpretation.* Princeton: Princeton Univ. Press, 1980.

Theissen, Gerd. "Itinerant Radicalism." *RRel* 2 (1975): 84–93.

Thompson, William G. "An Historical Perspective in the Gospel of Matthew." *JBL* 93 (1974): 243–62.

———. *Matthew's Advice to a Divided Community: Mt. 17.22—18.35.* AnBib 44. Rome: Biblical Institute Press, 1970.

Tompkins, Jane P., ed. *Reader-Response Criticism: From Formalism to Post-Structuralism.* Baltimore: Johns Hopkins Univ. Press, 1980.

Trevett, Christine. "Approaching Matthew from the Second Century: The Under-Used Ignatian Correspondence." *JSNT* 20 (1984): 59–67.

Trilling, Wolfgang. *Das wahre Israel: Studien zur Theologie des Matthäus-Evangeliums.* SANT 10. 3d ed. Munich: Kösel-Verlag, 1964.

Turner, Nigel, *Style.* Vol. 4 of *A Grammar of New Testament Greek,* by James Hope Moulton. Edinburgh: T. & T. Clark, 1976.

Uspensky, Boris. *A Poetics of Composition.* Eng. trans. V. Zavarin and S. Wittig. Berkeley and Los Angeles: Univ. of California Press, 1973.

Van Tilborg, Sjef. *The Jewish Leaders in Matthew.* Leiden, Neth.: E. J. Brill, 1972.

Vawter, Bruce. "The Divorce Clause in Mt. 5, 32 and 19, 9." *CBQ* 16 (1954): 155–67.

Vermes, Geza. *Jesus and the World of Judaism.* Philadelphia: Fortress Press, 1984.

Walker, Rolf. *Die Heilsgeschichte im ersten Evangelium.* FRLANT 91. Göttingen, W. Ger.: Vandenhoeck & Ruprecht, 1967.

Waetjen, Herman. *The Origin and Destiny of Humanness: An Interpretation of the Gospel According to Matthew.* Corte Madera, Calif.: Omega Books, 1976.

Weaver, Dorothy Jean. "The Missionary Discourse in the Gospel of Matthew: A Literary Critical Analysis." Ph.D. diss., Union Theological Seminary in Virginia, 1987.

Wilckens, Ulrich. "*Sophia.*" *TDNT* 7 (1971): 496–526.

Witherup, Ronald D. "The Cross of Jesus: A Literary-Critical Study of Matthew 27." Ph.D. diss., Union Theological Seminary in Virginia, 1985.

Index of References
to Matthew